God, Guts, and Guns

GOD, GUTS, AND GUNS

Phillip Finch

Seaview/Putnam
New York

For C. David Burgin
Finally

Library of Congress Cataloging in Publication Data

Finch, Phillip.
  God, guts, and guns.

1. United States—Politics and government—1981-
2. Conservatism—United States—History—20th century.
3. Radicalism—United States—History—20th century.
4. United States—Politics and government—1977-1981.
5. Fundamentalism. 6. Moral Majority, Inc. I. Title.
E876.F56 1983   322.4'4'0973   82-19415
ISBN 0-399-31012-6

Printed in the United States of America

God, Guts, and Guns Made America Free
Let's Keep All Three

—KKK bumper sticker

Acknowledgments

Thanks are due to the staffs of the Montgomery County Library in Bethesda, Maryland; the Multnomah County Library in Portland, Oregon; and the Library of Congress, for extraordinary assistance and forbearance, routinely rendered.

The material on COINTELPRO was copied from files maintained by the Center for National Security Studies in Washington, D.C., an important source of public-interest materials obtained under the Freedom of Information Act. The Center's files on right-wing activity were also helpful.

Special thanks are due to the directors and staff members of the Wilcox Collection of Contemporary Political Movements, which is housed in the Spencer Library at the University of Kansas. The mass of the collection is daunting: nearly a quarter-mile of shelving laden with hundreds of file boxes, all full of extremist political tracts, periodicals, and other publications. Such a repository is a true treasure for anyone who knows the value of primary research, yet the sheer size would have been stultifying if not for the superb organization and efficiency of the library staff. I'm certain that I found material there which simply does not exist anywhere else. It would not have been there for me or for anyone else to find if Laird Wilcox had not saved it and the librarians had not catalogued it.

Thanks to Olivia and Leon Mandel for their friendship, for bed and board, and for all their help.

Finally, I'm grateful to everyone who took the time to talk to me, preach to me, and answer my questions along the way.

Introduction

On most maps it is a big ugly blot, ill-defined and featureless, dark and scary and impenetrable. Terra incognita. Abandon all hope. . . .

The project took on aspects of some foolhardy expedition, Columbus sailing off toward the abyss. Warnings from friends (who, like most of us, had heard rumors about the place) became a dolorous good-bye chant: Be *careful,* this is *dangerous,* you must be *crazy,* why fool with the *Radical Right?*

So this is the log of a journey into a land largely uncharted. There are a few guidebooks for the territory, but most have the unsettling vagueness of an armchair adventurer's tales, the way *Moby Dick* might have read if Melville had been afraid to go near the water. Observation from a safe, comfortable distance just won't do; to map the philosophical fringes from an office lined with political-science texts is to describe China by peering from the Great Wall through a pair of cheap binoculars.

The territory and its denizens have long deserved close examination, careful description. Now they may be more important than they have been for decades. Those fringies on the right, without anybody noticing, may have helped in their fractious and belligerent fashion to put Ronald Reagan in the White House.

Herewith, a model for the changing political sentiments of an electorate. Imagine a huge iron wrecking ball—the populace at large, inert and ponderous—sitting in an open field. Surrounding the wrecking ball are political zealots of all stripes, each pushing and shoving the ball (which is to say,

7

the hearts and minds of most of us) in one direction or another. The big
iron ball describes an aimless, meandering path. Its movement is slow. But
the ball does move, in a direction that suits those zealots who have mus-
tered up enough strength and sense of purpose. Never too far, of course;
the weight of the ball is always too great for anyone to oppose for long.
Then other zealots regroup and heave and move the ball in another direction. But for a while, a few people working hard and believing even harder
have pushed us closer to where they want us to be. Consider then the
common theory that the nation's political conscience began to tilt right-
ward several years ago, and suddenly there is good reason to want to
understand those zealots at the radical edge of the movement.

The journey is easier if you travel light, shuck off all the standard
notions about this so-called Radical Right. Presumptions are excess bag-
gage. The term itself is a hindrance that means little. Radical Right: It rolls
easily out of the head and off the tongue, a fine alliterative label of convenience that is useless without definition. It is based on an artificial
scale—you know, the one we all learned in high school, the old left-to-
right index of political thought that had the Communists at one end and
the Nazis at the other end and everybody from socialists to Tories to
Jeffersonians somewhere in between—a scale that long ago lost whatever
relevance and meaning it might have had, if only because the extremes at
either end so strikingly resemble one another in their intolerance of
human freedom.

So the term is unsatisfying. But what is better? Those within like to call it
the "patriotic movement." Characteristically enough, that precludes the
possibility that anyone outside the movement is motivated by love of
country.

Bob DePugh, who twenty-two years ago founded a paramilitary resistance group, the Minutemen, has an observation worth noting: "Radical
right doesn't mean much. You could call it the American nationalist movement, but not everybody who's part of it is really a nationalist. A lot of
people call it the patriotic movement, but you're being generous to call
some of these people patriots. That brings us back to 'radical right,' and
maybe that's as good a term as any, if you're going to use one."

Might as well make it uppercase, then. Radical Right it is, but with a big
stipulation. Let it be understood that this is an aggregation in name only.
There is no homogenous, monolithic Right. Its members generally share
the patriotic symbols of cross and flag, and there are a few nebulous ideals—economic liberalism, traditional social values, an abhorrence of collectivism—that are to be found in varying proportions in most right-wing
philosophies. It is a sort of ideological gumbo, for no two batches are ever

identical. In fact, those of the right find much to separate them. The multiple variations on a few basic political themes are important to them. Details count out on the borders. The liberal and leftist coalitions of the Sixties, however fitful and uncertain, would be impossible for most of the people in this book. They are independent and happily disagreeable. Accommodation is not in their nature. They're willing, eager, to scrap over small things. That is easy to understand if you realize that every one of them believes with head and heart this article of life: *There is a single correct way, and I know what it is.*

That is how they look at the rest of the world. It is the skeleton that supports all that they say and do and believe. Take it away and their hard, chiseled principles collapse into so many puddles of rhetoric. That kind of confidence is strange and even a little frightening to those who see life in neutral gray tones.

It will be necessary to get personal here, briefly. An unpleasant business. The author would like to keep himself out of the book entirely, but that can't be done. A book like this takes form through thousands of subjective, intimate judgments: what to keep and what to discard, what's important and what's trivial, what's startling and what's routine. Somebody else would make some of those calls differently.

The facts, then: white male, married, age thirty-three; Roman Catholic upbringing; oldest of five children, father an old-line blue-collar union man; never marched, never gave money, and one day discovers himself that most contemptible of creatures—a complacent bleeding-heart liberal; realizes that things are tough for all sorts of bleeding hearts these days and is willing to listen to alternatives.

The Radical Right couldn't have asked for more, really, than this political virgin, fresh territory, willing to restrict prejudice only to that which he observed, not what he had been told elsewhere.

One of the first things he notices is that this Radical Right is less a movement than a menagerie, a political taxonomist's nightmare. Contradictions abound. It defies bracketing. It refuses to sit still and be counted. It is amorphous, nebulous, slippery. It is frustrating. With every answer come at least a couple of new questions.

I got my first hint of this when I talked to a man I'll call Sam Potter. He was the first person I interviewed for this book. He was, in fact, the only real right-winger I knew, and that was a most tenuous kind of acquaintance.

Every other name in this book is real. Sam Potter's isn't. He didn't want to be part of this book at all, but I've changed his name to include him because he is perfect, so typical, I would learn, of the way those on the right qualify as unique breeds of one. It's a good human story, and I use it here for that reason as well. Politics in its purest (which is to say, most extreme) forms really is a way of life, and there is no comprehending the ideology without first understanding the people.

Finally, what happened to Sam Potter when he moved to a place I'll call Fremont County is instructive because it tells us something about the Radical Right's ambiguous place in our society, even in places where you'd think it ought to be welcome.

Anyway, Sam Potter. His name is a fiction, but everything else about him is as real as a pebble in your shoe. He is stubborn. He is a loud and insistent patriot. He is strong and upright; he would have to be, to have survived so many collisions with immovable authority. Somehow he never learned the neat feint, the pirouette around an obstacle. He has spent his life seeking them and colliding with them, head-on.

Sam Potter has a basic problem with the world in which he finds himself: He chafes against regulation that the rest of us accept without pause. Something about building codes, zoning laws, census forms, fishing licenses rankles him. These are all surely good devices in our day. They keep things in order, and order is important in a crowded fast-moving world. Maybe he is just a sour old crank for letting these good devices disturb him. And maybe he is a relic from another time, like a Stegosaurus at a lawn party, who can't do anything right where he finds himself. Good intentions are no help; his nature does him in every time. He shrugs, he tries to scratch his back or unlimber his legs—disaster! Disruption follows him like a bothersome little dog, yapping at his heels.

His reputation, in a particularly malignant form, preceded him to Fremont County. The sheriff's office was ready for him: a dossier, files of newspaper clippings, the real skinny, all courtesy of the last jurisdiction where Sam lived.

Sam had sold his business in the city. Now he was bringing his wife and children to live in the country, among the pastures and the piñon pines and the sagebrush of Fremont County. He is a different sort of man, not like the rest of us, and he hoped to find comfort in the space and the silence and the good hearts of the country people that he remembered from his childhood on a farm.

The people of Fremont County knew none of this about Sam Potter. But they did know what the sheriff's deputies were letting slip about him even as he arrived: that he had been to prison, that he belonged to a secret subversive organization, and that he was a troublemaker.

This is probably the place to talk about Fremont County, where Sam

Potter bought 100 acres bare of everything but rocks and some scrub trees. By quirks of geography and weather, of regional economy and history and chance, Fremont County has fewer than one resident for each square mile of land within its boundaries. It is a place of cattle ranches and high awesome mountains. Fremont County grants no dispensation from taxes or court orders, but its space does give the illusion of freedom.

Sam Potter was looking for some space, and some peace for a change, and a little room in which to stretch his legs without upsetting the tea cart and the pastry tray. Maybe more important, he came expecting kinship and welcome from people who understood him. Why not? Big spaces appeal to the tough and independent mind. You have to be secure in yourself, the way Sam Potter is, to be happy for long in a territory where the landscape swallows up little bits of humanity. If he looked for trappings and symbols, Sam Potter could see plenty of pickup trucks with gun racks and American flag decals in the window, owned by mavericks just like himself.

A few years before Sam Potter chose it for his home, Fremont County had united to defend itself against invaders—homosexuals. Because of an article in a big-city daily newspaper, some of the county's citizens became convinced that hundreds of gays were about to descend upon them. If the invaders had been coming to admire the mountain scenery and to fish in the streams, they would likely have been greeted by a welcoming committee, for Fremont County's economy depends on a fickle tourist trade. The article in the newspaper, however, suggested that the gays were planning to stay, register, vote, and to replace the county's incumbent officials with a gay slate in the next general election—to form, in effect, the first specifically homosexual municipality in the nation. That possibility was real enough, since Fremont County's population is so small that a few hundred identical ballots would sweep an election.

Fremont County reacted. Locals pressured businessmen to resist supplying the conquering hordes when they arrived. There was a drive to register all friendly residents (even, it was rumored, the out-of-county families of friendly residents). And, though Fremont County is sheepish about it now, there were at least a few self-deputized committees of vigilance—cowhands from the county's ranches, mostly—patrolling the roads that enter Fremont County, ready to intercept the carloads and busloads of metropolitan homosexuals that were expected at any moment.

They never arrived. Some of the locals judged the story a hoax perpetrated by a newspaper with nothing better to do than make trouble. Others believe that an advance party noted the snow and ice that burden the county for several months of the year, noted as well the equally frigid attitude of the residents, and decided to try the idea another place, another time.

The county's reaction was, at any rate, exactly the sort of self-reliant display of local independence that might have encouraged Sam Potter a couple of years later when he looked for a new place to live.

That is where Sam Potter bought his bare 100 acres, and where he rented a house for himself and his family. He surely thought that he had found sanctuary. Instead, he was getting into as much trouble as he had ever known.

There is in Fremont County, as in most rural areas, an informal but clearly established network for gossip. Usually, news finds its way to the community's points of intersection—a bank, a couple of bars, a general store—and radiates out from there. New faces in the county are always sure subject for speculation, dissection, analysis.

When Sam Potter and his family moved to Fremont County, the lines of gossip overloaded. In a place so insular, secrets rarely stay kept. Soon after Sam Potter arrived, the contents of his dossier were the prime topic of chatter. There had been a donnybrook with sheriff's officers elsewhere in the state when deputies tried to enforce a court order allowing union recruiters on private farmland. ("A matter of principle," Sam Potter would say much later. "A judge can't take away a citizen's rights to use his property the way he wants.") Then ten months in a federal penitentiary for failure to file a tax return. And, finally, membership in an organization called the Posse Comitatus—soon known in Fremont County simply as "the Posse."

Fremont County knew just enough about the Posse to be frightened of it, and not without reason. The Posse can be frightening to outsiders. Its members often carry guns. They speak with the fervor of revolutionaries. And unlike many other groups on the Radical Right, which seem moved more by publicity than by principle, the Posse Comitatus is reclusive, cautious with the public if not entirely secret. Most of Fremont County did not know that, but there was a common understanding that the Posse was different, threatening, something to be shunned. And before he and his family had lived there a year, the residents of Fremont County became convinced that Sam Potter and the Posse Comitatus intended to seize control of the county by registering hundreds of its members to vote in the next general election.

Here the truth gets slippery. Sam Potter has a version of it, and so do Fremont County's district attorney and most of its citizens. Sam Potter says it was only a coincidence that a friend from a big city moved to

Fremont County, registered to vote, and entered the upcoming election for sheriff. Most of Fremont County, however, figured that was Sam Potter's first step toward taking over.

They saw more: Sam Potter presenting to the county planning commission a plan for a subdivision that he called Constitution City. Fremont County decided that Sam was going to sell lots to Posse members so that he could load voter rolls.

More: unfamiliar faces at the county clerk's office, registering to vote.

More: a classified ad in the right-wing tabloid the *Spotlight,* asking for donations to help finance "the first real Constitutional government in America." The ad listed a post-office box in a town just fifteen miles from Fremont County, and a deputy who watched the box saw it emptied by a man who had been seen with Sam Potter.

It is traditional in Fremont County that, about a month before local elections, the candidates meet the voters at the County Hall to answer questions and debate the issues. It is also traditional that these functions have all the verve of a quilting bee. This time was different. This time, the pickups with gun racks filled the hall's parking lot. Sam Potter and a few of his friends faced maybe half of Fremont County's adult population.

Sam Potter wasn't on the ballot, but he spoke to the crowd anyway. He told the people that they were mad at the wrong enemy; that he and they thought alike; that he was a real American just as they were, and that they ought to be cooperating with him instead of battling him.

Someone who was there remembers that "everybody listened to what he had to say, and then when he was finished, every redneck and every cowboy in the county stood up, one after another, and told him and his buddies that they shouldn't expect to live too long after the election if they kept up with what they were doing."

The account is probably accurate. A few days later, Sam Potter's friend withdrew from the race for sheriff and returned to the big city. Not long after the election, Sam Potter was convicted of conspiring to illegally register voters. After he had served his time, Sam left Fremont County and rented a tract home in the flatlands. I talked to him there for the first time. I had known him mostly by his Fremont County reputation, which by then was awesome and terrifying. But it was no junior Martin Bormann in a hood who opened the front door. Sam Potter had a big antic grin and a vigorous handshake.

He had rented a small house. The living room had space for a love seat and a console color TV. In one corner, a gold-fringed Stars and Stripes hung limp on its staff. On top of the TV was a three-volume quarto-size set of the *Christian History of the Constitution of the United States of America.*

Sam is tall, big-boned, not at all fleshy. Gaunt-faced with deep-set eyes, he looks as if he could have been plucked right out of a Mathew Brady photograph. He is unembellished, unornamented. He talks and acts the same way. When I made the standard pleasantries about his home—a nice, comfortable place, I said—he snorted and said, "This? This place is awful. The construction is pitiful. Look at how small the rooms are. The federal prison was nicer than this," he said, and he laughed.

Sam has an unrestrained burst of a laugh that he uses for punctuation and ironic underlining. It is a laugh loud enough and intense enough to startle a small child. He can shade it with bitter tones or modulate it to suggest delight, depending on how he is feeling about the folly he sees around him. And the folly within himself, sometimes.

"One thing for sure about people like me," he said after a few minutes. He stopped and laughed; he knows the rest of us think his ideas are strange. "There's no two of us the same. That's why we can't ever get together on things. People think we're taking over, but it'll never happen. We keep forming circular firing squads."

That was an apt enough subject on a day less than three weeks after the national elections of 1980. I asked him if he was a Reagan man.

"Not me. But I'm glad he beat Carter. That man is no good. He did his best to ruin this country. I voted the American Independent ticket for president and I split my vote between Democrats and Republicans the rest of the way down the ballot.

"Mostly I looked for people who were running for their third or fourth terms, and I voted against them. Something happens to politicians when they get elected. They have great ideas and they say they want to work with the people who put them in office, but then they get a taste of the power and they change. They go back to Washington or they go to the statehouse and they join the club. They forget who put them there in the first place. So when I see some guy who's been in office six or eight years and wants to get elected again, I vote against him, whoever he is or what he says he stands for."

But that, I said, doesn't sound like any way to sustain the right's momentum.

Sam shook his head. Obviously, he had been over this ground more than once. "This 'right' and 'left' business is all a mess," he said. "Same with 'liberal' and 'conservative.' They're just words, they don't mean anything. Most school books diagram out 'right' and 'left' and they put the Communists and the fascists at opposite ends. Well, that's ridiculous. [A big laugh, real foolishness here.]

"For me, communism and fascism are the same. They're both totalitarian systems that don't allow room for the freedom of the individual. That's what it's all about, if you want to draw a diagram, total personal freedom at one end and totalitarianism at the other.

"That's why I call myself a liberal. [Another laugh; this is a calculated shocker.] That's right, a liberal and a constitutionalist. I'm liberal the way most of our Founding Fathers were liberal with individual rights. They wrote that freedom into the Constitution. That's why it's a sacred document, as far as I'm concerned.

"I don't believe Reagan is a real constitutionalist, but he does think American, and that's something. If Carter had won again, I think the Russians would have been over here before the end of winter. I mean it. I think we were that close. They'll put it off now that Reagan is president. I think with Reagan we'll have two or three years, maybe, to get ready for them. But it'll happen, sooner or later, bet on it."

There was no laugh at the end of that sentence. Sam Potter expects a Russian invasion sometime in this decade and he is convinced that the U.S. military will be unable to stop it. That will leave the question of freedom in the hands of Americans who are willing to fight for it, right in their own towns and fields. For Sam Potter, that will be a moment to relish. Perfect! The very best of American freedom-lovers (all the others now fleeing the country or collaborating with the enemy) taking up arms to repel the invaders.

"There are more of us than people think," he said. "Not just thousands, but several million of us. We can do the job. The armed American civilian is the most formidable fighting force the world has ever seen. I remember in forty-two in San Diego, there was a scare that the Japanese were going to be invading. Thousands of people showed up on the beaches with shotguns and rifles, ready to take on the whole Japanese Army.

"A lot of good Americans today don't want to take orders from a commissar, and they're prepared to do whatever it takes to keep that from happening. But they have to get ready, and they have to get organized. The military won't do it for us, that's for sure. [Loudest laugh of the day.] It's in our hands, and we've got to get ready."

Sam Potter was ready. In the garage of his rented tract home was canned food to last him and his family for six months. He boasted that he could shut the doors and board up the windows and not leave the house for weeks.

"I've got some water, too," he said. "Not enough for six months, but I know where I can get more when I need it."

The mountains, he felt, weren't really secure. For best strategic advantage, he said, he'd have to withdraw to the Midwest, though even here he was in far better shape than some of his friends who were foolhardy enough to have stayed in the cities.

Later, when I tried to describe my conversation with Sam Potter, I compared it to talking with someone who is wearing a pair of prismatic lenses that turn the world into inconceivable images. To talk with that person, you must slip on an identical pair of lenses; then it's possible to look at an object and discuss it, because you're now seeing the same image.

Talking with Sam Potter was like that. It was a sensation that would become familiar as I spoke with some of the most radical, the most serious and committed people in this book. They see the world differently from most of us. To talk to Sam Potter on his terms means putting on a set of perceptions that show the Russians ready to hit the shores next week, perceptions that have American presidents cooperating with the KGB, that give an urgency to the chore of stockpiling food and water to survive the impending crisis.

We ate lunch from Sam Potter's survival cache. He heated a can of tomato soup and a can of pork and beans, made a sandwich with canned tuna. He looked relaxed. He talked about the fundamental church that he had discovered nearby, about the new church building that he had helped to construct, about his family: grown sons and two disabled children that he and his wife had adopted.

It seemed a good time to ask him about Fremont County.

He put down his spoon and looked at me. I could see his mouth tighten.

"I never met country people like that before," he said. There was a quaver in his voice. "I grew up in the country, and the people I knew were the best, the finest people you could imagine. When a new family moved in, everybody else from farms miles around would be there to greet them, make them welcome. They'd bring food and they'd come ready to help with whatever needed to be done to the place.

"I just wasn't ready for what happened up there. Nobody who wasn't there would believe what I went through. When I walked through town, nobody talked to me. They either stared at me or crossed over to the other side of the street when they saw me coming. My children got treated so bad at school that I sent them to live somewhere else in the state. Just because they're my children, Sam Potter's kids. And they're good kids. All the lies and all the malicious stories that were told about me up there, nobody dared to say a word about my children. That would be too much even for those people.

"There's no church up there, do you know that? Not in the whole county. That says it all about them, as far as I'm concerned. They're devils, they're evil. That is a bad place, and it's got some divine retribution in store. The Bible says, 'Let no man put himself above another.' That's what they've done. And it'll come back to them. They'll get back what they gave.

"When I was in prison," he said, "I heard blacks talk about how they were discriminated against, how they were persecuted or repressed. I thought they were making too much of it. But after what happened to me up there, I know what they meant. Now I know what the blacks in this country and the Mormons a hundred years ago must have experienced, the kind of hatred they were up against. It is a terrible thing."

I've tried to understand Sam Potter, first his crimes and then his politics, which don't spring so much from his mind as from his heart and the foundation of his being.

He said that he scuffled with the deputies over the court order because the judge was wrong and he, Sam Potter, was right. It had nothing to do with the union, he said; it had to do with things that no judge can touch. There is only his word on that.

But his conviction for tax evasion is enlightening. Sam simply did not file a tax return one year. There are many ways of avoiding taxes. The right accountants and lawyers can make a millionaire's tax bill look like a pauper's, and without risk of jail or even reprimand. Others simply cheat in ways both crude or sophisticated, and then hope to escape attention. But Sam Potter did none of these things. For him, no subterfuge, no conniving, no stealth. By failing to file a return, he virtually guaranteed that he would be noticed, and prosecuted, and jailed. That is what happened. He waited to be brought to court, and he was. And he served his ten months, minus nine days' credit for teaching a prison course on the U.S. Constitution.

A matter of principle, he said. No matter that without our taxes the nation would be in a mess. No matter that part of Sam Potter's tax bill goes for guns and bullets and airplanes to keep the Russians from walking up on the beach at Malibu and Carmel. No matter. The income tax is wrong, he insisted. Unconstitutional. And he kept insisting the point all the way to the penitentiary, and he still says it, though he now files his returns. He missed his family and he's made his gesture.

There is no way of knowing for certain whether Sam Potter ever intended to install his own version of a constitutional government in Fremont County. After a year of poking around the Radical Right, I do know now that while the Posse Comitatus may be a lot of things—nettlesome, absurd, self-important, quixotic, overblown, maybe even subversive—it isn't cohesive enough or strong enough to begin to occupy even so vulnerable a place as Fremont County. Typically enough of groups on the feuding, fragmented Radical Right, there is a single Posse Comitatus in name only. It really exists in isolated clumps that tend to act both independently and ineffectively.

But Fremont County didn't know that, which is typical as well. The Radical Right operates behind a one-way mirror; it sees the world outside (even if the vision is sometimes faulty), but what goes on in the right's tight, closed system never gets to the other side. We go on what we read in newspapers and what we see in TV news reports, and that is a pitifully shallow, ill-informed melange of myth, rumor, and random fact.

Sam Potter was genuinely perplexed, mystified, by what happened to him in Fremont County. So is every liberal city-dweller to whom I've told the story. "It should have worked," they all say. "They should have gotten along."

It would have been different, I think, if Fremont County had stopped to listen to Sam Potter and if Sam had judged more acutely the people among whom he chose to live. There's a lesson in this. It comes from both ends. Most of us are scared of extremes and we shun extremists. Their words slide past us and don't penetrate. Extremists on the right don't understand that. They overestimate their own strength, at the same time scorning all the varieties of thought out there in mass America. In ideological debate, they will fix on an arcane point of disagreement and blithely dismiss a dozen points of concordance. This is one of the reasons that the Radical Right is perpetually estranged from the bulk of us who live and work and vote in this country (which is not to say, however, that it has failed to influence us in some profound ways).

What happened in Fremont County was that Sam Potter and the ordinary folk never understood each other, and never tried. The union never had a blessed chance.

That still leaves open the question of whether Sam Potter actually tried to set up his own government in Fremont County. At first I was sure that Sam had been the victim of a xenophobic lynch mob in panic; he seemed too bright to have seriously considered such a ridiculous enterprise. I haven't changed my opinion of his intelligence. But the more people I've met who think the way he does, the easier it has become to imagine Sam Potter and a few of his friends sitting together one night and convincing themselves that they needed to do this deed for the good of the nation. It is the very kind of dumb and hopeless enterprise on which dozens of men on the Radical Right like Sam Potter have wasted their time and money and energy.

In a way, I'd like to think that he did try what everybody in Fremont

County thinks he tried. If it's true, then I know that Sam Potter really is a man born out of time, that he doesn't really belong in this modern age. He isn't like the rest of us. He won't back down. He spurns compromise. There's no place for him now; he can't even run to the mountains for sanctuary. But 200 years ago, he'd have had no trouble in this country. If the world he saw had been wrong, he would have marched west into the woods with an ax and a rifle and he would have made his own world, one that suited him exactly. And when that one started to go bad, he'd have marched off and done it all over again, another fifty miles farther west.

That's why I pity him instead of fearing him. And that's why the people of Fremont County—mostly decent and good people, whatever he says about them—were wrong to shun Sam Potter. On closer examination, Sam Potter seems not so much a monster as a relic.

That's a romantic and softheaded notion, maybe. I mention it here only to underscore the point that I struck out on this journey into dark and secluded places expecting to encounter ghouls, and I found much, much more. There were sinners and saints, geniuses and dolts, men cunning and men obvious.

Occasionally it was even possible to know who was which.

1

A thicket of names, a confusion of voices. The White Students League and Women for a Constitutional Government. Citizens Alert for Morality, Citizens for Immigration Reform, Citizens for God and Country, Citizens for the Republic. The Green Mountain Riflemen and the Yellow Dog Political Fund. National Association for the Advancement of White People. North American Anglo Alliance. Committee for a Free Estonia, Committee for Godly and Profitable Living, Committee to Establish the Gold Standard, Committee of Ten Million. Happiness of Womanhood, Inc., and Free Nationalist Commandos.

A couple of glances at Laird Wilcox's *Directory of the American Right* is enough to dispel forever the notion that the Radical Right consists mainly of Klansmen and Nazis. The directory lists 1,596 organizations in the United States that identify with one aspect or another of what are generally accepted as right-wing positions. Within that group is a distinct division between truly radical and conservative—"kosher conservative," as some extremists put it, with considerable enmity. This book is about the radicals of the other side of that surprisingly clear line. The distinction bears explanation later; for now, note that it exists, and note as well that even with the movement reduced to its most extreme elements, there still remains a bewildering variety of viewpoints with an organization to accommodate every one. Details of ideology are crucial. It is not at all uncommon for a radical to start his own group after rejecting several established ones.

None, he will have discovered, has grasped the particularities of understanding quite as deftly as he.

Those armies of one are inconsequential. Many exist only as long as the single term of a post-office-box rental. But while they appear and vanish, there are perhaps fifty groups that seem to endure, that are important within the movement's confines. Listing and classifying them is worthwhile, since on the Radical Right, knowing the game—let alone the players—is often impossible without a program.

Start with the oldest and best-known of America's purveyors of intolerance, the Ku Klux Klans. Use of the plural is intentional, since there may be as many as forty separate Klan groups around the country.[1] They are distinct from one another. They rarely cooperate. They recognize no central authority, since there is none to recognize. There is no licensing or franchising board that grants the brand name Ku Klux Klan. Becoming a Klan leader is as easy as outfitting oneself and several friends in robes and hoods (satin is preferred) and ordering stationery with a blood-red KKK logo. That is precisely how it has been done, a score of times or more in the last dozen years.

For that reason, referring to "the Klan" is inaccurate and misleading, though it is an almost universal practice among journalists.*

There are two important Klan groups, each closely identified with a single aggressive leader. Bob Shelton and his United Klans of America in Tuscaloosa, Alabama, led segregationist resistance to civil-rights activity in the South during the Sixties. As late as 1977, the UKA was thought to outnumber all other Klan factions.[2]

But beginning in 1975, when he broke with a rival, Bill Wilkinson has been steadily drawing men and money into his Invisible Empire, Knights of the Ku Klux Klan, which is based in Denham Springs, Louisiana. Wilkinson now claims that he has surpassed Shelton's UKA in membership.[3] The Invisible Empire is by far the most active and most visible Klan.

Wilkinson formed the Invisible Empire after splitting from the Knights of the Ku Klux Klan, then headed by David Duke, with headquarters in Metairie, Louisiana. Duke was a media darling: Grand Wizard at twenty-six, tall, blond, and handsome, college-educated and reasonably articu-

---

* The Federal Bureau of Investigation took advantage of the confusion during its counterintelligence program against some Radical Right groups in the Sixties. When an official of a small splinter Klan was arrested for sodomy, the FBI leaked the news to some of its press sources. An FBI memo from the period speculates that this would help to discredit all Klans, since press and public rarely make a distinction between the organizations. In fact, while the general rhetoric is standard, there often are drastic differences in strategy and purposes among the various groups.

late. By 1977, Duke estimated that he had appeared on more than a hundred television and radio talk shows, with eighteen appearances in New York alone.[4] He has been interviewed by Barbara Walters, photographed by Candice Bergen, the subject of articles in *Playboy* and *Oui*. He was, however, unable to consistently muster attendance for his Klan's public appearances. All light, no heat, was the general appraisal from Wilkinson and Shelton. In 1980, Duke left the K-KKK to his former Grand Dragon, Don Black, and founded the National Association for the Advancement of White People (NAAWP), in New Orleans. Within a year, Black and several members of his Klan had been convicted for conspiring to start a revolution in Dominica. The group is insignificant now.

The National Knights of the Ku Klux Klan, led by James Venable in Decatur, Georgia, at one time was a strong challenger to Shelton's UKA. The National Knights may have closer connections than any other Klan faction to the original Klan of the nineteenth century, but pedigree counts for little in these circles. Wilkinson claims to have siphoned off the militants from the National Knights; these days, Venable's group is heavy on trappings and ceremony, but light on the marches and confrontational politics that are important to Wilkinson's strategy. "Venable's into socializing, not mobilizing," is the way one self-professed Klansman has put it.[5]

There are a few other Klans worth mentioning, if only once. The California Knights of the Ku Klux Klan, in Fallbrook, California, once were associated with Duke's Klan. Now the Californians are independent, led by Tom Metzger, a TV repairman who won the 1980 Democratic nomination for the state's Forty-third District seat in Congress. Dale Reusch's Ohio Knights of the Ku Klux Klan and the Independent Northern and Southern Klans (based in Indiana) are both splinters from Venable's National Knights.

The Southern National party, organized in Memphis by Robert E. Lee McCampbell, shares the nominal Klan goals—e.g., an end to affirmative-action programs and to forced school-busing; welfare reform; strict (and small) immigration quotas; and revival of segregation—all without explicit racial rhetoric, however. The SNP stresses separatism and states' rights; its literature proclaims that it is "dedicated to the creation of an independent southern republic." The SNP claims 4,000 members on its mailing list; and one party leader, oil and gas attorney Elmore Greaves, plans to run for governor of Mississippi on the SNP ticket.[6]

The National States Rights Party is led by two men: Edward Fields and lawyer J. B. Stoner, who briefly represented James Earl Ray, assassin of Martin Luther King, Jr.[7] Stoner was indicted in the 1958 bombing of the

Bethel Baptist Church in Birmingham, but for more than ten years successfully resisted extradition from his home state of Georgia.

The NSRP uses for its logo the lightning-bolt insignia of Hitler's Waffen SS corps, and its monthly newspaper is called the *Thunderbolt.* The party and its paper are almost exclusively racist, with lesser emphasis on an anti-Communist message. Many stories in the *Thunderbolt* are reprinted items from other periodicals, usually about sensational crimes committed by blacks against whites. "News Media Suppresses News on 'Missing and Murdered' Whites," one recent issue was headlined. Articles inside were titled: "Kills Girl with Acid," "Slow Painful Beheading," and "Will Race Mixing Doom Mormons?" A story that had received brief national attention a few weeks earlier—an argument between a taxi driver and CBS anchorman Dan Rather that included a high-speed run through city streets in Chicago—got a special twist in the *Thunderbolt:* "Negro Terrorizes Dan Rather" was the headline on a story that went on to suggest that Rather "feature this personal experience with African behavior on his '60 Minutes' Sunday night show."[8]

Stoner asserts that he is a "white racist,"[9] and his antipathy embraces both Jews and blacks so forcefully that the NSRP takes on aspects of a plainclothes Nazi group. A number of articles in the *Thunderbolt* in the past three years have been sympathetic to the pro-Communist Palestine Liberation Organization: "Jews Dynamiting of Arab Homes Ignored by World Press," said one headline.[10] Criticism of Russian Communists, meanwhile, often hinges on charges that they are dominated by Jews and linked to Israeli interests.*

There are subtler shadings of radical thought. Liberty Lobby is an anti-Zionist (though not explicitly anti-Semitic) political group based in Washington, D.C., best-known for its weekly tabloid, the *Spotlight,* with a circulation of over 300,000.[11] Though his name never appears on the masthead of the *Spotlight* and only rarely anyplace in the newspaper, Willis Carto is the founder of Liberty Lobby and owner of its publishing operation. He is also the major sponsor of the Institute for Historical Review, which attempts to disprove that Nazi Germany set out to systematically exterminate the Jews.[12] Articles about the institute and its work, written by IHR

* Nobody on the Radical Right has yet successfully confronted the apparent fact that Russia is anti-Zionist and that Israel's Arab enemies, especially the PLO, Iraq, and Libya, all have strong associations with the USSR. The most popular solution to the quandary is to claim that Israel is actually allied to Russian Communists, and that Middle Eastern tensions are therefore a sham engineered by conspiratorial Jews to mislead the free world—an unlikely proposition, considering the evidence. Here every Jew-hating anti-Communist doctrine chases its own ideological tail, and looking past the apparent contradiction posed by the evidence requires a true act of faith.

employee Tom Marcellus, frequently appear in the *Spotlight,* although the Carto connection is not usually mentioned.

The *Spotlight*'s wide circulation confers considerable power on whomever is ultimately responsible for its editorial slant and content, so Carto's goodwill is important on the right. In the last several years, Carto has looked favorably on the Reverend John Harrell with his Christian-Patriots Defense League, and on Lyndon LaRouche with his U.S. Labor Party, National Caucus of Labor Committees, and an assortment of front groups.

Harrell is a former Methodist minister whose gospel has become a combination of extremist politics, segregation, and that version of biblical prophecy which has become known as the Israel Identity movement (of which, much more in chapter 5). Beneath a single umbrella, Harrell has gathered a system of five different religious and right-wing organizations. The central one is the Conservative Churches of America, which sponsors all the others through its status as a nonprofit religious organization.

Of the four entities that the church supports, only one charges dues: the Paul Revere Club, which asks $5 a month, in return for which the member and his family are said to be guaranteed sanctuary at any of the several survival bases that Harrell's groups maintain in the Midwest in case of a national crisis. The Citizens Emergency Defense System and the Save America Gun Club are both adjuncts of the Christian-Patriots Defense League. Once or twice a year, the C-PDL holds survival seminars called "freedom festivals" in southern Illinois. Usually they attract about 1,500 people, an enormous gathering on the Radical Right. The seminars include instruction in the Identity faith, with its strong anti-Jewish emphasis, along with three days of somewhat perfunctory paramilitary training for a smaller number of members.

The *Spotlight* and Liberty Lobby's radio shows (daily on 470 stations) have given Harrell's groups favorable coverage. Liberty Lobby representatives, in turn, have addressed the assembled multitudes at Harrell's "freedom festivals."

Of all the curious manifestations of political thought on the American right, none is more startling, more Byzantine, more improbable than those advanced by LaRouche's National Caucus of Labor Committees and various front groups, including the U.S. Labor party, the Fusion Energy Foundation, the National Anti-Drug Coalition, and the National Democratic Policy Committee. The NCLC operates an international Teletype system[13] and publishes the periodicals *New Solidarity, Campaigner, Executive Intelligence Review, Investigative Leads,* and *Fusion*—this last a polished monthly magazine full of highly accurate technical information about nuclear-energy research.[14]

NCLC operatives gather intelligence material for use in the group's New Solidarity Press Service and the publications. They are most memorable when they stand in the lobbies of major airports hawking copies of *Fusion* and bearing hand-lettered pronuclear signs: MORE NUKES, LESS KOOKS; MORE PEOPLE DIED AT CHAPPAQUIDDICK THAN IN NUCLEAR PLANT ACCIDENTS; THREE MILE ISLAND IS BUILT BETTER THAN JANE FONDA.

This is especially striking because LaRouche and the NCLC were thoroughly identified with the militant left until 1973. LaRouche formed the NCLC from activists who had been part of the 1968 student strike at Columbia University.[15] The group originally was part of the Students for a Democratic Society (SDS).[16]

In 1975, LaRouche began to make contacts across a wide spectrum on the Radical Right. One of the most important was with Carto. Some sources claim that Carto funneled right-wing contributions through Liberty Lobby into LaRouche's 1976 presidential-campaign accounts.[17]

The approval of Carto, who is influential and respected on the right, would be a boon to anyone attempting to establish himself as LaRouche seems to be trying. Carto's publishing enterprises have sold NCLC material, and the *Spotlight* endorsed the NCLC.[18] Their association became so controversial within the movement that in January of 1980 Liberty Lobby issued a position paper defending the USLP as a legitimate ally of right-wing interests. The *Spotlight* still reprints occasional articles from the New Solidarity Press Service.

Still, it would be a mistake to make too much of the LaRouche-Carto connection, or for that matter, of any association on the Radical Right. Alliances in the movement tend to be brief and perfunctory. Carto is known to be cautious in his alliances, protective almost to the point of jealousy when he guards his reputation and his interests. Given his wariness, and the universal fragility of coalitions on the Radical Right, there is little chance of a deep and lasting bond between Carto and LaRouche.

Carto, Bob Shelton of the UKA, Robert Welch of the John Birch Society, and Bob DePugh form the core of what might be called the "old guard" of the extreme American right. Welch and the JBS are discussed more fully in chapter 9. It is enough to say here that the organization is precisely as it has often been portrayed: utterly anti-Communist and conspiracy-minded, very much a reflection of Welch, its founder and director.

DePugh has been an ideological leader on the right for more than twenty years. In 1961, he formed the Minutemen, a group that was supposed to operate as an underground resistance system, but which sought national publicity in its early years with public weapons training and military exercises. DePugh called the Minutemen a "counterinsurgency group"; others termed it simply "subversive" and "revolutionary." With his bent for inflammatory words, his penchant for intelligence-gathering, and his weakness for harassing his enemies, DePugh became detested and feared by the left. For more than a decade he reigned as a political bogeyman of the most fearsome variety.

DePugh served four years in federal prisons during the Seventies for convictions on firearms charges and bond-jumping. (He was a fugitive for more than a year.) Since then, the Minutemen have been far reduced in numbers and much less active. DePugh's main political enterprise now is the Committee of Ten Million, which he envisions as a gathering of right-wing interests. Though he asks only $10 for a lifetime membership, he has achieved far less than 1 percent of his optimistic membership goal.

Still, DePugh remains a real force on the Radical Right. His *Blueprint for Victory* handbook, in its several editions, is as close as anyone has come to setting down a manifesto of the Radical Right, and leaders of small single-issue groups on the right often seek his help and advice. Several years ago, he led a fruitless effort to form a right-wing leadership council. DePugh is especially popular within those single-issue groups that advocate tax revolt and oppose gun-control legislation.

Among the so-called tax-strike organizations are the U.S. Taxpayers' Union, the National Taxpayers' Union, Americans for Constitutional Taxation, and Your Heritage Protective Association, all of which advocate some form of tax rebellion, usually on a constitutional basis.

The National Rifle Association is by far the largest and most influential of groups opposing gun-control legislation—so large and powerful in fact, that it has outgrown the Radical Right. The Second Amendment Committee and the National Association to Keep and Bear Arms are smaller, even more vocal versions of the NRA. The National Pistol and Rifle Association is the creation of Dr. John Grady, a physician in Benton, Tennessee, an activist notable not only for his opposition to gun control but for his alliances with "pro-life" and "pro-family" groups. He is a quiet but considerable influence within the movement, and a rarity in bridging the gap between conservative and radical factions while retaining the respect of both.

The more radical elements of the tax-revolt and firearms organizations often overlap in the Posse Comitatus. Though the group claims membership in every state except Hawaii, its actions are notable only in Missouri, Wisconsin, California, and Oregon. It is strongest by far in Wisconsin, where members of the group are reported to have served unofficial subpoenas on forty-three state and county officials, ordering them to appear before a "Christian Citizens' grand jury." (None did.) The Citizens Law Enforcement and Research Committee (CLERC) is an offspring of the Posse;[19] CLERC and the Posse both hold that national taxation is unconstitutional, that elected representatives and bureaucrats have overstepped their constitutional bounds, and that the only legitimate power to make and enforce laws belongs to entities at the county level. Bearing arms without restriction is a constitutional privilege, they say. Thus, there is a considerable mixing with the Posse of tax-strikers, gun-control opponents, and remnants of the Minutemen.[20] Through CLERC, the Posse is said to be tied to the Reverend William Gale, cofounder of the Identity religious movement.

Then there are the Nazis. The temptation is to omit them altogether, so negligible are they in numbers and credibility. They operate out on the nether edges of the right, virtually impotent except for a phenomenal ability to attract press coverage far beyond their real significance. That magnetic effect helps to explain the only success that a National Socialist has ever enjoyed in a popular election here. Harold Covington, then leader of the National Socialist Party of America (NSPA) won 43 percent of the vote in the 1980 Republican primary for the attorney-general race in North Carolina. Covington received far more press attention as a Nazi than any other twenty-six-year-old political unknown ever could have expected.*

American Nazis are divided into at least six fragments grouped around two poles. At one end is the National Socialist White People's party (NSWPP), descended from George Lincoln Rockwell's American Nazi party. The NSWPP is probably the largest and best-organized Nazi group, though size and organization are strictly relative.

Opposing the NSWPP, and at least vaguely allied, are several groups, most prominent among them the NSPA, which provoked a national brouhaha in 1977 when it threatened to march in uniform through the Chicago suburb of Skokie, Illinois. The NSPA at the time was headed by Frank Collin, whose father later was revealed to be a German-Jewish immigrant named Max Cohn. Collin is serving a seven-year sentence in an Illinois penitentiary on a conviction of eight counts of sexually molesting young boys at party headquarters in Chicago.

---

* Covington has another explanation: "There are many closet Nazis in the Republican Party," he was quoted as saying in the *Kansas City Star,* May 8, 1980. "Most conservatives are closet Nazis. If you scratch a conservative you'll find a Nazi underneath, just as if you scratch a liberal you'll find a Communist underneath."

The National Socialist White Workers party (NSWWP) in San Francisco is the largest West Coast Nazi group. The party and its leader, Allen Vincent, got extensive publicity when Vincent rented a storefront in a San Francisco neighborhood and opened the Rudolf Hess Bookstore. The group got further publicity as the subject of a documentary film, *California Reich,* which received a 1977 Academy Award nomination.

There are more of them: more alphabet soup, much more ado about nothing. They all attract malcontents who drift over from the fringes of other groups—and the fringes of the Invisible Empire or the National States Rights party are very fringey indeed. That is virtually the Nazis' only connection with the rest of the Radical Right. This movement chooses its own heroes, and the Nazis just don't qualify.

WITNESSING

Left and Right

(LAIRD WILCOX has researched and written on contemporary political movements for more than fifteen years. He publishes annual directories and bibliographies of both the American left and right. During the mid-Sixties, he was a member of the Students for a Democratic Society and a leader among student leftists at the University of Kansas. He continues to study political movements of every stripe, but his sympathies have shifted.)

"I started out being liberal in my teens. My father is very liberal; he was a socialist when he was in college. But my mother is pretty conservative, and her mother was an admirer of Senator McCarran, so I got it from both sides. And I found myself being sympathetic with the left because it seemed so exciting and adventurous, although it also felt a little crazy. I had internalized the point of view that intellectual people, sincere people, were all liberals and leftists, while only Neanderthals, bigots, and reactionaries were right-wingers or conservatives.

"I functioned under that premise for three or four years. I was editor of a leftist student paper and active in the civil-rights movement. Then I began to analyze this stuff, and I never could get really caught up in all of the selfless and self-sacrificing bullshit. I did it for a while, but it never felt right. I broke with the SDS in 1966 because of increasing signs of totalitarianism, nihilistic behavior, and drugs. I detected an awful lot of really heavy self-destructiveness, real self-hatred, suicide real and symbolic. And there was this crazy kind of immediate identification with anything that was an enemy of their own culture, whether it was the Viet Cong, acid-rock groups, other races, other cultures, whatever.

"As a participant and observer in both movements, I'd say that leftists generally tend to be much more other-directed. They tend to value other cultures, other races, and other countries over their own. They tend not to identify with their own self-interests. Instead, they're altruistic and self-sacrificing. They are also ever so ready to sacrifice their own people and anybody else in the service of their ideology. A typical example of this is busing, which has been an intolerable misery for thousands upon thousands of white families and a lot of black ones, too. Yet busing has been a moral imperative of the left.

"They're not pragmatic in that sense; instead, they're rigidly idealistic and ideological. There is probably a more rigid orthodoxy among some elements of the radical left—and I'm not even talking about the Marxists here, just doctrinaire liberals—than you would find among Jerry Falwell's Moral Majority types. The right tends to be much more individualistic and inner-directed. There's a funny kind of egotism on the right, maybe even a selfish egotism.

"Generally, conservatives and right-wingers have a great deal of faith in the market system, economic freedom, although there are a lot of exceptions, like self-serving businessmen who support import quotas. But in general, conservatives have a very healthy self-esteem. They're willing to take care of themselves, and they think other people should take care of themselves, too. They really do see it as the better system. It's not a niggardly selfishness like 'Let the bastards work or starve.' They just believe that in the long run the only kind of system that will really work is enlightened self-interest.

"I've noticed other differences. Leftists and liberals are very comfortable dealing with abstractions and intangibles, but they seem to get nervous as hell when you start trying to get concrete. Right-wingers, on the other hand, don't want to hear about abstractions. The only thing they want to know is 'How does this affect me, right now?' Recently I had a long discussion with several members of the Socialist Workers party, and I picked up again on leftists' willingness to identify themselves with a movement that's bigger than themselves. You don't see that on the right. The closest thing to it is patriotism and a love for America—but even there, America is not a movement, it's a nation with pluralist values, and right-wingers realize that.

"The nationalism you find on the right seems jingoistic, but it's really more intelligent than it looks. On the left, it's different, this need to merge with some sort of mass movement, to subordinate your own interests to the interests of a cause, a social cause, a collective cause. The right has no equivalent of that. The kind of rightists you find in a group like the Christian-Patriots Defense League, for example, are basically working-class people, pragmatic and goal-oriented. They're interested in their belief system because they think it will make their world better immediately. There's none of this pie-in-the-sky 'when the revolution comes.' They want less inflation, they want their kids to go to neighborhood schools, they want to have jobs and not have to compete unfairly with blacks because of Affirmative Action. Maybe they don't like blacks, and they want to be free not to like blacks and not to have to live next to them. That differs from the typical member of the Socialist Workers party, who basically is not interested in the present at all, except to reject it. The right tends to be preoccupied with the present and the past, whereas the left is almost totally preoccupied with the future.

"On the right and the left both, you find a self-righteousness. With conservatives, it's a moral-superiority attitude. They feel they're right with God, and you're not. Whereas with leftists, it's that their motives are morally pure: They're not interested in profit, they're not in it for personal gain, they just want everybody to be happy, even if it kills them. It's a moral superiority of 'I am ever so selfless and self-sacrificing, and I'll sacrifice myself and my family and anybody else for the good of the whole,' while the self-righteousness among conservatives goes something like 'I am right with God. My beliefs are ordained as being sacred and pure, and therefore I am morally superior.'

"In 1966 I rejected the whole self-sacrificing guilt trip of the left, and I went off by myself and struggled with it for a couple of years, really agonizing over it. It was like losing faith, in a way. I realized that I had made a mistake. I had never really felt comfortable saying the things I had said, never felt as if I belonged with those people. Once I admitted to myself that it was okay to change some of the ways I had been thinking, I felt very free, like I was back where I belonged, in a place that was much more suited to the person that I am.

"I went through a period of experimentation and overreaction. I became very curious about the incredible excesses of the student left, why they did the things they did and why I had done it. I began to study ideological movements, read just tons of stuff, some of the best of which was the work of Eric Hoffer, especially *The True Believer* and *A Passionate State of Mind,* both very important influences.

"I went around two or three years sounding like a right-winger, and since then I've gone back to a neutral position. But I have to say that if I let the chips fall where they may, if I analyze all my beliefs and my tendencies and my personality, I probably am a kind of libertarian conservative if I am what I am without trying to be anything else. I'm liberal in some areas, like freedom of speech and the press, classic liberal positions which most liberals are not very consistent in. My economic beliefs and my foreign-policy beliefs are quite conservative, anti-Communist, anti-Russian. I think those bastards are out to get us. The evidence is stacking up pretty high, and a lot of people who were liberals in the Sixties are now becoming scared-shitless right-wingers in the Eighties because they've come to realize that we could get beaten in a war, largely through our own mistakes and self-deception. I don't think I'm alone in that respect."

2

Joe McCarthy, if he were alive, probably wouldn't belong to the Radical Right. Jerry Falwell doesn't, though some who admire him are close enough to bear mentioning. Robert Welch and his John Birch Society qualify, but just barely. Sure, Nazis and Klansmen are automatic members. But so are some other people whose politics are just as extreme, if not nearly as notorious.

A term like "Radical Right" poses pitfalls, questions. Where do you draw the line? Who gets in and who doesn't?

The calls aren't all easy. Instinct is no help, for "radical" is all a matter of perspective. What's outré to Tom Hayden may be the soul of rock-ribbed righteousness to a woman who spends four evenings a week working for a national antiabortion bill. She in turn has her own idea of unpardonable excess, while to others she is an object of contempt for having allowed herself to become sidetracked from the fight against America's real enemies. The point is that there has to be some standard beyond simply offending liberals, some absolutes that stand up to the vagaries of personal opinion.

Stare at the clutter long enough and patterns emerge. Labels are no help, but observation is. It becomes apparent quickly that hating communism is insufficient—that's a given in this territory. But to abhor the vaguest suggestion of socialism, not just as a matter of principle but with genuine visceral passion, is another matter. Between the true collectivist and the true individualist is a conflict of two sets of mind, two ways of living life, and everyone on the Radical Right feels that difference down to the bone.

Now the earmarks are more obvious. Look for energy and fastness of conviction; radicals know what they know. Look, too, for alienation and disaffection. Almost by definition, radicals are a minority. True radicals are on the outside looking in, disconnected from the sources of power. (The Reverend Falwell fails here, if for no other reason.) True radicals are the unwashed, political lepers. It is a delight to watch a mainstream politician squirming as they approach. They've gone too far, see, and they're grubby, unpresentable. Oh, he'll take their money and take their votes, if they promise to keep a proper distance. But he won't invite them to the party until they clean up and put on ties.

That suggests another standard. Everyone in this book is a revolutionary. Some prefer prayers and petitions to armed force, but all of them have a vision of a world that is greatly different from what prevails now. They are all perfectly serious about making it happen. Their beliefs are absolute. But filling in the shades of belief is another task yet. The Radical Right is a wild patchwork of ideology. Clash, not compatibility, is the rule. Many of the people in this book don't get along with one another, and they won't be happy keeping company within these bindings.

"An incredible variety of people" is the way one member described an early meeting of the Committee of Ten Million. "You name it, it was there. Smart people? I talked to very bright and very serious people, quite credible and very personable. Crazies? They were there, too, some of the damnedest nuts you ever saw, real screwballs. I got backed into a corner by this Ku Klux Klansman from Iowa spouting some of the wildest ideas I've ever heard. They're all here, whatever you're looking for. That's the way the right is."

Dogma, then, is at best a crude template. Just when you're ready to conclude that everybody on the right wing treasures the Constitution, you find one who, while nestling comfortably against all the other acute angles of the classic form, thinks the Bill of Rights is a mess and ought to be redone. One who sees a Jewish conspiracy behind the Bolshevik Revolution finds himself chin-to-chin with another who is convinced that Communists have made pawns of well-meaning Jews. Many of the people in this book mix their politics with an equal part of Christianity in some form, but there are at least a few who grumble that thinking too hard about God takes your mind off the job at hand.

One distinction, however, does hold up: To use racial terms when discussing politics or social ills is radical in our society. That's not an arbitrary judgment but an observation of matters as they are today in this country. We have no greater political taboo, and it's one that the Radical Right cheerfully, doggedly, resolutely violates. That helps to explain the movement's perpetual status as a pariah in mainstream politics.

The targets haven't changed a great deal since the mid–nineteenth century—blacks, Jews, and immigrants. There are minor differences, though. More than a century ago, the Know-Nothings despised Catholic immigrants from Europe and Ireland; today, their current equivalents are illegal aliens from Mexico and refugees from Haiti, Cuba, and the Far East. (Catholics, who inspired such fear three or four generations ago, now are accepted as members in several of the Ku Klux Klans.)

Understand that any generalization about a movement as diverse as this one is a rickety construct indeed. That said, it is generally true that blacks are only secondary targets for the Radical Right's bilious invective. Though they are despised and disparaged by some, the prevailing attitude in most quarters is a sort of benign distaste. "I don't like blacks, but I don't hate 'em, either," said a woman at a gathering of the Christian-Patriots Defense League last year as she interrupted a discussion of racial matters. "Those people need our help. There's no people on earth that's been used and manipulated more than they have." That drew a chorus of "Amen" and "You're right," to which she added: "And we know who's been pulling their strings, don't we?"

Enter the constant and abiding villain of the Radical Right, object of unfettered venom and enmity reserved for none other. The Radical Right is at war with Jews. In a year of research for this book, I heard Jews described as spoilers of Christian culture, as genetic offspring of Satan, as the ultimate source of evil on the earth. In various quarters, they are held to account for the spread of pornography, for the two world wars, and for high inflation. Within the Radical Right is a body of myth and spurious literature that advances the notion that Jews, over centuries, have organized a plot to control the world, and that communism is its latest manifestation.

For most of us, that is fanciful nonsense, but many on the Radical Right hold it as an article of faith, so strong and exclusive that it separates them from the merely conservative or reactionary. The John Birch Society, in all repects but one, is markedly conservative. It supports a reduced bureaucracy and reduced taxes, it espouses a free-market economic approach, it sees national strength in church and family, and it actively opposes the spread of Communist influence around the globe. All are standard conservative positions. But Robert Welch, the society's founder and director, also believes in an international cabal with roots in the eighteenth century. And while the JBS avoids all racial references, that belief in a master conspiracy is enough to put Welch and his organization on the other side of a distinct line between conservative and Radical Right.

The conspiracy theory is worth exploring here. Not everyone on the Radical Right subscribes to the theory—not in public, at least—but it is a fundamental part of the movement's polemic and politics. To understand the conspiracy and the world view behind it is to see clearly corners of the Radical Right that would otherwise remain hopelessly obscure.

Since 1776 (goes the theory) world politics has been manipulated by a secret elitist group that can be traced to the Order of the Bavarian Illuminati, founded at the University of Ingolstadt by a defrocked Jesuit named Adam Weishaupt.[1] This group, its goals and methods known only to a privileged few, seeks absolute control over the earth by one-world government. To achieve their ends, the masters of the conspiracy—termed *"insiders"* by Robert Welch—draw within their organization leaders in national politics, economics, education, and finance. In return for their cooperation and absolute fealty to the cause, the members are rewarded with glimpses into the depths of the conspiracy and with assistance in rising even higher in their fields.

Quoting Welch: ". . . deception within deception was the very essence of the system. There were echelons of power—and of corresponding illumination—all the way from a broad base at the bottom to a very small Inner Circle at the top. And many a man has met with horrible retribution for overrating the level to which he thought he had climbed within the hierarchy of the Conspirators. The Duc d'Orléans in the early 1790s and Richard Nixon in the early 1970s were outstanding and obvious examples."[2]

Such talk—more than his determined anticommunism—gives Welch credibility in some quarters of the Radical Right.

Some of the most effective agents of the conspiracy (the theory goes) have been international banking concerns, particularly those of the House of Rothschild, J. P. Morgan, and the Rockefeller family. In the nineteenth century, theorists claim, the Rothschilds became rich by provoking wars that they then financed, and this turmoil furthered the aims of the conspiracy by making nations dependent upon the financial resources of the banking giants.

The Civil War, according to this theory, was brought about not by slavery but by the conscious efforts of the Rothschilds and Benjamin Disraeli, whose chief agent in the United States was Judah Benjamin, first adviser to Jefferson Davis. But Abraham Lincoln upset their plans by refusing to take out loans to finance the nation's war debt; instead, he infuriated the Rothschilds by issuing his own bonds—"greenback dollars"—for which imper- tinence he was assassinated by a Rothschild agent, John Wilkes Booth.

Most versions of the theory put a racial cast on the conspiracy by noting that the Rothschilds are Jewish. The supposedly conniving and devious nature of the conspirators draws on racial stereotypes. Welch and the Birch scenario diverge from the others on this point.

"Anti-Semites have played into the hands of the conspiracy by trying to portray the entire conspiracy as Jewish," writes Birch researcher Gary Allen. "Nothing could be farther from the truth. The traditionally Anglo- Saxon J. P. Morgan and Rockefeller banking institutions have played a key role in the conspiracy . . . it is just as unreasonable and immoral to blame all Jews for the crimes of the Rothschilds as it is to hold all Baptists accountable for the crimes of the Rockefellers."[3]

Communism (the theory continues) is a tool of the master conspirators. Karl Marx's *Communist Manifesto* is actually a rehashing of Adam Weis- haupt's original program, and Marx was commissioned to do the work, having been instructed to attack the established orders and their founda- tions of religion, property, and nationalism. Conspiratologists claim evi- dence that an international banking consortium—including Morgan and Rockefeller interests, Jacob Schiff and Max Warburg of the Kuhn-Loeb investment bank, and Lord Alfred Milner of England—financed the Bol- shevik Revolution and kept it alive during its struggling years in order to further the aims of the conspiracy.

More conspiratorial connections, according to theory: Felix Warburg, brother of Kuhn-Loeb's Max Warburg, became prime mover in the estab- lishment of the Federal Reserve Board. Lord Milner, with financing from Cecil Rhodes and the Rothschilds, established a secret society known as the Round Table, which controlled President Wilson's trusted adviser, "Colonel" House. House's influence led to the formation of the League of Nations, the first attempt at a one-world governing body, and to a Treaty of Versailles that was responsible for World War II twenty years later. The American extension of the Round Table became the Council of Foreign Relations, and later the Trilateral Commission, with heavy financing from the Rockefellers. Welch and others claim that by supplying a steady stream of diplomats and advisers—Henry Kissinger, John Foster Dulles, Robert McNamara, Arthur Burns, Averell Harriman, and Dean Rusk among them—to successive administrations, the CFR has actually con- trolled a succession of American administrations. Thus, there's not only an external enemy but an internal one as well, each controlled from the same source.

And it is a malignant source, theory holds, a threat to basic goodness and morality. Welch lists what he calls the fundamental aims of the conspirators:

(1) Destroy all religion, all previously existing government, and all traditional human institutions. (2) Eliminate all conceptions of morality from the human mind. . . . Whatever helps our great revolutionary cause is good; whatever hurts it is bad! (3) Make the power of government absolute, and all-extensive over the lives, possessions, activities and even thoughts of all its subjects. (4) Make everybody labor under governmental planning and control. (5) Divide the products and results of that labor equally among the people. . . . (6) Do away as rapidly as possible with the family unit . . . and consider the life of the individual as of no more value or importance than the life of an ant, or of any other animal.[4]

There are a multitude of variations. One supposes a battle between Anglo-Saxon interests in the cabal (led by the Rockefellers) against Jewish interests (especially the Rothschilds). Another finds links between the Society of Jesus, Freemasonry, and the Illuminati. The U.S. Labor Party promotes its own bizarre version.

But the basic form is the same, and a neat, tidy package it is. The conspiracy is dedicated to secrecy, and thus can never be verified. It seduces the best and the brightest, subverting them to its own perfidious aims; thus, it can never be successfully opposed. It wages universal war against all the traditional values; thus, it provides a single enemy on the other side of the trenches, and it turns every conflict into a skirmish of evil against morality. And because it supposes decisions made mysteriously and darkly, it provides an explanation for all those events that frustrated individuals can't understand and can't seem to control.

The bad guys of the scenario are worth reviewing because they recur constantly in Radical Right arguments. They include the Rockefellers (with their associated subsidiaries, including the Chase Manhattan Bank); the CFR, the Trilateral Commission, and the Bilderberger conferences; virtually any Jewish banker, but especially the House of Rothschild; the Federal Reserve Board; national TV networks and most big newspapers (which, in conspiracy theory, are subverted either by reason of Jewish management or by key personnel belonging to the CFR); and the United Nations. It is an impressive shopping list, a catalog of power, and a nightmare for anyone given to a sense of helplessness. It posits the elite against the ordinary, the shakers against the shaken. It makes an adversary of the establishment, a step that most conservatives find difficult to take. Welch knows that.

"DO YOU WANT IT STRAIGHT?" he headlined one of his monthly bulletins. "If you really do, then be prepared to let us dish it out straight, without any watering down. For the key ingredient this time, of the verbal antitoxin which we intend to serve you at this dispensary, is that bitter word: *Conspiracy*. . . . Now if some of you good patriotic friends dislike our language, as being of too 'extremist' a nature, then you are already backing away from really 'wanting it straight.' "[5]

That's the Radical Right, an embattled minority, Cincinnatus at the gates, fighting not only the Vandals on one front but an apathetic and ill-informed majority at the rear. It's a role that many in the movement seem to relish. And when the enemy is Jewish, then the struggle is nothing less than a holy war. That makes the opposition more easily identifiable, and it defines more clearly the stakes: not just vague notions of decency and the family unit and free enterprise, but Christianity and God's kingdom on earth.

The holy war has produced—and has been sustained by—one of the century's most durable hoaxes, a book called *Protocols of the Meetings of the Learned Elders of Zion*. It purports to be (quoting a note in one popular English-language edition) "the program for Jewish conquest and world domination" in the form of minutes from twenty-four meetings of anonymous Jewish leaders. Quoting again from the Introduction: "the innermost circle of the Rulers of Zion . . . reveals the concerted plan of action of the Jewish Nation developed through the ages and edited by the Elders themselves up to date."

The document seems to have appeared first in czarist Russia, used as propaganda tool against urban Jews in the Bolshevik leadership. Translated into German, it figured in Nazi propaganda during the 1930s.[6] In this country, it remains a classic of conspiratological bigotry, despite an awkward and unwieldy translation.

The work is remarkable for using racial stereotypes in a careful and detailed strategy of subversive intrigue. Protocol eight, part two: "We shall surround our government with a whole world of economists. That is the reason why economic sciences are the principal teaching given to the Jews. Around us again will be a whole constellation of bankers, industrialists and—the main thing—millionaires, because in substance everything will be settled by the question of figures."

Too perfect, too good to be true. But the holy warriors aren't puzzled that conspirators so devious and clever could have allowed so sensitive a document to fall into the hands of a *goy* with a printing press. A few believers, when the point is pressed, will eventually admit that, okay, maybe the Protocols are suspect. But, they will add quickly, what the book has to say is accurate all the same.

Even that admission is rare. In certain segments of the Radical Right, the *Protocols* is as well read and as confidently accepted as the Holy Bible and the U.S. Constitution. Many can quote protocol and verse. And the *Protocols* serves as an ultimate rationale and justification: "You know you can't trust the bankers. Look what it says in the *Protocols.*"

The *Protocols* didn't create anti-Semitism in the Radical Right, but it did help to give it focus. For sixty years, it has served as a primer of the Master Conspiracy. There are thousands of Jew-haters who can recall with clarity, fondness, even nostalgia, their first encounter with the book. They remember their first reading as a moment of enlightenment, a turning point in their lives, a fork in the road marked with signposts large and clear.

WITNESSING

Extracts from Protocols of the Meetings of the Learned Elders of Zion

I, 3: It must be noted that men with bad instincts are more in number than the good, and therefore the best results in governing them are attained by violence and terrorisation, and not by academic discussions. Every man aims at power, everyone would like to become a dictator if only he could, and rare indeed are the men who would not be willing to sacrifice the welfare of all for the sake of securing their own welfare.

I, 11: The political has nothing in common with the moral. The ruler who is governed by the moral is not a skilled politician, and is therefore unstable on the throne. He who wishes to rule must have recourse both to cunning and to make-believe. Great national qualities, like frankness and honesty, are vices in politics. . . . Such qualities must be the attributes of the king-doms of the *goyim,* but we must in no wise be guided by them.

II, 1: It is indispensable for our purpose that wars, so far as possible, should not result in territorial gains: War will thus be brought on to the economic ground, where the nations will not fail to perceive in the assistance we give the strength of our predominance, and this state of things will put both sides at the mercy of our international *Agentur.* . . .

II, 3: Do not suppose for a moment that these statements are empty words: Think carefully of the successes we arranged for Darwinism, Marxism, Nietzsche-ism. To us Jews, at any rate, it should be plain to see what a disintegrating importance these directives have had upon the minds of the *goyim.*

IV, 4: In order to give the *goyim* no time to think and take note, their minds must be diverted toward industry and trade. Thus, all nations will be swallowed up in the pursuit of gain and in the race for it will not take any note of their common foe. . . .

VI, 8: In order that the true meaning of things may not strike the *goyim* before the proper time we shall mask it under an alleged ardent desire to serve the working classes and the great principles of political economy about which our economic theories are carrying on an energetic propaganda.

X, 2: The mob cherishes a special affection and respect for the geniuses of political power and accepts all their deeds of violence with the admiring response: "Rascally, well, yes, it is rascally, but it's clever! . . . A trick, if you like, but how craftily played, how magnificently done, what impudent audacity!"

XI, 4–6: The *goyim* are a flock of sheep, and we are their wolves. And you know what happens when the wolves get hold of the flock? There is another reason also why they will close their eyes: for we shall keep promising them to give back all the liberties we have taken away as soon as we have quelled the enemies of peace and tamed all parties. It is not worthwhile to say anything about how long they will be kept waiting for this return of their liberties. . . .

XIV, 4, 5: Our philosophers will discuss all the shortcomings of the various beliefs of the *goyim*. But no one will ever bring under discussion our faith from its true point of view since this will be fully learned by none save ours who will never dare to betray its secrets. In countries known as progressive and enlightened we have created a senseless, filthy, abominable literature. For some time after our entrance to power we shall continue to encourage its existence. . . .

XV, 22: We are obliged without hesitation to sacrifice individuals who commit a breach of established order. . . .

XVII, 2: We have long past taken care to discredit the priesthood of *goyim*, and thereby to ruin their mission on earth which in these days might still be a great hindrance to us. Day by day its influence on the peoples of the world is falling lower. Freedom of conscience has been declared everywhere, so that now only years divide us from the wrecking of that Christian religion. . . .

XX, 5: The tax upon the poor man is a seed of revolution and works to the detriment of the State which in hunting after the trifling is missing the big. Quite apart from this, a tax on capitalists diminishes the growth of wealth in private hands. . . .

XX, 31, 32: . . . It is obvious that with any form of taxation per head the State is baling out the last coppers of the poor taxpayers in order to settle accounts with wealthy foreigners, from whom it has borrowed money, instead of collecting these coppers for its own needs without the additional interest. So long as loans were internal the *goyim* only shuffled their money from the pockets of the poor to those of the rich, but when we bought up the necessary person in order to transfer loans to the external sphere, all the wealth of the States flowed into our cash boxes, and all the *goyim* began to pay us the tribute of subjects.

3

"I read and re-read this document within a week," Hillman Holcomb has written of his first encounter with the *Protocols*. "My world crashed to the ground and splintered into irretrievable pieces. The shock of disillusionment was complete and devastating."

That was fifty years ago. He was twenty-three years old then, living in a brownstone rooming house on East 82nd Street in New York. He had a bachelor's degree from Yale and a job with the Electrolux Company that paid him enough to permit occasional carousing on a Saturday night. That was how he found the *Protocols*.

"I came in rather late in the night," he remembers, "and I discovered that I had lost the keys to my apartment. I had to wake the manager of the apartment to get in. She was a rather stern woman, about sixty-five. She didn't say much to me then, when she let me into my apartment, but she did tell me that she wanted to see me the next day. That afternoon when I went to see her she said, 'Young man, I have someting for you to read.' And she gave me a copy of the *Protocols*.

"I suppose I was ready for them. I had found New York to be . . . pretty hard to describe, after growing up in the South. Completely different from everything I had thought a big city should be. It was teeming with Jews, swarming with them, and their whole outlook was different from anything I was accustomed to. I was always aware that I was a white man, and a Christian at heart, though I hadn't given it too much thought. So I was ready for the *Protocols*. And when I read them I said, 'Well, this answers a lot of questions.' "

This is a story about the strange and sometimes grotesque shapes that political thought can assume on the Radical Right. There are thousands of routings, detours, that a few basic ideas can take. They're cast out in the wind, these ideas, in hardy little spores like the *Protocols,* but what they grow into is largely a function of where they come to earth.

Hillman Holcomb is not a major figure on the American Radical Right. He is one of thousands of minor characters, and most people in the movement would disown him if they knew of his existence. He has an idea that smacks of dread collectivism, and his racial views are extreme even among the extremists. For example:

"A lot of Jews would like to escape from the tyranny of the synagogue, but they're afraid they would not be accepted by the white Christian race. They're bound in there, and the big Zionists have taken advantage of it. Other Jews are Satanists from A to Z, and I say exterminate 'em, get 'em the hell away from Western civilization.

"The thing that's preached as Christianity today is far from the teachings of Christ. I call it Churchianity. I want a noncompromise Christianity. The Christ that I know, he said, 'Those mine enemies, who would not that I should reign over them, bring them here and slay them before me.' Death was not something that he would cringe from. People say that you should love Jews. Love, hell. These people are destroying Western civilization."

One-man marching bands are no novelty on the Radical Right. The solitary zealot with a mimeograph machine in his basement is a cliché of the movement, and Hillman Holcomb is a paragon of the cliché. He is not at all unusual for having spent thousands of hours and thousands of dollars disseminating his personal vision of the truth, tossing out his own idea spores and hoping that they will bear fruit somewhere.

It has been twenty years since Hillman Holcomb gave issue to a political idea that can accurately (and not uncharitably) be described as unique, arcane, personal. At least part of its lineage is rooted in the old anti-Semitic right, and it reflects the Radical Right's Jew-hating in naked form, but Hillman Holcomb's special twist makes it something like no other idea on the Radical Right. Twenty years, and Hillman Holcomb is still waiting for the first bloom of the seeds he cast out. Still, he seems undismayed. He is a square-jawed man with features that haven't yet surrendered to gravity or to lines. A forthright face, a strong voice, and, when he talks about his idea, a manner that suggests only confidence.

His home is a big, beautiful split-level in an expensive neighborhood above San Francisco Bay. His second wife is dead, and he lives there alone. There is art on the walls, an Oriental screen in one corner of the living room, a row of Doulton character mugs on the mantel. When a visitor comes to talk one day about politics, and about the big book of ideas, Hillman Holcomb greets him wearing a slightly out-of-fashion brown suit (but still clean, pressed, and natty). His manner is formal but friendly. He begins by talking about his landlady in New York, in 1932.

Her name was Haviland Lund, he says. She had been a lecturer, trying to promote an American back-to-the-land movement. She chastened him the morning after he had forgotten his keys: "If you young owls of this generation are going to destroy yourselves with alcohol, to whom are we going to pass the torch?" She gave Holcomb a copy of the *Protocols* and she had a whole library waiting for him later. He read Nesta Webster, whose works are seminal in conspiracy theory. He read *Rivers Flowing Eastward,* another enduring anti-Semitic staple.

"She knew a lot of the people who were aware of the danger, who knew what was going on. These people did everything they could to enlighten me. I read every book on the subject that I could buy or borrow."

He remembers long nights of political discussions with Nazi sympathizers, acquaintances he had made through Haviland Lund. He attended meetings of pro-Nazi leagues, and sometimes he addressed the gatherings. He cheered at the movies while others hissed at newsreel images of Hitler and Mussolini.

Still, he says, he wasn't sure that fascism was an answer. It seemed a dead end, yet he had no alternative. Then he met Howard Scott and his life changed.

Howard Scott was an apolitical visionary with a plan for nothing less than a total revamping of North America's social and economic structure. Scott wasn't a racist; he had his own idea, something that was supposed to make race and political distinctions irrelevant. Industrial advances, Scott thought, had made nonsense of the supply/demand system. Instead, he postulated, goods ought to be priced not by supply but in proportion to the amount of physical energy that had been spent producing them. He conceived of a society in which workers were paid not in cash but in "energy certificates."

The organization founded by Howard Scott, Technocracy, Inc., survives today, but it had its greatest popularity in the Thirties.* It is nonpolitical, except in the broadest sense, and by no means racist, but it gave Hillman Holcomb the answer he had been seeking from Nazism. When Howard Scott talked about the outmoded price system, Hillman Holcomb remembered the economic tyranny plotted in the pages of the *Protocols*. He made the connection, even if nobody else did.

He embraced Technocracy. He traveled with Howard Scott on lecture tours, and they often talked through to the morning. Sometimes he tried to show Scott the vital link, that last leap of understanding that only he had yet taken.

"I called him 'the Chief,' " Holcomb says, his voice clear and distinct, his words precise. "I probably knew Howard Scott better than any living man. He was high-strung, a Stradivarius violin of a man. He was a scientist, an engineer, a mathematician. He was truly a genius, a great man.

"He was my teacher. He showed me what can be done about the social problems facing America, that the credit-value system was no longer useful because we had evolved from a system of scarcity to one of abundance. And I knew that we were in an oligarchy, that we were headed for despotism because of this money system that we've got.

"The Chief knew the way I felt. I tried to get him to come out against the conspiracy, against the Zionist Jews, but he wouldn't do it. He didn't want to go off on religious or philosophical concepts."

Hillman Holcomb married. He opened a real-estate agency. During World War II he went before a draft board and announced that he would not fight against Germany, that if drafted he would try to educate every white soldier he met about the dangers of the Zionist conspiracy. The draft board excused him, he says, with the stipulation that he take a job in a war industry. He took a job in a shipyard for the duration. After the war, he opened an accounting firm.

All the time, he was loyal to Technocracy and to Howard Scott, but frustration gnawed inside him. It had to have an outlet. The answer he had found, this synthesis of two great revelations, was too good to keep private. In 1958, he installed a used offset printing press in his basement.

"There were two men important in the development of Christian civilization," he says. "One of them was Jesus Christ, who perfected the meta-

* From Dashiell Hammett's *Thin Man* (1934): ". . . some woman came over and asked Phil—he taught at Columbia—one of the questions about Technocracy that people were asking that week."

physics of morality. But there was not enough calculus and modulus in all
of Christianity to erect a barn. Howard Scott, on the other hand, was
concerned exclusively with the physics of function. I brought the two of
them together, and I ended up with Christian Technocracy, which was the
only name that I thought fitted the ideology.

"Some things you just have to do. You get the urge inside you and you
explode if you don't do it. So I did it. I taught myself how to run the press
and how to make photographic plates. I rented a collator and I learned
how to use that. I took three years off, and I really didn't do much during
that time except to write my big book. I would work on it in the morning,
keep at it until late at night, every day. My wife couldn't understand why I
would do that."

His big book consists of 789 pages of single-spaced typescript. The cover
shows a cross and an American flag with the bold-type acronym G.I.F.T.
(Gentiles Incorporated for Technocracy). Hillman Holcomb needed almost
three-quarters of a million words to explain his leap of intellect from the
Protocols, though if he had gone lighter on the racial adjectives he could
have shortened his work considerably. As it stands, his book is about the
size and weight of a metropolitan telephone directory. The language is
dense and difficult, and littered with racist slang, improbable strings of
jargon: "The lying, talmudic, khazar, mongoloid Jew kike can only
approach his father, the nihilistic devil lie of money and the damnation of
communistic chaos, through the satanic price system triad of debt, credit
and value."

He printed 3,000 copies. Stacks of the book filled his home. He put a $25
price on the title page, but the truth is that he gave the book away to any
Christian who asked for it, and to many who didn't ask: to libraries, to the
Vatican, to bishops, to politicians. He sent one to Joseph Kennedy, with a
note that said, "Have your boys read this."

He was out in the open now. Continental headquarters of Technocracy,
Inc., expelled him for conduct unbecoming a Technocrat, charging in a
letter of dismissal that he introduced into discussions of Technocracy "a
personal subjective campaign of hateful vilification and racism." He rented
halls throughout the San Francisco Bay Area to share his enlightenment,
but the few who came to listen came also to ridicule. He tried to buy time
on radio stations, but his broadcasts were tolerated for only three weeks.
His wife divorced him; she never really understood why he was doing
these things, he says now.

Holcomb denounces money as "Jewscrip" and describes materialistic
Americans as "tumblebugs rolling up a big ball of dung," but he lives in

this fine house and keeps checking accounts in the banking system that he so despises.

"I live under this system," he says. "There are certain things I have to do, but I don't have to approve of it."

Though he once collaborated with others on the Radical Right (he remembers passing out leaflets beside Willis Carto in San Francisco more than twenty years ago), he is estranged from them now.

"If you use part of the body to represent different political outlooks," he says, "I represent the head, and the rest of them represent the anus."

He has a few dozen copies of the big book left in his basement.

"The time is coming when people are ready to listen," he says. "They weren't ready back in sixty-three when I tried it the first time. That was my mistake. After that, I thought it would never happen in my lifetime, but now I think the time is near. I have one more book in mind, something that will bring it all up to date.

"My problem is that I'm running out of time. I'm healthy, I've been lucky that way. But I've only got so many years. I'd like to find a couple of young fellows to take up where I leave off. I'm realistic. I know that even if this thing happens in my lifetime, I'll probably have a hard time adjusting to it, I'm so used to the old ways.

"But I know that all we need is for people to hear this message, and then they'll know that it's something we need. Just get the message out and things will start to happen awful fast. They weren't ready to hear it before, but that's changing. I can tell the difference. Now people are ready to listen to it."

WITNESSING

Graffiti

A scandal of major proportions has broken out. The Chicago *Sun-Times* has been caught red handed in fronting for the international dope cartel known as Dope, Incorporated.

After this exposé the *Sun-Times* will no longer be able to piously denounce "corruption" when the truth emerges about the protection racquet [sic] they are running for the drug peddlers of this city and the nation.

This scandal could very well finish off the *Sun-Times* once and for all for anyone who still believed it was a credible source for news. . . . By now it should be obvious that the Labor Party has caught these Dope, Inc. networks red-handed and who should come out of the closet to defend them but the pious and condescending *Sun-Times*. Could it be that most of their reporters are using pot on a regular basis? At least that would explain the level of integrity of that newspaper.

U.S. Labor party flyer, June 1979,
after a *Sun-Times* article about the USLP

Better Tried by Twelve Than Carried by Six
Slogan, *Vigilante* magazine

We believe our system is an old house riddled by rot, decay, vermin, and termites. It has passed the point of repair—due to greed, neglect, disinterest, and foreign infestation. . . . To those who say, "Let's take to the streets now while we have a semblance of Freedom and movement," we are a tempering influence.

Statement of policy, Christian-Patriots
Defense League

We received your letter. For newspaper it is available at $1.00. or package information, including the newspaper at $2.00. We discontinue the free sample due to high cost of postage and because to many people not of the white race constant demand for sample and others giving us names and addresses of people not interested and not white.
We are sorry for the other who are white and sincere. Newspaper subscription with mailing (come every quarter of the year) price is $5.00.
Sincerely yours,

Verbatim text of letter answering a
request for a sample copy of an
American Nazi newspaper

There is no greater law firm than Smith & Wesson, especially if it is backed up by a twelve-gauge injunction.
Member of the California Posse Comitatus

Woe unto you, IRS and collection agents, hypocrites! For ye pay tribute to dedication of service and sincerity, but have omitted the weightier matters of the law, mercy, faith, the Bill of Rights, and the United States Constitution: these ought ye to have done, and left the other undone.
Ye blind guides, which strain at a poor man's penny, but allow the millionaires to slip through planned tax loopholes.
Woe unto you, IRS and collection agents, hypocrites! For ye make every appearance of clean and righteous judgements on the outside, but within ye are full of extortion and excess.
Thou blind IRS, cleanse first that which is within your own offices that thy outward acts may be clean also.
Woe unto you, IRS and collection agencies, hypocrites! For ye are like unto whited sepulchres, which indeed appear beautiful outward, but are within full of dead men's bones, and of all uncleanliness.

Adapted from the Book of Matthew, chapter 23
by a fundamentalist minister who is
active in the "tax revolt"

Jewelry policy
It is the policy of the Invisible Empire, Knights of the Ku Klux Klan, to sell only fine quality Jewelry. The quality is reflected in the price of our items. We feel that anything bearing the symbol of the Klan should be heirloom quality and that nothing less would be acceptable. The Ku Klux Klan is to us, something which can be passed on from generation to generation and it is this concept that we view our merchandise.
CLOISONNE—This ancient art of enamelling (Not Paint) was developed in China. The process is a delicate and time-consuming event which results in some of the finest workmanship known throughout the world. . . . All of our Blood Drop symbols are manufactured in this process. . . .
KKK blood drop belt buckle. $6.00
Rope necktie with blood drop symbol. . . .$6.00
LADIES' pierced gold dangle ear rings with blood drop symbol. . . .$13.00
KKK blood drop pendant. . . .$6.00.

From 1978 gift catalog of Invisible Empire, KKK

As far back as I can remember, I have been helping Bob DePugh and his right-wing activities. It started in 1962, when the Reuther brothers jumped on his back and demanded that Bobby Kennedy investigate all of us. I was already a member of McIntyre's movement; Hargis's movement; Goff's movement; John Birch Society—and so I joined the Minutemen too! I felt right at home with them for years. Speaking at many "DePugh meetings" all across the nation, I soon became his National Chaplain. Honor was high, but salary was low. And so it went for nearly 20 years. This is my third (and hopefully) final split with Bob DePugh during the past twelve years.

Open letter of resignation from the
Committee of Ten Million
by the Reverend Bob LeRoy, former chaplain
of the Minutemen

Techniques of Harassment
Techniques of Harassment Vol. 1 and Vol. 2
Home Workshop Silencers
Life After Doomsday
Take My Gun—If You Dare
Improvised Munitions from Ammonium Nitrate
Evaluation of Improvised Shaped Charges
Automatic and Concealable Firearms Design, Vol. 1 and Vol. 2
Guide to Viet Cong Boobytraps and Explosive Devices

Book titles offered by survivalist equipment catalog

When I am threatened with "the end of civilization as we know it," I try to look grave. But inwardly I'm cheering.

Letter to the editor of a white nationalist monthly

4

The candidate, freshly confirmed by his party, addresses the faithful from a podium in the convention hall. With this speech, he sallies forth into the fray of a presidential campaign. Thousands watch from the floor before him, millions more by television. He reaches the end of his prepared speech, but his last few phrases lack the requisite climax. He stops; there's a pause, as if for a snap decision. Then his jaw juts. His eyes narrow for a moment. His mind is set. He tells the audience that he has something else to add, something that isn't in his text. Maybe he'll be criticized, but he's going to say it anyway.

"God bless America," Ronald Reagan intones boldly.

To most of those who heard his words at that moment, the display was either pure hokum or good politics, or good show business, or pleasant sentiment. But in a considerable segment of the Radical Right, Reagan's words that night struck a deep and intimate chord of harmony. To many in the movement, the notion of a supreme being anointing this nation is real and concrete. They make no distinction between patriotism and religion. Love of God, for them, is manifest in loyalty to country. To fail one would be to blaspheme the other. They are certain, moreover, that this nation and its government are God's special creations, conceived in divine inspiration with the commission of doing the Lord's work.

It is a potent combination, religion and politics. The trappings of daily life in this country affirm the connection. In God we trust, our currency tells us. At least one popular TV evangelist preaches with a row of Stars and Stripes in the background. The national flag hangs from a staff beside the altar of a Catholic church in suburban Maryland, just as it does beside the altar of a Lutheran church in Portland, Oregon, and as it surely does beside the altars of thousands of other churches elsewhere. Innumerable public and civic functions begin with a requisite prayer of benediction, and students at hundreds of private schools begin their days with a prayer and with the Pledge of Allegiance: ". . . one nation, under God . . .". Protests by atheistic patriots, or patriotic atheists, seem to have little affected the assumption that national and religious impulses both spring from the same blessed source.

The Radical Right—at least, much of it—has embraced that idea, though religious patriotism is by no means the exclusive property of extremists. But when the Roman Catholic Father Coughlin railed against banking tyranny in the 1930s, he spoke as a Christian, not as an economist, and his message was intended for an audience unquestionably Christian. His successors as America's favorite political preachers, Carl McIntyre and Billy James Hargis, were able to move from anti-Communist vitriol to scriptural Christianity without pausing to draw a new breath. The ranks of the Radical Right are full of ministers (some ordained, others not) who bless America's faithful and damn her enemies as a matter of religious doctrine. Among the most effective right-wing campaigns in the 1950s was a series of rallies known as the Christian Anti-Communist Crusade, and literally dozens of smaller campaigns since that one have used the Savior's name.

On the Radical Right, even those groups that are essentially secular and political regularly invoke the Lord. To do so is considered highly judicious, and there is almost no greater slur than the accusation that one is not a good Christian. In 1978, the National States Rights party newspaper, the *Thunderbolt,* criticized the Minutemen's Bob DePugh with a bill of particulars that included the charge that DePugh was not a Christian. DePugh responded in an open letter that he had been baptized more than thirty years earlier into the Reorganized Church of the Latter-Day Saints, and that "those of us who believe in the Book of Mormon as well as in the Holy Bible do consider ourselves as Christian." De Pugh signed his letter with the phrase "For God and Country."

Bill Wilkinson (who has closed his correspondence with "For God, Race, and Country") explained the requirement that members of his Invisible Empire also be Christian.

"You must believe in the tenets of the Christian religion to become a Klansman," he said. "Now, that's very vague. It doesn't mean that you have to be active as a churchgoer. But it does mean that you must believe that there's a God, and that Jesus Christ came and died for our sins, and that sort of thing. We believe that that background alone gives us something of an advantage over other organizations."[1]

An early pamphlet distributed by the United Klans of America was almost apologetic in noting that the organization's religious requirement would exclude Jews: "At every Klavern meeting Jesus Christ is lauded and his teachings expounded. . . . Therefore, it would be unjust to allow the Jew to enter into the fellowship with the Klavern by appealing to his patriotism, and then have him cease to attend because every meeting would be out of harmony with his religious convictions." (There is, however, no evidence that any Klan meeting was ever mistaken for a New Testament study group.)

Some leaders on the Radical Right privately decry Christianity's effect in extremist politics. To do so publicly, however, would mean virtual banishment from the movement.

"It [religion] takes away more than it gives back," one man said after he had been promised anonymity. "It's true, over the years guys like Hargis and McIntyre brought a lot of people into the right by talking about politics. Those are the people who started listening because they wanted to hear religion, and they ended up getting interested in politics. But the preachers drain off so much money. They tell the people they need money to fight communism, but it really goes into their churches and schools, and sometimes their own pockets. None of these guys can point to anything they've done that definitely has helped the right wing politically. They're doing it for God, though, so it's all right for them to ask for money. But if I do the same, I'm milking the patriots for a buck. I honestly feel that they do more harm than good."

The man's envy is understandable, predictable, and far from unique; to most organizations on the Radical Right, simply producing and mailing a monthly newsletter presents an imposing financial challenge. But the complaint ignores the powerful attraction of a religious philosophy that might best be termed "conservative Christianity," a complex of ideas that could rework America to a degree far greater than the Radical Right has ever been able to manage. This is one of two conflicting strains of Christianity that today dominate religious thought on the Radical Right. The other is the Identity movement, which gets treatment of its own in the next chapter.

Conservative Christianity has a long history in this nation. It is a greater social and political force now than it has been in the last half-century or more. The philosophy is often termed "fundamentalism," though the strictest of fundamentalists like to reserve the term for themselves. It presents, by any name, an unyielding and absolute moral standard derived from Scripture. It leaves no slack for arbitrary judgments. Right is right, according to the code, and sin is sin regardless of the circumstances. Further, each is easily identified. Conservative Christianity has no patience with the equivocations of situational ethics.

An important corollary of conservative Christian thought is that values are ultimate because they are ordained by a higher order; and that without direction from that power, humans are incomplete and unfulfilled. Man alone is a most faulty instrument, this line of thinking goes. That assumption places it squarely against the humanistic system of belief.

Jerry Falwell, today the most prominent conservative Christian, writes in his book, *Listen America:* "Man by nature is not good. . . . People are living and dying for money. We see drug addiction and alcoholism and people worshiping the idol of and the god of sex."

A radio preacher in Kansas, one Sunday morning in the summer of 1981: "We're sinful, we're wicked, we can't help ourselves. We're dying, we're condemned. We're born with the innate nature of doing evil and wickedness. You can try to help yourself and try to do good, but there's something in you, there's sin in you, that won't let you. Little children, you'd think they'd be innocent creatures. But they're spoiled brats, they want their way, they scream their heads off. They'll tell you lies, they'll cheat. Where do they get all this? They're born with it. This is Adam's nature. It came upon us from Adam's sin in the Garden. That's why we need a Redeemer, to restore us back into the order, where God wants us to be, so that we can walk honestly and correctly. But we can't do it without God's help. We have to open up our hearts and let him in."

And a member of the Virginia delegation to the 1980 Republican convention: "Religion and politics are one. Religious people are delegates. I'm a Presbyterian and we believe in man being unregenerated without Christ. If you're not regenerated, you're basically evil. Christian philosophy is that man is basically evil."[2]

That philosophy has had an impact—blue laws and strict alcohol regulations, for example—in areas where it has dominated religious thought. And until the startling emergence of the Identity theory, it was the sole and traditional religion of the American right. But never before has it enjoyed the national influence that some politically aware activists like Jerry Falwell have given it.

Falwell has been called a "fundamentalist," and he seems not to have avoided it. But the term applied to Falwell may be misleading. Others who claim the title say that Falwell is far from a true fundamentalist. Real fundamentalism, they say, is separate and reclusive—two adjectives that are rarely used to describe Falwell.

Ron Branson, for example, is a fundamentalist gadfly in Los Angeles who has tilted at such religious figures as Hargis, Oral Roberts, Billy Graham, and Bob Jones. Branson, who describes his philosophy as "fundamental, separatistic, independent," has criticized Falwell for associating with religious charismatics and Evangelicals, for having been photographed with Elizabeth Taylor, for using the media in his ministry.

"Dr. Falwell is appearing more and more like Billy Graham with his hob-nobbing with every shade of religion and high government officials," Branson writes in a tract titled *Dr. Jerry Falwell: King of the Mountain, His Spirit of Compromise.*

Esoteric, maybe, and not worth noting, except that Falwell's departures from the fundamental norm have helped to make conservative Christianity a genuine political force in just a few years. Fundamentalists abhor ecumenism; Falwell embraces the conservative elements within all the Protestant denominations, the Catholic church, the Mormon church, even politically conservative Jews. "Hob-nobbing with high government officials" offends the fundamentalist ethic, maybe, but it is the way to political influence. And he has achieved that without trading away the essentials of absolute ethics and divine power.

Under the umbrella of the Moral Majority Falwell has brought: political activists like Paul Weyrich and Richard Viguerie, whose direct-mail fund raising has helped dozens of candidates sympathetic to the causes of conservative Christianity; hard-line conservative politicians like senators Jesse Helms of North Carolina and Jeremiah Denton of Alabama; loosely confederated single-issue associations that have campaigned nationally in the past against the Equal Rights Amendment and abortion; dozens of small local groups that have attacked sex education in public schools, pornography, legal tolerance of homosexuality, and what they perceive as licentious literature in public libraries; and a huge, formless, and previously ineffective mass of people who have grown restive with the sweeping social and moral changes of the last two decades.

All were disaffected, unhappy with things as they had been. And all shared at least a general belief in the absolute values of conservative Christianity. To credit Falwell and the Moral Majority alone with bringing them together would be absurd; the mechanism surely ground on more than one cog. What is significant is that so many disjointed elements found coherence so quickly, and that Falwell, being the most prominent of all, was there in the vanguard. With help from the media, he held the banner high so that even the most distant stragglers could keep sight of it as they hurried to front up.

He did more. Along with a few secular activists, most notably Weyrich and Phyllis Schlafly, Falwell turned his followers' dissatisfaction into militancy. They could fight man's natural iniquities, he told them, at the polling places and in the legislatures.

This is a book about the Radical Right, and while Jerry Falwell is an activist, he is no revolutionary. Some of his followers are, however. They want to change this nation, they want to change the way we live, so drastically that the result would be revolutionary in every way. Some support the proposition that the United States was instituted as a Christian Republic, and that unless our leaders seek divine guidance and govern by divine principle, we will never fulfill our manifest destiny. Their extrapolation of the traditional view of church-in-state is sufficiently spectacular that they are not out of place in this arbitrarily limned Radical Right.

"The faith of the early Republic . . . was hostile to the establishment of a church from above, or religious controls from above," writes the Reverend R. J. Rushdonny in the foreword to *The Separatist Illusion* (Milford, Mich.: Mott Media, 1977), which attacks the supposition that the First Amendment excludes Christianity from state affairs. "The idea," Rushdonny writes, "was to create a situation in which Christianity would be the established faith from the ground level and free to prosper accordingly. The purpose thus of the Constitution was not to express Christian faith but to allow such faith freedom from the state in order to dominate society, law, and education."

Many conservative Christians are convinced that the Constitution is a divinely inspired document, and that the freedoms it expresses are tools to be used to institute a proper and devout national life—that they are, in effect, freedoms to live a pious life, but no other kind. By this view, the use of constitutional freedoms to protect a pornographer, for example, is corruption of a divine instrument. The line of reasoning goes something like the following:

A. There is a single, clearly defined and easily discerned way of life that is pleasing to the Lord.
B. All other behaviors are repugnant to him and are therefore not to be tolerated.
C. The Lord brought forth the United States, and inspired the Constitution, so that his believers would have a place and the guaranteed freedoms to live as He wishes.

D. Those freedoms are now being used for perverted purposes.

E. Therefore, the present state of affairs is unpleasing to the Lord, and all who would do His work must take every measure to restore the Republic to the holy and purposeful state for which it was created.

This is a critical confluence of implacable ethics and electoral politics. To understand their sense of mission, remember that these people hold a code. It is at once inflexible and yet appropriate for every facet of life. It guides them in the greatest decisions and the smallest. They apply it to all that they encounter, and today that includes politics.

They have enormous power when they act together. Consider the way the Equal Rights Amendment was shut down in the state of Nevada.

It was 1974. Janine Hansen, newly graduated from Brigham Young University with a degree in child development and family relations, knew that ERA was going to be an issue in the state legislature that year. She had no doubts about the amendment—it was bad, she believed. She waited for opposition to form against it. She knew politicians. They would do the expedient thing, which would be to ratify the amendment if nobody spoke against it. They would need encouragement to do what she knew was the right thing.

"Nobody was doing anything," she remembered years later. "So I called a friend of mine, and I said, 'Sylvia, be my co-chairman.' And she did. That was where my real solid commitment began. I've been working on those family issues, hundreds and thousands of hours since."

Janine Hansen, then twenty-three years old, helped to turn the ERA into an issue in Nevada. She and her friends all knew others who felt as she did. Some of them were willing to give hours and some money. This was not politics so much as a conviction about the way things ought to be, life as it ought to be conducted by good people in these United States. It was something they felt, more than thought.

Janine Hansen organized her friends and the friends of her friends, almost all of them political neophytes. They wrote letters and signed petitions, and they were always there to testify when testimony was needed in the statehouse. When the matter went up on a state referendum in 1978, they campaigned to have it rejected. ERA by then was a hot issue. The amendment lost by a 2–1 measure—an impressive display of clout.

The same thing was happening elsewhere; the religious right by that time was finding strength in numbers and looking down the gun barrel of their convictions at the liberality and social changes that displeased them most. They were discovering strength in unified numbers, and lawmakers around the country were discovering that out there among their constituents was a sizable body of people willing to see legislation in moral terms, and willing to get involved on just those terms. Dangerous stuff, passion in politics. The professionals knew—Martin Luther King and Vietnam had proved it again most recently—that the old rules were useless when righteousness got tossed into the pot.

For the Hansens, it all came together so naturally: presidential elections, the Bible, creeping socialism, the Book of Mormon, back and forth across the dinner table in the family's little bungalow in Sparks, Nevada, the house where Janine still lives with her parents, her husband, and her son. There were Oliver and Ruth, four boys, and the one daughter, Janine. They were all smart people and they all learned at the dinner table how to argue a point. They did not avoid the large issues. The Commandments and the Constitution, Jack Kennedy and Barry Goldwater, civil rights, George Wallace, Nikita Khrushchev. One thing the children learned early from Oliver and Ruth: The Lord may pose puzzles, but never imponderables. There is always an answer.

"It started when we were just kids," says Janine Hansen Triggs. She holds her two-year-old son, Zachary, on her lap; he does his own monologue into the microphone of a tape recorder. "At the dinner table, reading about politics in the newspapers. It was always encouraged. I got involved in it for the first time when I was twelve years old. I remember we had about seventeen Goldwater stickers on our car and I used to go with my mother down to Goldwater headquarters every day to help out and do what I could do."

The Hansens, understand, did more than talk. You may judge their activity by the impressive thickness of the pile of newspaper clippings that have chronicled their doings. Just a sampling:

1940—"Elder Oliver F. Hansen returned to his home in Sparks this week after completing a two-year mission in the North States Mission for the Church of Jesus Christ of Latter-Day Saints. He followed the custom of all missionaries of the church by paying his own expenses."

1964—Oliver Hansen of Sparks, for five years a bishop in the LDS church, files to run for justice of the peace.

1964—Joel Hansen serves a two-year mission in Uruguay for LDS church.

1967—Janine Hansen is named "outstanding girl" at Sparks Junior High School. She is cited for her membership in the National Honor Society, her place on the school's honor roll, and "a perfect citizenship record."

1970—Daniel Hansen draws 4.5 percent of vote in election for governor.

1971—Chris Hansen becomes Eagle Scout.

1974—Joel Hansen, Reno schoolteacher and former winner of Fleischman State Department scholarship, wins 8 percent of vote in race for seat in House of Representatives.

1974—A letter to the editor of the *Nevada State Journal*:

Thank you for publishing the picture of me and my horse, Yeska, and for the article about my objective of saving gasoline during the service station shutdown.

But it seems that I did not make my points clear to your reporter-photographer. My main objective in riding my horse from Sparks to Reno to work was to protest President Nixon's folly in regulating the price of gasoline. That objective was not printed with the picture.

Price regulation of this nature is socialistic. In other words, it is anti-American. All Americans ought to object to evil forces which tend to destroy our splendid freedoms under the Constitution. The socialists have been whittling, then chopping away our Constitutional blessings for a long time now.

I was riding for Americanism and in opposition to socialism.

Sincerely,
Oliver F. Hansen.

1976—Janine Hansen files as Independent American party candidate for House of Representatives. She will reach minimum age of twenty-five just a few days before swearing-in would take place if she wins. (She loses.)

1977—Janine Hansen is chairman of Stop-ERA Committee of Nevada (later Pro-Family Coalition of Nevada).

1980—Janine Triggs is elected delegate to White House Conference on Families in raucous meeting at Reno City Hall.

"It just sort of grew," Janine Triggs says. "As we became more interested in the Constitution, and in constitutional principles, our commitment grew, and our investment in different campaigns grew. Dan really got us involved in the third-party movement. He ran George Wallace's campaign in Nevada one year, and I was involved in the Wallace campaigns when I was a teen-ager. Our ability to do different things grew, and we went from campaign to campaign, issue to issue.

"I was twenty years old when I first spoke before the legislature. That was in 1971, when the first hearings on abortion took place in this state, when they were trying to change the law. That was when I first really felt committed.

"A lot of people don't have any political beliefs. They may have some general feelings, but most of them won't spend the time and effort to do things like going door to door. I think a lot of people would say that I'm not very tolerant. But I have a lot more tolerance for a committed liberal than I do for someone in the middle who's uninformed, who hasn't got the interest or the brains to make any commitment."

She is a nice lady, sort of plain and sort of pretty at the same time. No makeup, librarian-prim. A good, quick mind. And while this observation won't please them on either side of the fence, it has to be made anyway: She resembles many of the women against whom she has fought so hard on issues like abortion and the ERA. Like many of them, she seems to care more about what she thinks than how she looks. She scurries to find time in her life for family and for the cause, just as many of them do. And just like the most ardent feminists, she practices politics more as a crusade than as a campaign.

They still can't stand her.

"To Democrats and liberals around here, she's just a monster, an ogre," said someone who has been close to Nevada politics for the last five years. "They can't talk rationally about her. They'll get red in the face, just apoplectic. She really does something to them."

When I met her for the first time, just a few days after the 1980 elections, they were as angry at her as they had ever been. She had enraged the party regulars by switching affiliations one day before the deadline and running in the Democratic primary against an eighteen-year incumbent in the state assembly. Her opponent called it "absolutely the dirtiest race I've ever been involved in."[3] Triggs accused her opponent of tearing down her signs and posters; he accused her of circulating libelous literature. The state party chairman threatened legal action to have her name removed from the ballot. What she had done, he said, was "morally reprehensible. This person is so far out of the Democratic mainstream you'd have to say she's up in the mountains somewhere."[4]

She lost the primary by thirty-seven votes.

In the general election, she and others in the family worked for a conservative judge running for election to the state supreme court, for a conservative assembly candidate in Reno, and for a conservative candidate to the state university's board of regents. Having the Hansen family take your side in an election can be no small boon. They know how these things work. They can write a brochure and get it printed and have it put on every porch in the precinct. They know where to order lawn signs and how to put the touch on volunteers.

Through the summer of 1980, until the last ballot had been marked in

November, they maintained a bank of telephones in their garage. They can deliver votes. Before every election, they scan the wasteland of politics, casting about for a candidate here, another there, who shows promise. They seek an assemblyman, a judge, a college regent who might make the world a little more like the Hansens would like to see it. But politics are an imperfect means for change, because it is a rare politician who sees the Hansens' vision as clearly and brightly as they do.

"People that get elected might have political strategies, but they usually don't have any committed beliefs or philosophies," Janine Triggs said after that 1980 election. "They blow the way the wind blows. They just aren't committed, for instance, to preserving the Constitution and the freedoms that our Founding Fathers sought to give us."

She told about a man whom she had helped in a statehouse race. When she and her husband talked to him a few days after the election about proposing an antiabortion bill, he told her that he didn't intend to be a grandstand politician. Which meant that he would steer away from controversial issues like an antiabortion bill.

"And he had always been committed," she said. "But after the election, he started working on getting elected again. When people get elected, they sometimes get mesmerized by staying in office. That's the problem with this country: Instead of governing, they're campaigning. You have to listen to what your constituents say, you have to keep in touch with them. But a lot of politicians fail to do that.

"It's extremely hard to buck the tide of the process. Some people do. I know them. I've met them, liberals and conservatives both. But it is difficult. Sometimes the voters who put you in office forget about you, and the ones who remember are the lobbyists, the special-interest groups, the people with all the money. It's easy to lose touch."

There is a remedy, though. That is to work even harder, to make the organization even stronger, and to command so many votes that the politicians can't afford to forget. This is an important difference. In many other quarters of the Radical Right, the balkiness of public systems has been reason to fling up hands in disgust and walk away. But even the most extreme of conservative Christians seem to have a limitless reverence for institutions.

So six nights after the 1980 elections, Michael Triggs and his wife, Janine, carry a movie projector through the Nevada chill into the home of a woman who is an officer of the Nevada Pro-Family Coalition. The woman has invited more than twenty of her neighbors to come for the evening and watch a film on the dangers of humanism in public schools. Four arrive, all women, and one of them is already a member of the coalition. The film—for which Janine and Michael personally paid $200—features a woman standing at a podium and speaking in a heavy Texas accent. Humanism, she says, is a godless philosophy which teaches that there are no absolute values, that all authority is to be questioned, and that man need not look beyond himself to find answers for his problems.

When the lights go up and her husband rewinds the film, Janine Triggs tells the women about the corruption she saw at the 1977 International Women's Year Conference in Houston. (She had run as a delegate from Nevada, was defeated, but attended on her own anyway.) There had been lesbian information booths, she says, and vendors selling vibrators and sex aids—all extensions of the humanist, value-denying philosophy. While the hostess for the evening brings around fruit punch and oatmeal cookies, Janine passes out free literature: a newsletter of the Nevada Pro-Family Coalition; a photocopy of a letter to the editor of the *Reno Gazette,* critical of Planned Parenthood; and copies of a poem titled "Precious Feet," accompanied by a photograph of the perfectly formed feet of a ten-week-old fetus. The poem reads, in part:

TINY, PRECIOUS BABY FEET
You're loved because you're mine
And no one else can make YOUR PRINTS
Across the SANDS OF TIME

For maybe twenty minutes the women talk. Mostly, it is Janine who talks. She warns the women to be wary of any school course called "values modification" or "values clarification." What that is, she tells them, is the humanists' attempt to make children question all authority and all fundamental values in their lives, to persuade them that they should reject the natural ties of church and family.

The women nod, but the only enthusiastic response is from the woman who already knows Janine and the message. She has a story of her own about her thirteen-year-old son's junior-high sex-education class.

Then there's a pitch, not for money but for help. She wants to do more of these meetings, Janine says. It would be nice if every one of the women who attended tonight would hold one and invite her own neighbors.

There are no volunteers. The women look uneasy. There's a feeling that this shrill alarm in the night has been too much, too fast for a poor housewife. And anyway, it's hard to imagine a philosophy with the nice, benign name of "humanism" being all that evil.

Janine presses on. Take the literature home, she says. Read it and consider it, and think of how important the ideas might be for friends and neighbors with families of their own.

No, she tells an onlooker after the guests have gone, she isn't disappointed by the results. She would have liked to see twenty couples instead of four women, but she isn't complaining. She says the Pro-Family Coalition holds two or three meetings most weeks around the Reno area, and they are profitable; they provide names on telephone lists, more volunteers, eventually more votes and more stragglers brought into the fold.

She is a determined and energetic woman, by no means unique in the conservative Christian movement. There are thousands who are just as committed and as energetic as she is, who are working just as hard for the same goals in other parts of the country. Its bedrock convictions may be the heart of conservative Christianity's new power, but people like the Hansens and their daughter are its bone and sinew. They helped to elect congressmen—maybe even a president—of their preference in 1980. They have helped to defeat others who displeased them. That they will eventually change the texture of American life is indisputable. That process of alteration is under way already; the only questions are how broad and how durable the changes will be.

WITNESSING

One Way
(From interviews with Janine Hansen Triggs, November 1980)

"I saw a story on television the other day about a gay rodeo being promoted in Reno. It really irritated me, that we should have that kind of thing going on, telling people that homosexuals or sympathizers should even be tolerated here. Homosexuals, what they want to do in a closet, I could care less. But if they get out and start promoting this as acceptable, in absolute opposition to what the Bible teaches, in absolute opposition to what we know from history, then that jeopardizes my liberty. It jeopardizes my freedom for my little boy to go to and from wherever he wants without them being able to influence him, or whatever the heinous crime might ultimately be."

"In this new movement, the New Right, people are committed to issues first and then they get involved in the political process, like against ERA or abortion, where religion is such a big part. Most of the people I work with—whether Mormons, Catholics, Baptists, or evangelicals—are all committed religious people. They believe in God, and most of them are Christians, although we have cooperated with the Jewish community. I saw a survey once that said of people against ERA, about eighty-five percent feel that religion is important in their lives. And it was just about the opposite for people who support ERA.

"For me, religion and politics are really cohesive. They can't be separated. I guess I'd have to say that my first commitment is to my God and my religion. But my religion teaches us to be involved in civic matters. We believe that the Constitution was divinely inspired by God to provide a nation in which we could have freedom of religion. We believe that God brought Columbus to this land. And that He raised up the Founding Fathers so that we might have freedom of religion, to provide an opportunity for the gospel to be restored. The restoration of the gospel of Jesus Christ is based on having a place to do it. God is involved in the affairs of man. In that way, the two things are inseparable.

"There's a big argument about the separation of church and state. Liberals use that to exclude religion from government. The purpose of it, if you study Thomas Jefferson and what he did, was that Congress should have no law regarding the establishment of religion. They didn't want government interfering with religion, but that didn't mean that individual people, God-fearing people, shouldn't have an influence in government. Read the works of the Founding Fathers. All of it refers to God and to the Creator, and it shows that they felt that it was their divine destiny to have freedom in this land.

"The only time that liberals scream that there shouldn't be religion involved in government is when it's the kind of religion they don't believe in. If it's humanism—the worship of man and his greatness, really atheism, which has been defined as a religion by the Supreme Court—you can have that in the textbooks, you can promote that in the schools. But if you believe in God, and you believe God created the earth, and you're against abortion because you think that's taking a human life, then your form of religion should be abridged, because you're not supposed to be involved. The National Council of Churches can be involved, and Martin Luther King could use religion to promote his personal philosophies, but when it comes to somebody like Jerry Falwell, oh, no, that's not right, you can't do that.

"Without the morality which God has given us to live by, without the morality of religion, we can't have freedom. You can't have freedom without morality because immoral men will enslave one another. I think our Founding Fathers knew that. They recognized that without God they have no hope. When you look at the beginnings of this country, you wonder how it ever got off the ground, unless God did have a hand in it.

"Good government is a tool of God that He uses to open a way up for His children to be free."

"The basic humanist tenet is situational ethics; that there are no absolutes. They have the attitude that if it feels good and it doesn't appear to be hurting anybody too much, go ahead and do it. I think we need to improve what we start with, try to do what God asks us to do, improve our lives. We have to rise above some of the basic animal instincts, toward God's level, where he has a pure love and a pure desire to do good, not a selfish desire.

"Humanism is kind of selfish, doing something for our own selves instead of helping others. I've seen it in the women's lib movement, in the unhappiness it has brought to the lives of those women who have embraced it. Instead of feeling like the purpose of life is to share and to grow, like by having a child, they downgrade and denigrate the position of mother. They exalt the position of individual, liberated women.

"I've seen a lot of them in this state because I've been involved in it for a long time. They just go downhill. They end up getting divorced or losing their family. Their whole life gets changed from a positive point of view where they wanted to help women to a kind of selfish anti-man point of view.

"People are looking for absolutes. They're floundering. Just like with children, who need to know how far they can go, so they can feel secure. They need limits, and I think grown-ups feel that way, too.

"Religion gives you the basics, someplace to start. To figure out all the dos and the don'ts and the gray areas, you've got to do considerable thinking. If you believe in God, you've got a pretty good foundation. You believe that and you don't have to spend your whole life searching to figure whether that is right. You accept that and go from there.

"I operate on that system every day. I see that it works, I see that it's right, and I feel good about it. We're human, we can't possibly see the whole perspective, but on the whole my decisions have been correct. Before I've made my decisions, I've prayed about them. I've tried not to do anything until I felt good about it."

"I keep saying I want to get out of politics, because I'm tired, I'm really tired. But then I see something on TV or in the paper, and I just know I have to do something. It's sort of like an addiction. I'll feel compelled, absolutely compelled, that I must do something. Because if I don't do anything, maybe nobody will do anything. I try to get people involved, but I do feel the responsibility of leadership.

"I want people to put their faith in a cause, not in people. People are fallible. We cannot put our faith in an individual candidate. We must put our faith in the principle and in the cause. It doesn't matter who is leading it, as long as they are right and others follow. If they get out of line, there's nothing sacred about any single person."

5

Popular wisdom is not much help these days in negotiating the strange religious landscape of the Radical Right. Everything is akilter and out of place. Old assumptions head to detours and dead ends. The paths are strewn with anomalies, and unlikely noises of protest arise from among folks who are supposed to embrace that old-time religion, hard-nosed fundamentalism.

Example: A pamphlet, making its way by the thousands across the Radical Right, asks, almost petulantly: "My Minister, Is He Wrong AGAIN?"

Example: Five men, right-wing activists all, discuss one evening the enemies of the nation—Communists, bankers, Jews, conspirators, and turncoats. "And the preachers are the worst of all," one of them says. "Any minister who keeps on preaching one day after he finds out that he's running with a pack of rats must be a rat himself."

Example: A tract entitled *An Open Letter to Jerry Falwell*, widely circulated among the faithful of the Radical Right, charges that the evangelist is either "blinded in ignorance . . . unknowingly teaching gross scriptural error . . . or . . . knowingly and willfully deceiving millions of honest Christian people and leading them into a pit."

Example: A Baptist minister, who has made a career of lecturing fundamentalists about the evils of world communism, has a season's bookings canceled when he publishes a notice that he must take a stand against "the true enemies of Our Lord." Now he preaches to another flock. "I'm still a Baptist," he says, "but now I'm an Identity Baptist."

What's happening here is a war, no less, for the religious loyalties of the Radical Right. That means high stakes in money, in membership rolls, and—maybe most important—in the future direction and character of the right. Never before has conservative Christianity faced even a nominal challenge to its primacy as the religion of the Radical Right. But the Identity faith fits the psyche and the philosophy of the movement as no other doctrine ever has. In fewer than twenty years, Identity has captured some of the most extreme elements of the Radical Right, and has helped to create some others. The doctrine has made amazing advances and has created considerable turmoil within the right while escaping notice beyond it.

The crux of its teachings is that white Christian Americans are the spiritual and genealogical descendants of the Old Testament people called Israelites—God's chosen people, and his nation on earth. Thus the names by which the belief is known: Israel Identity, Christian Identity, the Kingdom Message. By any name, it is a drastic interpretation of Holy Scripture. Theologians have generally assumed that the Israelites of the Old Testament were Jews.

The ramifications of the theory are manifold. It gives the Radical Right a single racial, religious, and national identification, something that fundamental Christianity, for all its austere fundamentalism, never was able to do.

There is much more. Because of its literal and traditional reading of Scripture, conservative Christianity has held that Jews, as God's chosen, are ordained to exist as a nation with lands under their own dominion, exactly as the Bible stipulates. This has made at least nominal Zionists of conservative Christians.* (Some do appear ambivalent on this point—torn, perhaps, between scriptural dicta and personal sentiment. On September 17, 1980, the *Dallas Morning News* quoted Dr. Bailey Smith, president of the Southern Baptist Convention and a member of Moral Majority, saying that God "does not hear the prayers of the Jew. . . . For how in the world can God hear the prayer of a man who says that Jesus Christ is not the true Messiah? That is blasphemy. It may be politically expedient, but no one can pray unless he prays through the name of Jesus Christ"). But even the most generous version of Identity teaching holds that the modern nation of Israel is a historical fraud, and that the ancestors of modern Jews

---

* Israeli Prime Minister Menachim Begin seems to understand the connection. When Israeli planes destroyed a nuclear reactor in Iraq in 1981, Begin first notified President Reagan by telephone; the second American he called was the Reverend Jerry Falwell. And when Begin visited Washington, D.C., in September 1981, his itinerary included a private meeting with Falwell at Blair House.

were little more than bystanders in biblical history. God's chosen, they say, already have their promised nation, the U.S.A.

That is the more clement of the two major strains of Identity thought. The more popular version, known as the "two-seed-line theory," hypothesizes that throughout history there have been two genetic groups in direct opposition. One is the white race, favored by God and subject to his laws. The other is a race spawned by Satan in the Garden of Eden, now called Jew, responsible for all evil and upset throughout history.

Those are the rudiments of a knotty and intricate system of ideas. Beyond that are telling nuances that are important to understanding the doctrine and appreciating its attraction on the Radical Right. What follows the next two paragraphs is an introduction to Identity, a truncated version of a three-hour monologue that an Identity pastor, Clyde Edminster, delivered to me one afternoon. It is strange and fantastic stuff, maybe, but worth the effort for the pings and echoes of Radical Right philosophy that resound through it. And that is important: Though inspired by a similar idea in Britain, America's Identity movement was conceived and first spread by three men with ties to the Radical Right: Wesley Swift, Bertrand Comparet, and William Gale. In a sense, then, it is a creation of the Radical Right, an indication of fundamentalism's shortcomings as a politically militant religious doctrine. Identity was, literally, tailor-made for the Radical Right, in ways that become increasingly apparent as Identity theory becomes clearer.

I had found Clyde Edminster's name in an issue of his monthly magazine, *Christ Is the Answer*. It was a puzzling little publication, a mix of health-food advice, photos of the pastor's family, and a long, dense tract on Revelation prophecy that seemed to imply that the United States would soon find itself in a war against Russia and China, a war that would be part of divine plan. I sent in a subscription (and received a Hallmark Thanksgiving card signed "Clyde and Bea Edminster"), but after reading five issues of the magazine, I still found the theology impenetrable, a bewildering labyrinth of prophetic visions, biblical references, and phrases like "Serpent Seed" and "the End Time message." I wrote to the reverend asking for an interview. He assented, in a letter noting that he had "no personal hatreds against any person, persons, or groups of persons who represent any philosophy, ideology, or political persuasion." Later I would understand why he included the disclaimer.

His home and his church are on a three-acre tract near Rainier, Washington, in the shadow of a beautiful big mountain of the same name. He took me to the outbuilding that he uses as a printshop, where he produces his monthly magazine, various pamphlets and tracts, and at least one book

a year. He stoked the fire in a wood stove there, checked to see that the
tape recorder was working properly, and then settled in to tell the story of
mankind, from the Creation to Armageddon.

"In the second chapter of Genesis, God has already created mankind as
a whole, all the colored races. There's a number of species of mankind, in
fact several of the black man alone. There's the brown race, the red race,
which are all different species as well. Some of them are quite primitive
and some are pretty well developed. After God had created all of these, he
said, 'Be fruitful and multiply.' He placed them in different areas of the
earth—the yellow man over in China, the brown man in India, and so
forth.

"On the third day, after God had created all of these, he saw that they
were good, but they weren't perfect. They're bushmen, they live in the
woods, they pick the fruit off the trees and they eat it. He said, 'There is
not yet a man to till the ground.' No one is to the point where he can till
the ground and plant and harvest.

"So the Lord God, Yahweh Elohim, formed man out of the dust of the
ground. He's a species that God has created to supervise, to supersede, all
that He has created, to bring harmony and peace. He formed this man and
He breathed into his nostrils the breath of life, and Adam became a living
soul. Adam's life was not contingent upon his bloodstream. He was of a
higher order, a higher intellectual order. The Eighth Psalm says he was
created a little lower than the angels, a little lower than God himself. In
other words, He was creating a race of people to be his sons. In Luke 3:38
we trace the genealogy of Jesus right back to Adam. Adam was a different
race. And God saw loneliness in Adam's heart and gave him a help-
mate.

"They were innocent creatures doing God's will. Then this creature, the
bright and shining one, this Lucifer or Satan, came to Eve because he knew
that she was the weaker of the two sexes and he knew that he would have
more influence over her. He told her that God was holding out on her and
Adam, that she could bring forth children like these other creatures did, if
she would eat of the tree of knowledge and use her own wisdom. So she
did. And she had—I believe it was an affair, in the Garden with this creature. The Shiny One showed Eve all about sex. She partook and she saw
that it was good, something to be desired. And with this affair, a seed was
planted in her womb. When she went back to Adam to show him what she
had learned, another seed was planted in her, Adam's seed.

"When God learned what they had done, he called them all together,
Adam and Eve and Satan, and he put a curse on them all. He cursed Satan

first for having tempted the woman and deceived her. He told Satan, 'On your belly you will crawl all the days of your life.' He said, 'I will put enmity between thee and the woman, between thy seed and her seed.' I think this was a symbolic picture of a race of people that was going to come across the face of the earth, eventually. And he said, 'There shall be controversy between the two races of people that shall come forth out of this, continual conflict between them.'

"Then he told Eve that she should bring forth children in sorrow, and that is why white women have such a terrible hard time with childbirth. It's part of the curse. And the curse for Adam was that he had fallen from his high estate, down with all the other creatures with blood in their veins. But he says they will be delivered eventually. And we will, when God restores us back to where we were with eternal life again.

"The main thing is the controversy between these two seed lines. There's the seed of the serpent race that was first planted in Eve, and the seed from Adam of the white race. In the fourth chapter it says that Eve brought forth two children. And it's very likely that they were twins with different fathers, because there was animosity between them right away. Two different kind of people altogether. Cain didn't want to work. He wanted to live off his ingenuity, live off somebody else's sweat, and this is typical of the serpent race of people. Then Satan saw that he had a chance for his people to be able to gain power if Cain killed Abel. Then Cain took off into the jungle, and went into the Land of Nod, and took a wife from one of the other races out there. He built an empire, and this became known as Babylon, and these were the beginnings of the serpent race of people.

"Wickedness became great on the earth. Everybody was integrating, mixing up, and this is what God didn't want. He created them separately so that they would mate with their own kind. But the wickedness became so terrible that God knew he would have to put an end to it all. So God called Noah, who was the only one he could count on, the one who was keeping his seed line pure, who hadn't mixed in any way. After the Flood, God started a new order. But apparently Noah had taken on some of the serpent seed.

"Now, Yahweh Elohim told Abraham that he would have a son. He said, 'Isaac shall thy seed be called.' The seed of Isaac. Isaac's sons. Saxons. Anglo-Saxons. That's the genealogy of this race. Isaac was the father of Esau and Jacob. They were twins, and I think the same thing happened, the serpent seed got in there somehow, because Esau was born red and hairy.

"What happened in Jerusalem was that the Judah kingdom was wicked, backsliding. That's where the serpent line, the Canaanites, came in. They integrated, they took over key positions—the ministry, the scribes, the priesthood. The Canaanite group, the descendants of Esau, is a hybrid race. They're always looking to mate in with somebody of a higher order to improve their bloodline, to bring in more intellect, more sharpness. So they integrated in Judah; and by the time Jerusalem was built up, the Canaanites had infiltrated, taken over. So when Jesus came, He wasn't welcomed. He said he came into his own but his own received him not.

"These people had their own plan, their own religion, called the Babylonia Talmud. Most of these people are what we now call Jews. Jesus spoke to a lot of these Jews who came up to Him and tried to question Him and antagonize Him. He said, 'I know who you are; you're of your father, the devil.' He called them a generation of vipers, serpents. They're the ones who crucified Him. Pilate said, 'Shall I crucify your king?' They told him, 'We have no king but Caesar.' They rejected Him then and they reject Him today. God said, 'I come but to the lost sheep of Israel.' That's who He's for, and that's who receives Him. Some others don't have the capacity to receive Him.

"Meanwhile, in 721 B.C., the Assyrians had carried off the ten northern tribes, but some of the Ephraimites escaped. They went up between the Black Sea and the Caspian Sea to the Caucasian mountains, where they found a pass and got through. That's why we're called the Caucasian people, because we've traced the white race of people back to that area. They went over that pass and for several hundred years they trekked to the north and the west. This is what God said they should do. The prophecies in Isaiah are all about how God would lead his people north and west. It took them several hundred years, but they finally settled in Western Europe and the British Isles.

"I think you have to study what happened to Jacob to see what God has in store for America, because we're the modern Jacobites. Jacob had been many times blessed: He had wealth, position, power, sons. When he was ready to return to the promised land, he put all his wealth in a great train and he set out for home. But on his way there, he learned that his brother, Esau, was jealous of what he had and was on his way with four hundred armed men to take it all away from him.

"Jacob was frightened. He didn't know what to do. Then one night he met the Lord, and he wrestled all night with the Lord, but he couldn't beat him. So Jacob said, 'Lord, you've beat me. I know I can't do anything without you.' And the Lord had Jacob right where He wanted him then. All the Lord wanted was for Jacob to realize that his own strength wasn't enough, and to put himself in the Lord's hands.

"When Esau met Jacob, he didn't fight him. The Lord took care of that. He took care of Jacob because Jacob gave himself up to the Lord.

"And that's what the Lord wants from us. We're the modern Jacobites. We have the birthright. We have it all: wealth, forests, valleys. We can grow anything on our land. We can do anything, not because we're better than anybody else but because we're a chosen people. We're a servant nation to God, because God wants to show what people can do when they live under His just and equitable laws. But we've been backsliding. We haven't been obeying God's laws. Other nations are jealous of our birthright. We're in big trouble. We've utterly failed.

"Now God is going to complete His plan. He's going to set the Red One against Jacob again. Except this time it won't be Esau with four hundred armed men. It'll be Gog and Magog, Russia and China, with two hundred million. They'll be loaded down with bombs and all the implements of modern warfare. Some of them will come straight over the North Pole. It's all in the thirty-ninth chapter of Ezekiel. We don't know what warfare is. We've never been invaded. And when we see those masses of people, we won't know what to do. The unions are going to strike and deprive us of our food supply. Millions of people will die. It'll be horrible.

"What are we going to do? Well, we of the white race have been programmed so that when the bottom falls out, when we've tried everything else and nothing works, then we'll turn to the Lord. Why is it that way? Why do we always wait to the very last before we ask for His help? But that's the way we do. That's what America is going to do when all seems lost. Those who don't embrace God will be wiped out. Those who do, He'll spare. It will be like the Angel of Death in Egypt, slaying the firstborn of every family except the Israelites who put the blood of a lamb on their lintels. Those who survive, God will use to build up his new order of the ages. God will deliver us. He'll restore us to Adam's former estate. We'll have dominion again the way Adam did, only this time we won't want to lie or cheat or offend God. The Lord is going to do all this for His chosen people who call out to Him and put themselves in His care.

"The Israelites were in Egypt for two hundred and ten years before they crossed the Red Sea and traveled to the promised land. Since our nation was founded in 1776, I feel our time to cross the Red Sea will come in 1986. It's almost upon us. You can see the signs. Things are bad and they're going to get worse.

"We need to be delivered. Like the Israelites in Egypt, we're under some strict exploitation. This time it's from the international banker, who's the seat of the serpent race. The Israelites in Egypt made brick without straw. The Egyptians tore them to bits and told them what to think. It's the same today with the mass media preparing people's minds. I think the same element is in charge of the media.

"There is a group of people, an elite, that's in control. The poor Jew that isn't in the elite, he gets exploited the same as everybody else. He's controlled, too; they exploit him so they can keep the Jew together as a whole. This elite that's always been in charge, they're the international bankers, the Bilderbergers, the CFR, the Fabians, the Illuminati. That's where the seat of the satanic order is. Most of the people in our government are Fabians. Communism was built by this same group of people. They created the Bolshevik Revolution. Don't you see how godless and terrible communism is today?

"Now it's manifested in world Zionism, the plan to build a super one-world government. The United Nations is the framework of the whole thing. They plan to build a U.N. Tribunal building over in Palestine. Integration is part of all this. This elite group, they're constantly trying to upbreed themselves. The philosophy of the land is to integrate. They're forcing integration. Mrs. Roosevelt encouraged this. She said we want to build a super race, a homogenized race. They called him 'the UNESCO man.' There's a statue of him in the rotunda of the U.N. Building in New York. He's olive drab, a mixture of everybody. This is wiping out the races, especially the white race of people.

"Some people say when you talk like this, you're biased, you're a racist. Well, Jesus was a racist then. And God was a racist, because he put divisions between us like this."

Other Identity ministers might quarrel with some of the particulars, but Edminster's version of the message is true to the essentials. These basic motifs recur constantly in Identity tracts and sermons:

1. The image of Identity believers representing the last embattled few who will remain faithful through adversity. Identity congregations sometimes refer to themselves as "the Remnant," in reference to the 144,000 stalwarts who preserve the faith and the kingdom during the Tribulations in the Book of Revelations.
2. The distinction between an absolute law of God and man's faulty regulations. Identity believers often justify civil disobedience, especially tax rebellion, on the grounds that they are obligated only to divine law.
3. The assumption that, by flouting God's law, the nation has moved to the brink of disaster. Identity believers are convinced that an epochal cataclysm is impending. To them, the Russian invasion of Af-

ghanistan, the explosion of Mt. St. Helen's, high interest rates, violent crimes, even erratic weather patterns, are a telling portent, not disconnected occurrences. The corresponding assertion is that nobody owes allegiance to institutions that have become so corrupt as to incur God's wrath. This is a real contrast to the lingering respect for civil establishments that is characteristic of conservative Christianity.

4. The conviction that the white race in its present state has been reduced from an elevated glory, while other races were created as subservient physical beings and can aspire no further. I once heard a fundamental Baptist minister discussing the evils of race-mixing with a gathering that was largely Identity. The minister at one point cited a biblical law that seems to banish for ten generations those of mixed blood. A man in the audience interrupted to say, "The thing is, you're talking about these other races as if they're people like us."

   "I know what you're getting at," the minister said. "You're going on the idea that all the other races are pre-Adamic, like beasts of the field. I can't say I see that when I read my Bible, but if that's going to help you keep your family bloodlines pure and white, you go right on and believe it."

   Later, the minister said privately: "What these people [Identity believers] are saying is that God had to practice for a while on the other races before He finally got it right. And I can't buy that. It's blasphemy to me."

5. The assumption that Jews are inherently evil, that they have been imbued with a cunning and a sense of purpose which is really beyond normal human capacity, because this is all part of God's plan. The implication is that God created Jews as a natural enemy of the white Christian.

6. The conviction that Jews in the midst of white Christians creates inevitable friction. The most extreme conclusion is that Jews ought to be removed from the earth to end this turmoil. I've never heard an Identity minister advocate such an extreme, but it is a conclusion that I have heard some believers voice after listening to a particularly rousing sermon.

7. The premise that for white Christian Americans there is no distinction between race, religion, and nationality. This is a most potent combination: Maybe the best recent example of the fervor that it can produce was in mobs that captured the U.S. Embassy in Teheran. They were at once Persians, Moslems, and members of the Iranian nation; to be one was to be the other, and there was no question of divided loyalty.

How popular is the movement? There is no national Identity church, and thus no national list of congregations. But one compilation shows more than fifty ministers identified with the doctrine. The most important of those whose message evokes some strain of the Identity belief are William Gale of Los Angeles, one of the earliest Identity preachers; Dan Gayman of Schell City, Missouri; Richard Butler of Hayden Lake, Idaho, whose church was bombed in early 1981; James K. Warner of Baton Rouge, Louisiana, a leading white nationalist; Bertrand Comparet of Metairie, Louisiana, who joined the late Wesley Swift to produce the first Identity sermons less than thirty years ago; Sheldon Emry of Phoenix, who has a national following through a mail campaign and a radio network, and who leads the minority of Identity ministers opposing the two-seed-line approach; and Robert Miles of Cohoctah, Michigan, onetime Grand Dragon of a Michigan Klan,[1] who uses elements of Identity theory in preaching a philosophy he calls "dualism," and whose congregation has been addressed by West German racist Manfred Roeder and Matt Koehl of the National Socialist White Peoples party.[2]

Identity's implications are broad. It provides answers to political, moral, military, and racial issues. It careens from religion to politics to cosmology, touching virtually every subject of interest to the Radical Right as it goes. Fusing the two-seed-line Identity doctrine to conspiracy provides an explanation and a villain for virtually every social ill.

Identity's differences with conservative Christianity? Because it holds that Adam was specifically white, and of a higher order than any other creature, it makes dogma of racism; conservative Christianity, while it may harbor some racists, is not an inherently racist philosophy. Identity also contradicts the fundamentalists' literal biblical interpretation that the Jews are God's chosen. Thus, it provides a focus and a rationale for the hatred of Jews so prevalent on the Radical Right (though, in truth, the Radical Right has never seemed to need any encouragement or justification for that hatred).

Like some conservative Christians, Identity preachers have emphasized the apocalyptic prophecies of the Book of Revelation. But there is a crucial difference in the interpretation of those prophecies.

Militants on the right have long criticized a belief in a divine act called "rapture," popular among conservative Christians and fundamentalists. They hold that before the Tribulation occurs, God will snatch away, or "rapture out," his true believers, to keep them out of harm's way. Rapture has infuriated the activists of the Radical Right, who feel that the belief enervates the political impulses by encouraging pure religious faith rather than political works.

Identity, however, teaches that the faithful will have to survive the Tribulation before they can enter the promised kingdom, and that suits the militants perfectly. It also accounts for Identity's impressive representation among survivalists who are preparing for a global disaster.

"Rapture has been used to neutralize a lot of people," says Jack Mohr, the onetime fundamentalist who now calls himself an Identity Baptist. Mohr says: "I used to believe in rapture, and I used to preach it, but after studying my Scripture, I don't believe it anymore. I was giving a talk in Kansas City not long ago about communism and its threat to Christianity, and after I was finished a woman came up to me and she said, 'I agree with most everything you said, but I don't have to worry about that, because Jesus is going to come back and take me away before all that happens.' I asked her what about all those Christians in China and Russia that ended up getting killed in concentration camps. Didn't they feel the same way? I told her, 'You might discover, when it's time to leave, that you're going to get zipped up in a shroud of your own self-righteousness.' People get mad when you tell 'em that. I've had preachers lambaste me for storing up guns and ammunition against a time when I might need them."

It is a deep schism. Conservative Christians regard Identity doctrine as pure heresy. Identity's preachers and believers look with contempt at conservative Christians. By failing to acknowledge the hard truths, they argue, evangelists are diverting souls and energy from the fight at hand. So there is a hard and bitter edge to their voices when they talk about *the churches* and *the preachers,* who are accused of refusing to use their power and their influence on behalf of the race, of refusing even to debate the issue. *My Minister, Is He Wrong AGAIN?*

The fight is dividing the Radical Right along roughly the same lines as the issue of racial conspiracy. It's the same question, actually, posed in slightly different rhetoric: Are Jews our natural enemies? Those who say no tend to group comfortably with those who respect institutions, who choose accepted methods, who are willing to hazard at least a glimmer of optimism about the future. Those who would answer differently are the disenchanted, the disenfranchised, the restless. Within this group—and it may very well be the larger, dominant one within the Radical Right— Identity doctrine in some form has taken firm root.

WITNESSING

Seeing the Light: Three Conversions

(AILEEN LENT was personal secretary to Senator Joe McCarthy for nearly two years when McCarthy was chairman of the Senate Permanent Investigating Committee.)

"In my opinion, the senator was one of the greatest Americans who ever lived. He was like one of us, real natural. He didn't have the social graces that a lot of senators have. He was as real and kind and thoughtful as he could be. He was devoted to this country, he would fight for America, but he wasn't vindictive. I never heard him say anything against other people, except the Communists, yes, what they stood for. He was deadly serious about saving this country. Many of us were really patriotic then. That was America. This country was full of loyal, patriotic, Christian Americans.

"When I left the government, I went to Savannah, Georgia, and started the Conservatives of Savannah organization, and I published a weekly newsletter called the *Bulletin Board of the Conservatives*. I sent it to subscribers in forty states. It was mostly about national legislation. I would read the *Congressional Record*, the bills before Congress, and I would write a résumé on where you should stand on these issues, so people could write their congressmen. In those days I thought you could save the country by understanding the law and getting our senators and representatives to vote right. I published every week for six and a half years. At the same time, I organized the American party of Georgia.

"Later I moved to Florida, and I became chairman of the party there. I used to call meetings of the state party and a man would come to me saying, 'Can I see you for ten minutes before the meeting, just ten minutes?' He'd come in with his Bible and he'd say, 'This is what the Jews are. They're not Israel, we're Israel.' And I'd tell him that I didn't have time to listen, so he'd send me some material and I'd put it aside. Six years in Florida and I never did wake up.

"It was the same later when I moved to Arkansas. My husband and I kept meeting people who'd say, 'Do you know who you are?' And I'd say, 'Yeah, I'm a Christian, don't bother me.' I joined a Baptist church, then another Baptist church, but all the time I kept thinking that something was wrong. I've been an Episcopalian, been a Methodist, and it always seemed like something was missing.

"So finally I decided to listen to some of this Israel business, and, you know, all of a sudden I realized what I was. I told my husband we had to go to Pastor Emry's meetings, but God got me sick so I couldn't go to Arizona to see Emry. Instead, we went three times to Dan Gayman's meetings in Missouri.

"Then God told us to move to Missouri, so we sold out in Arkansas. We had two houses, we had wells, we had guns, we had food, everything stocked up to last through the holocaust or whatever. But God said, 'You go up there now. This is the most important thing you'll ever do.' So now we really work for Christ and country, for Dan Gayman's church. I act as his secretary. I type up his newsletters. My husband is his treasurer. We give one hundred percent of our time.

"Pastor Gayman has been on tour in California. He says the people out there are crying for information about Identity. The last time I talked to him it was six-thirty in the morning out there, and he had been talking until one-thirty the night before. He said that he had gotten a whole Pentacostal church accepting the Christian Identity message, and he had all sorts of material he wanted me to bundle up and mail out there. He has a terrific turnout wherever he goes. This is beautiful. See, God is working now. Really, in the last days, He begins to work so fast."

(GORDON "JACK" MOHR estimates that he has spoken in 3,000 communities in forty-nine states, and in five foreign countries. The targets of his lectures have included gun control, humanism, drugs, and the unhealthy influence of rock music. He is a retired colonel in the U.S. Army, now a military adviser to the Christian-Patriots Defense League, and he is said to have been the first American soldier wounded in the Korean War.)

"About 1948, a year and a half before the Korean War began, I was in Korea as an adviser to the South Korean Army, and I was captured by Communist rebels in an attempted military coup. The plan was that they were going to take over by coup instead of by invasion as they tried in 1950. I was held prisoner for about three weeks until I escaped. I watched the take-over of Sunchon, a community of maybe 175,000 people, and I watched as the Communists very brutally slaughtered over thirty-eight hundred people.

"I was pretty badly mistreated while I was held captive. I was tortured, stripped naked in front of a crowd of several thousand people, with wires hooked up to my genitals as they turned the electricity on. I was sentenced to death by a firing squad. A Korean sergeant made quite a show of roughing me up, beating on me, while I was on trial. He was friendly to me, although I didn't know that at the time. After I was sentenced, he asked for permission to execute me, and he must have convinced them that he was the man for the job, because they allowed him to take me out of the city to shoot me. Instead, when we were out of sight, he fired some shots over my head and let me go. I went to the home of an American missionary and I stayed there until the government troops recaptured the area.

"It was horrible. I never thought I'd get out of it alive. What happens when a guy gets into a situation like that is that he starts making a lot of promises to the Man Up There. And when I came out of it, I felt pretty strongly about things. Until that point, I had never known very much about communism. I had watched the military propaganda movies about the siege of Stalingrad and I admired the Russian people for the way they stood up to the Germans in World War Two. And I pretty much felt that the Germans were the bad guys and the Russians were the good guys, the way we'd been told. I came out of my experience in Korea with strong feelings against communism, though, and I tried to learn all that I could about it.

"After I got out of the army in sixty-four, I started doing some speaking. Service clubs and Rotary clubs would invite me to talk about my experiences, and it started to escalate as I got better known. In 1968 I joined the John Birch Society speakers' bureau. I was with them for about twelve years, and while I think the organization itself is attempting some worthwhile things, I didn't like the dictatorial control that was coming down from headquarters. I was more or less told that there were certain areas that I should steer clear of and not talk about.

"I had been brought up in a church to believe that the Jews are the chosen people of God, and never to say anything against them. As I began to study the communist conspiracy, I realized that there was a very strong Jewish influence in the background of the conspiracy. I began to mention this occasionally, and I would get called on the carpet and was told I was not supposed to say this. The Society doesn't tolerate anything at all that could be construed as being anti-Zionist.

"After I left the John Birch Society, I began to study more deeply the Zionist connection with the communist conspiracy. I did more research. I've always hated hypocrites, somebody who would come in and sail under a false flag. I'd done a lot of work in fundamental churches, and I thought it would be wrong for me to go into a church where the pastor was teaching that Jews are God's chosen people, when I believed they weren't. So I wrote a letter laying out my views and what I had discovered, and I sent it to about two hundred fundamental church leaders.

"I immediately got about ninety-eight percent blackout. I had fourteen weeklong crusades scheduled for that year, and all but two of them were canceled. Those that have stayed with me, I don't go into their churches and mouth off about Jews, but the pastors know the way I feel. I try to keep away from the radical end of it as much as possible. I can talk about somebody that's had a bad influence without calling him a dirty kike or something like that. I've heard people curse the Jews, but I don't see what they gain from that.

"Recently I got a letter from a guy who thinks the way I do, except that he was angry because I use the names God and Jesus instead of Yahweh and Josueh, and he said I was going to go to hell because of that. But that's unusual. On the whole, I get along fine with the Identity folks, because now I'm an Identity Baptist."

(CLYDE EDMINSTER preaches the End Time Doctrine—his term for the Identity message—to a small congregation in Rainier, Washington.)

"You should have seen me before I got saved. God had to throw me over a cliff to save me.

"I used to go to church, but I wasn't a Christian. I smoked, cussed, went out. I had to get half loaded before I went off to work. One day after I got married, the Lord allowed me to work on a big dam, working on the side of a cliff, four hundred and fifty feet deep. We had ropes and a safety belt; I would hang down with a jackhammer and drill holes for dynamite into the cliff. One day I broke hold of a rope that had a cut in it. It broke, and I started falling. I could see the bottom, I was gone. I blacked out, and when I came to, I was holding on to another rope, up on a little ledge.

"The next night or two, I went to a revival meeting with my wife. The preacher started talking, and he showed me that I could have gone to hell, could have burned in hell forever. It scared the pants off me when I saw what could have happened. When he asked for people to come down and give their hearts to Jesus, I turned to my wife and I said, 'Honey, we're going down there.' We did, we invited Him into our hearts.

"You can't believe what a change come over me. I quit drinking, I quit cussing. Dirty jokes, I used to tell them by the hour. But it wasn't long before I couldn't remember a dirty joke. I just wanted to remember my Scripture and to sing Christian songs.

"When I went into the service, the Lord called me to the ministry. I used my veteran's benefits to go to seminary. I was ordained in forty-eight, and I've been a preacher ever since. For a long while I preached just as I was taught in the seminary, but I had a feeling that something didn't measure up. I studied my Scripture inside out, read the book until I wore the pages out. I knew something was wrong, but I couldn't figure out what it was. Then my brother told me about this fellow, Conrad Gaard, and told me that I ought to visit him and talk with him. It was Conrad Gaard who taught me about the kingdom, about how we're Israel, and that was what I started preaching, just the way I do today.

"Some of our denominational brothers didn't like that. See, the enemy has gotten into the church. So we don't have much fellowship with the denominational congregations in our area. I hold services every Sunday morning, with Bible study and Sunday School. We don't get a real big crowd, mostly family and people that see my warped way of seeing things. I try to get the word out. I preached for a long time, but the written word is more powerful, and I can express myself better by writing than by speaking. Scripture says, 'This gospel of the kingdom must be preached as a witness to all nations.' So I try to get my witness in there. I do work hard. There's a lot of work still to be done. There's a kingdom to be brought in."

6

"I fired the bastards," the man says. "You understand what I'm saying? I fired my government. They don't work for me anymore."

He is a small man, with deep-set haggard eyes, and he talks in a tone that could start a brawl if it were used in the wrong place at the wrong time. He brings cigarette to mouth, draws on it harshly, expels the smoke noisily through tight lips.

"When they got me into court, I got up and said, 'I have fired all persons on the public payroll. You shouldn't have to be here today, you should be out playing golf. You don't work for me anymore. I found out you didn't mean what you said when you took your oath.'

"The hardest time in jail I did was county jail time. I saw that no matter how much I didn't want to go to jail, I was there. So, I determined that I am subject to the despotism that Christians tolerate as law. The many-membered body of Christ, all us Christians, we are sick. We are divided. We are not in tune with our God. So, while the body is sick and in disarray, I am subject to that illness."

This is the frontier of the Radical Right, where talk comes in fighting words, where anger and disillusionment and bitter spleen are the common tender, where a stretch of jail time is proof of honor, where books of law are valued for the heat they will generate when burned on a cold night. This is a tough place full of hard men. It is a state of mind, but real enough for all that; its inhabitants live among us, but they are no longer with us.

82

Circumstance in the form of unpalatable law is partly responsible for that. But inclination is part of it as well. What's palatable, in law as in food, is very much a matter of personal taste. Listen to enough of the outlanders' hot words, learn enough about what they have done with their lives, and the conclusion is inevitable: These are not happy people and they are bound to live apart from the pack.

They break laws, but to call them lawless is flip and misleading. Most of them would say that they observe a code, but one different from ours— God's law, maybe, or personal insight, or a U.S. Constitution that has been carefully sifted to remove offending amendments and disagreeable Supreme Court rulings. They claim a moral prerogative, and they refuse to acknowledge that they are criminals.

Call it the Renegade Right, if you will. Its desperadoes may be distinguished from the rest of the movement by the enemies they proclaim; their principal villains are as likely to include the U.S. government as Russian Communists. Sometimes the focus is narrow: The IRS, FBI, or the now-defunct Bureau of Alcohol, Tobacco, and Firearms (BATF) have all bedeviled the militant right in the past, and they are now targets of its acrimony. Others reject the federal government in parcel, and find no redeeming qualities. They damn national institutions as completely and forcefully as any Yippie or Weatherman ever did.

When Robert Miles writes about the government, he usually calls it "the cesspool." Washington, D.C., is "the cesspool of cesspool of cesspools." FBI agents are either "redfeds," "satanists," or "federal dogs." Government informants are "rent-a-finks." Jimmy Carter was "the devil's peanut vendor." The terms are all from Miles's newsletter, *From the Mountain,* and nowhere within it is there any suggestion that he intends ironic overstatement. Miles means what he writes.

Miles preaches what he calls "dualism" to his congregation near Cohoctah, Michigan. He believes that God and Satan, nearly equal in power, are waging a cosmic battle and that we on the earth have been choosing up sides since Creation. He leaves no doubt about which side America's leaders and their minions have taken. The U.S.A. and the USSR, he writes, are "twin sisters of hell."

Miles is a former Grand Dragon of a Ku Klux Klan in Michigan. He served six years in federal penitentiaries for the burning of school buses in Pontiac, Michigan, after federal courts ordered busing of schoolchildren in 1971. Now his newsletter frequently carries the names and mailing addresses of jailed Klansmen and Nazis. One recent issue proclaimed: "No government other than that of God. No obedience except to the laws of God. No submission except to the will of God. No nation except that of our race given to us by God. For we war against princes and principalities which, being of this world, are creations of the devil."

The renegades of the right commonly invoke religious privilege. As Miles does, they cite a law of God, a higher authority, that takes precedence over man's regulations and strictures. Sometimes they appear sincere, but more often they simply sound opportunistic; conveniently enough, the fine points of divine statute are far less distinct than those of criminal code.

Most of this is of recent occurrence. Before 1960, the ideological forebears of what is now the Radical Right were almost uniformly respectful of authority and the national establishment. J. Edgar Hoover and the FBI were heroic symbols; Hoover's book *Masters of Deceit* (later revealed to have been written by his subordinates) was widely read and quoted by the conservative anti-Communists who dominated the movement, and at least two former FBI agents, W. Cleon Skousen and Dan Smoot, gained national reputations on the right. Even the Ku Klux Klans, which operated within the hazy penumbra of legal light in the South, made blacks—not federal authority—their targets.

The new militance can be traced to several factors. One is the accusation by Robert Welch that the government was riddled with Communists and that Dwight Eisenhower was a conscious agent of the Communist conspiracy. The charge was made in a private manuscript circulated in 1958, and was made public in 1960. Welch later claimed that his was a personal opinion, not official policy of the John Birch Society, but the effect was still sensational. The JBS at that time was spawning the Radical Right's leadership for the next two decades. Welch's remark—and maybe more important, the perspective that produced it—helped to shape the attitudes of men who in a few years would introduce a new stridency to the rhetoric of the right. Bob DePugh, for example, belonged to the John Birch Society before forming the Minutemen. Later he was dropped from the rolls; many of Welch's early admirers soon grew too contentious for the old master's tastes.

This was a time, too, when the right felt threatened by a liberal Democratic president, by growing pressures from the civil-rights movement, and by a national legislative approach that tended to take power from local government and concentrate it in Washington. The reactionaries of the right became louder, angrier, and increasingly impatient with federal government.

Impatience turned to hostility when the Justice Department began to investigate and prosecute right-wing militants. The techniques of infiltration that the FBI had against the Communist Party U.S.A. served just as well when applied to the United Klans of America. DePugh always claimed to suspect infiltrators in his organization, and his suspicions proved well founded when an agent of the Alcohol and Tobacco Tax Unit testified in 1966 about firearms violations he had witnessed while masquerading as a loyal member of the Minutemen. It would be years before Bob Shelton, DePugh, and other extremists learned the full scope of the FBI's counterintelligence program (COINTELPRO) through releases obtained under the Freedom of Information Act, but those documents only confirmed what the right's most extreme sector had long suspected: that for years some federal agency systematically had been using extralegal measures to harass it and to prevent its growth.

All this convinced the Radical Right that its relationship with American government was one of adversaries, not partners. The extremists' reasoning went further, in some cases. Since the government was now turning against genuine patriots (in their view) and actually was carrying out policies advocated by leftists and Communist sympathizers, then government itself obviously had become subverted. It was no longer to be trusted or supported, but instead was to be regarded as an enemy. The FBI, which the right once regarded as democracy's defense against the evils of international communism, now takes much of the movement's rage. It is a safe bet that America's used-book stores are well stocked with copies of *Masters of Deceit,* which once sat prominently on the bookshelves of right-wingers.

This means that a massive restructuring of a common image is long overdue. Those who associate the Radical Right with flag-waving patriotism and unquestioning loyalty to the Republic are much mistaken. Some in the movement yet cling to the trappings of old-fashioned patriotism; others reject even that. But the important point is that a significant portion of the Radical Right regards official government with as much outright anger as leftist radicals did fifteen years ago.

The renegades gravitate toward the single-issue groups that oppose gun control and taxation. They are the loud and radical element in groups like the National Alliance to Keep and Bear Arms and the U.S. Taxpayer's Union. They dominate some such groups. This is especially true of the more militant "tax revolt" organizations. Nowhere else on the Radical Right is there such a concentration of activists who willingly offer themselves in virtual sacrifice to the cause.

As usual, there are distinctions to be made between moderate and extreme approaches within the tax-revolt movement itself. The difference is straightforward enough here: There are those who want to lower taxes through legal means, and there are those who wish to pay no taxes at all, who almost by definition are in defiance of law. The moderates include Howard Jarvis and his American Tax Reduction Movement, which several years ago successfully sponsored Proposition 13, a property-tax ceiling in California. The moderates' tools are petitions, lobbyists, and political action groups. They are careful to make clear that they consider themselves part of the established order. And they are, although there is surely some crossover from the radical groups: Jarvis's organization, for example, very likely includes militant tax-strikers among its members or sympathizers. Generally, however, the plodding work of legislative initiative is dry and pale stuff for the renegades. They crave action, and there is no surer way of finding it than by failing to pay federal income tax. That is the path that many of them choose—nothing less than contempt for the system and open rebellion against it.

Within this group, the current debate is over just how open the rebellion must be to succeed. One argument holds that the best course is for a relative few to openly boycott the tax system, thus to encourage others. The opposing line is that quiet but widespread resistance alone will be enough to forever foul the works.

The following exchange, recorded at a tax-protest seminar in the summer of 1981, suggests the essentials of the argument—and its tenor, as well. This took place as one self-professed "tax fighter," a member of the Posse Comitatus, lectured a gathering of perhaps twenty people. He was about ten minutes into his discourse, hair flying, arms waving, voice rising and falling, when someone broke in.

FIRST VOICE: How can we abolish the income tax?

SPEAKER: Stop paying, number one!

VOICES: Tell us how to do it.

SPEAKER: Are you salaried people? Then you've got to go to your employer, you identify yourself as a constitutionalist and a sovereign American citizen. You have to get him to stop withholding your taxes. You take this piece of paper here [*waving a statement prepared by the Posse*] and you say, "I, Joe Smith, am not an artificial person created by any level of government, such as—"

SECOND VOICE [*with some assurance*]: You file something like that, you're going to have the IRS on your back in a minute.

SPEAKER: You don't think they're going to give up easily.

SECOND: But the thing is to keep the scum off your back while you're learning. Take two or three years to learn the stuff before you do anything. Get out of banking, so you won't have any financial records. What does the IRS do if they audit you and you're the least bit resentful of it? They grab your bank records. Ninety-nine percent of all your records, all your expenses, all your income is in your bank account. If you're a corporation, dissolve. You have to file two returns, they've got you in double jeopardy.

SPEAKER [*nods, resumes reading statement*]: "I categorically deny that the Internal Revenue Service has any jurisdiction over my life, liberty, or property in any way whatsoever without my knowledge, consent, or voluntary permission, which I specifically deny or withdraw if tendered mistakenly without knowledge and understanding." Sign it and give it to your employer.

SECOND VOICE: The IRS is going to come get you if you try that.

SPEAKER: You have to declare your independence. You're in no position to do anything until you've done that. Last week on TV I saw an IRS district manager in New York state that in the past year there were over a million people who either refused to file or refused to pay their income tax. Now, listen to what he said then. Only a thousand of these, only a thousand, were apprehended or audited or what have you. That's one one-*thousandth*.

FIRST VOICE: But I don't want to be one of those one one-thousandth.

SPEAKER: Now wait a minute. Then he said only one hundred of those were penalized. Now there is where you have to get down to the nitty-gritty, where you have to start working and fighting.

FIRST VOICE: Are there any groups that are getting together? That's a lot stronger than an individual.

SPEAKER: No! There's nothing stronger than the individual. You've got to recognize that we are sovereign. We don't need organized groups. But I can point you to many, many individuals who have gone this way and will help you. I mean, there are a lot of brave patriots who braved jail, went to jail for their beliefs.

SECOND VOICE: That's the reason we need a network of groups, people who have done research and know the ways of getting around this another way. The individual is going to go out and make the same mistakes everybody else makes and they're going to go to jail for it.

SPEAKER: Hell, they can't put us all in jail.

SECOND VOICE: No, but they can put some of us in.

SPEAKER [*loudly*]: All right, then, by God, they killed, they destroyed the signers of the Declaration of Independence. Let's lay our lives down for our country if we have to do it. Let's not chicken out.

[*A few cheers*]

SPEAKER: Last year there were only three hundred people in the whole United States that got sent to the crowbar resort. And I mean, it is a resort. And for heaven's sakes, don't get a lawyer to represent you when you go to court. This is fatal.

SECOND VOICE [*incredulous*]: It is? You must be joking.

SPEAKER: Listen, the lawyer is going to try to make a deal if you'll plead guilty. Don't do it! The worst gangster in the world pleads not guilty. Get up there and have your say, you make use of your constitutional guarantee of a trial by jury.

SECOND VOICE: You're going to make cannon fodder out of a lot of the people listening to you.

SPEAKER: That's probably so.

The tax rebels contend that the system they're fighting is ready to be toppled. They see it as a behemoth balanced on matchsticks. Pull out a few matchsticks here, a few there, a few more elsewhere . . . and the thing will come tumbling down, they claim, since neither the IRS nor the court and criminal system has the means to punish millions of offenders.

So the tax rebels see it as a battle of numbers. As long as they appear to be a minuscule and isolated group of crackpots, they're losers. But, they believe, if they can appear to offer numerical immunity from prosecution, that guarantee—not to mention greed—may be enough to entice millions into otherwise forbidding waters.

Thus, they try to persuade anyone they can that income taxes can be sneered at, that thousands are doing so already and are untouched. And the IRS is trying to show otherwise by pursuing heavy sentences for visible offenders. Until recently, IRS officials had refused to comment on claims by some tax rebels that they had successfully evaded filing for ten years or more, and that up to sixteen million people are successfully avoiding taxes. But a report by the General Accounting Office in 1981 urged the IRS to make public the tax returns of such self-claimed scofflaws. The report also encouraged the IRS to publicize the tax returns of those who claim to be innocent citizens illegally harassed and persecuted by vicious agents. The GAO claimed that the number of tax protesters identified by the IRS computers rose from 7,700 in 1978 to 20,800 in 1980. And while that was fewer than .05 percent of the forms filed, IRS district offices will spend a disproportionate 2 percent of compliance budgets pursuing the offenders, the report estimated.

That is testimony to the doggedness, the inventiveness, and frequently the plain intransigence and hostility of committed tax rebels, for whom the battle is usually a lifetime calling.

Some rebels—identified by the IRS as "illegal tax protesters," or ITPs— take the direct course and simply do not file a return. Others rely on a variety of subterfuges, schemes, and ploys, all of dubious legality and effectiveness. Among them:

Family trusts (also known as "living trusts" or "prime trusts"). By deeding all their possessions and wages into these legalistic contrivances (usually constructed at a cost of several hundred dollars or more), tax protesters hope to avoid all but a small percentage of taxes due. In theory, the trust pays out all its income in family living expenses, and thus also owes no taxes. Not effective in practice.

Mail-order churches. Some tax rebels obtain divinity degrees by mail and then use their "ministry" to avoid taxes. They may donate as much as half of their income to their own "church," which then pays its minister's living expenses. Others take a vow of poverty and transfer all possessions and income to the church. (IRS rulings and court precedent have called that tactic illegal, and recently, the IRS has been much stricter in granting tax-exempt status to new nondenominational churches and ministries.)

Barter. Though the bookkeeping alone is a mammoth undertaking, some tax protesters have set up barter markets through which goods and services can be exchanged without a transfer of money. Income from barter is taxable, but the trade can be difficult to trace. Even those protesters who do report barter exchanges may greatly underestimate the true value of what they've received. Many ITPs seem to feel that barter just isn't worth the trouble.

Cash transactions. If it isn't written down, tax rebels claim, then income is almost impossible to prove. Adherents of this tactic advocate dropping out of the banking system (since banks keep microfilm copies of every check and deposit processed) and dealing strictly in cash or money order. Again highly impractical.

Overstatement of allowances and exemptions. Some tax rebels who are wage earners file false W-4 (witholding) forms with their employers' accounting offices, claiming as many as ninety-nine allowances or exemptions from withholding. Then they refuse to file returns, a tactic used by organizers of 3,500 workers at a General Motors plant in Flint, Michigan, several years ago. The leaders of that protest drew jail terms ranging from two to three years, and the IRS now requires employers to file notice of anyone claiming more than nine exemptions.

Federal Reserve protests. This has become a frequent tactic since the treasury stopped issuing paper money as silver certificates. The argument is that since Federal Reserve notes are not redeemable in gold or silver, and since only gold and silver are constitutionally taxable, income received as Federal Reserve notes doesn't need to be claimed on a tax return.*

"Conscience adjustment." Tax rebels seem to have borrowed this tactic from antiwar protesters of the 1960s who declined to pay a percentage of their taxes based on the average amount that would be used for defense spending, usually about 40 percent.

Constitutional objections. This is a favorite of protesters affiliated with the Posse Comitatus. Claiming that the IRS has overstepped its constitutional authority, these tax rebels will file a Form 1040 with name and address only, and an attached statement that details their constitutional beliefs. IRS agents sometimes refer to such returns as "Daly types," after an early tax rebel, Jerome Daly, who unsuccessfully cited Fourth and Sixteenth Amendment issues in refusing to complete his form.

---

* In *U.S.* v. *Wangrud,* the Ninth Circuit court ruled that "it has been established by statute that Federal Reserve notes, on an equal basis with other coins and currencies of the United States, shall be legal tender for all debts, public and private, including taxes."

Fifth Amendment returns are a variation. The protesters supply name and address, but write "object" on every other line, and attach an explanation claiming that the tax form itself violates their right not to incriminate themselves.*

Most of these methods are transparent and the IRS has internal rulings or court judgments that negate all of them. The truth is that tax protesters who advocate such tactics don't expect them to succeed. They seem to be hoping for massive disobedience, not isolated successes. The real fight for most tax rebels begins after they've filed an illegal return. Then they do all they can to delay, frustrate, and overburden the process. Commonly they will make and then break appointments with IRS agents, and flood the agents' desks with requests for information and questions about legal rights and authority. When they finally do meet IRS agents, they frequently come ready to debate political dogma or constitutional rights, not the specifics of a tax return.

Still, the system grinds on. When the protesters go to trial, they almost always demand juries. Many try to plead their own cases without attorneys. On evidence alone, their cases are usually hopeless, but with juries—especially in tax cases—there is always the Big Joker, the element of doubt, the possibility that a tax rebel will make an appeal so emotionally irresistible that the jury will ignore the evidence and refuse to convict. That is usually the last hope of tax rebels, and usually it is a vain one. Tax rebels go to jail every year in numbers great enough to keep most Americans at least reasonably honest, and great enough to keep the tax-protest movement fully stocked with martyrs to the cause.

WITNESSING

Not a Nickel

(RON BOGGS was convicted in 1979 of failure to file an income-tax return. Now he is a frequent speaker at meetings of tax rebels, and this is the story he tells.)

"It happened when they sold the wheat to Russia in seventy-three. Up until then I had been a little bit antagonistic toward the government, not real satisfied with what was going on. I thought it was real stupid, to give

---

* The U.S. Supreme Court, in 1927, ruled in the landmark *U.S.* v. *Sullivan* that a taxpayer could not refuse to file a return on Fifth Amendment grounds.

away our wheat and have food cost more in this country. But when the Russians sold it back to us at an increased price, that really ticked me off. I thought, that's it, now you've done it.

"I was having lunch with some fellas after that happened and I told them how strange it was that we have to take something like that. Then one of them said to me that he had been to a tax-rebellion meeting in Orange County and that a fella there had said that you don't have to pay taxes. Let me tell you, I was in such a stage of fear in those days that when he said those words my heart jumped up in my throat. I was conditioned, oh, yes. That guy just said the magic words and the blood drained out of my face, and my throat went dry. But I had to find out what this guy was talking about. So I asked him where I could find that meeting. I wanted to be there.

"I thought it was going to be one of these cell meetings, and here they're meeting out in a public restaurant. The first speaker gave a dissertation, and he started answering questions, and he told me things that I just couldn't believe. I hadn't even been a student of the John Birch Society, I hadn't even been educated that far on it. I was cold turkey.

"I kept going to the meetings. I got a little bit active in the tax rebellion. Now, I can only absorb so much. I found that I was a rather dense person. I had become conditioned to getting my news from the papers and the boob tube. It would be hard. I'd go to meetings, and the speakers would rattle on and on and on, and all of a sudden, bango, they'd hit something, and it would stick. I began to find out that this thing called the Internal Revenue Service operates under the laws of the Communist Manifesto. Our laws, as far as the Constitution, say that Congress has the power to coin and collect the money. But the IRS is of the executive branch, not out of Congress. Congress gave up its hold on the money system.

"Something else happened during this time. After one of these meetings, a fella invited me to go hear Colonel Gale speak. From Colonel Gale, I began to hear that the white race is the chosen people of the Bible. I started to get the Identity message. Then I really began to realize my ignorance. Jesus said, 'Know the truth and the truth shall make ye free.' And I thought, I must be a slave, because I really don't know the truth.

"See, you're raised in this system to know that there's two things that are positive: death and taxes. Those are two brokagious [sic] lies. First, I am a man of life. I am eternal. That's one. Two, taxation is only a necessary punishment for disobeying the commandments of God. I cannot receive His blessings and deny His commandments at the same time. If you will not follow His government, there's only one other way to go, and that's taxation and despotism.

"I took my wife to a few meetings. I tried to hear different speakers in different parts of the city—in North Hollywood, Orange County, Los Angeles—trying to get a variety of speakers and a variety of ideas. But my wife wasn't too enthusiastic about it. We ought to back off, stay out of the limelight. She didn't like me getting out and being exposed in places where there might be an IRS agent.

"This was seventy-four. I'd go to the Identity church and I'd go to the tax meetings after that. For about a year, all through seventy-four and part of seventy-five, I was really in a quandary. I was thinking, Is the answer tax rebellion, or is it the John Birch Society sort of conservatism, or is the answer really in the Bible? My wife wanted me to stay away from all the trouble that these people were getting into. I wasn't into any trouble yet, but I was learning about it. The answer was, you cannot serve God and Mammon. He didn't leave me any middle road. I had to make my choice. Finally I became determined that I was not going to tell someone else's story. Either these things were true or they were false, and I was going to live my own story.

"On January 1, 1974, I had decided that I could file a W-4E and be in no quandary with the Internal Revenue Service. This would give me a year of study and stop the flow of cash going out of my pocket. I thought I would take the year of 1974 and see what I had learned, and after a year, if I wanted, I could cash in all my chips, pay all the money I owed in what they call 'taxes' and I call 'extortion,' and sign the annual confession form, and that would be it.

"I continued to work; my boss was willing to go along with whatever I wanted to do. I began to feel like a great burden had been lifted from me. I was enjoying a pay increase of between a hundred and a hundred and fifty a week. I worked for that money. And at the end of the year, I was ready to tell 'em I wouldn't support any more of their nonsense. I had to overcome the situation of believing that what we were fighting was communism. I knew it to be nothing other than an evil course. Satan has thrown so many damn dead ends in there, you start out saying where's the answer and you fall into a pit.

"In January of seventy-five, the IRS came to my home. They happened to drop by on an evening when I was holding a Bible-study class. I had no idea they were planning to drop in on me. But, see, I didn't answer their threatening letters. They'd send me letters and I'd just throw 'em in the trash can. So when they came to the house, I had 'em wait out on the porch. It was a chilly evening, but I didn't want 'em in the house. And when I went and talked to 'em, I went out with a gun on my hip. I didn't intend to do anything, but I do like to mouth off.

"We talked a long time, and I answered a lot of questions, and I didn't answer a lot of questions. They were real nice boys. I'll tell you, Al Capone would have been proud of 'em. Nice business suits—you couldn't see their guns. They asked me some questions that really weren't demeaning, like how many children I had, and they wanted to know how much money I earned. I said I didn't know, that my boss gave me a piece of paper but I threw it away, never even looked at it. I don't keep any books and records, so I have no idea. I told 'em, 'Whatever you guys say, I'll buy.' When they were finished, I invited 'em into the house for Bible study, but they said no, they'd rather not. See, I didn't owe a tax. I'm a citizen, not a tax-payer.

"Every so often, I got one of their nasty letters. Never read 'em. So seventy-five was bookin' along pretty good. My wife had filed a W-4E with her employer in April. In the early part of the year, the state sent me a letter. I just wrote on it, 'Deceased, Return to sender,' and they spent a whole six or eight months trying to find out if I was alive. When they finally figured out I wasn't dead, they called me up at work. I had a little go-round with the guy. I told him, 'I will not pay you a bloody nickel, understand that. Kill me, put me in prison, do what you have to do, but you're not getting any of my money.' When I hung up, I told my boss that an order would be coming for him to abscond with my money. Garnishing, extortion. They use a bunch of corkscrew names for all the Jew-Jap-Gypsy crazy bullshit. I said, 'I will not give them a nickel, so tomorrow, pay me up in full and we'll call it a nice day.'

"So I quit my job. They weren't bothering my wife yet, so she kept her job and supported us for the better part of another year. Finally, by October of 1976, we were being notified that we had to go to court.

"During all this time, I'm learning the different ways a guy can go. I watched many sincere patriots—concerned for their country, concerned for their families, concerned for their race—go to jail. They'd go to trial and they'd point out, Here's the law, judge, here's what it says. Ladies and gentlemen of the jury, they have no right to do this, blah-de-blah, on and on and on. And they were making very little headway. Some of them could stall a bit, but, basically, when the IRS decided they were going to pick on a guy, they could just about count on the fact that he was going to jail.

"This upset my wife at these meetings. She wanted to know why the speakers at these meetings didn't prepare the people for the fact that they were probably going to end up in jail. Because most of these guys will tell you, 'Aw, you don't have to go to jail. Use this packet and that packet, this one's five dollars, this one's ten, this one's a hundred, come on over and take my law course,' and all that.

"I had been going through this information. It looked good to me. I thought, Well, somebody ought to be able to go free on that. But people were going to jail. One guy goes free and the next guy goes to jail on the same thing. So we're not really dealing with law, we're dealing with the statutes of Omri. He was a king, and whenever he wanted to do something, he wrote a statute to cover it. And his statutes got as big as probably the L.A. law library. Same old scam. Our boys wrote the book.

"During seventy-seven we knew that the government was going to come down on us, in total, and when they did, we were going to lose everything we had. We knew that. Maybe not the first year, but the year after that another bill was going to come due, and the year after that another bill, and that eventually they were going to get it all. So we did a very logical thing. We gave the house away to my mother-in-law. A daughter can give anything to a parent; there are no laws covering that yet. And my mother-in-law sold the house, and bought a house trailer, which she later gave to her daughter. A friend of mine had some land up north that I could put my mobile home on. And that's what I did. One day I got a letter that I had to sign for, and it was notifying us we had to appear in court.

"So we started our melee in the courts. I wanted to go *pro per,* but they wouldn't let me represent myself. They gave me a lawyer. I told him right from the start, that there was nothing he could do to alter my guilt. I said, 'I am guilty and there is nothing you can do about that. I won't sign their papers. And if I won't sign their papers and pay off their extortion ring, you can't save me from a bloody thing.' I told him, 'You do what you have to do, we'll go down there and spend some time. But I can't go down there and plead guilty to something that isn't a crime.' But I told him to go down there and give it his best, just like he intended for me to win, just like he thought he could convince the jury I was innocent. Oh, yeah.

"We were sentenced to a year and a day on each of three counts, to run concurrently. The crime was willful failure to file for seventy-three, seventy-four and seventy-five. And I made this statement, it's in the record. I said,' I'll willfully never file anything again. 'I won't support 'em. They can put me in prison, that's all right. If I have to spend the rest of my life in prison, I'll accept that. But I won't tolerate being a party to this system. I told the IRS, 'If you catch me with ten thousand dollars in my pocket, I'll burn it before I ever give any of it to you. Not a nickel. I may never enjoy it, but you're not going to get any of it.'

"I never got involved with any of them again. They did the appeal thing without me. I wouldn't even sign the paper for that. I wouldn't even give 'em one drop of ink, you understand? I did my time, I got cut loose. And they knew I'm never gonna pay 'em again. Will they send me back to jail?

I don't know. Are they loaded dice? Do they want me back? I don't know. But I cannot pay taxes. I cannot receive God's blessings and pay taxes. He forbids that.

"My wife gave our daughter the mobile home, and I stay in that now. It's paid for, and I live in it, but it doesn't belong to me. I have no claim to anything. My son bought a vehicle for me to drive. If he hadn't done that, then I suppose I wouldn't have anything to drive. I don't have quite enough faith not to work at all, but I have cut it down to such a minimum that I have a little bit of difficulty surviving on it. I feel that when more of the body of Christ joins me, then it will be a little less difficult to take another step and show them that we only need to work a month every year, and if they come a little bit farther with me, maybe we can show 'em a week. I really don't do a hell of a lot all year. It's sinful, really, that I have such an easy life."

(Ron Boggs's wife died before she entered prison. He lives alone now in northern California.)

7

To complain of official injustice is one thing. To take up arms in complaint is quite another. Some of the renegades on the right have been doing just that. At least two organizations of note on the Radical Right—the Christian-Patriots Defense League and Bill Wilkinson's Invisible Empire, Knights of the Ku Klux Klan—have made no secret of buying guns and training some of their members to use the weapons in what amounts to armed resistance. A third group—the loosely affiliated hyperconstitutionalists who go by the name Posse Comitatus—has embraced the gun as a political talisman.

This is frightening news on the face of it, but old news in a way. Individuals on the Radical Right have been arming themselves for at least twenty years as a matter of personal action. What is changing is that the leaders of at least three groups are urging some of their members to do so now as a matter of policy.

The three cases should be examined individually. They are distinct groups, with ostensibly different purposes. In the case of the Invisible Empire, the organized cadre that the Klan has touted appears far less threatening than the unofficial army that for years has existed within its ranks, in fact if not in name. For the moment, however, the subject at hand is the apparent existence of trained, ideologically committed shock troops within Radical Right organizations. And all indications are that panic

96

about battalions of the right secretly girding themselves for a battle is probably misplaced.

One telling clue is that both the Wilkinson Klan and the C-PDL have eagerly divulged their military training and have even encouraged press coverage, which suggests that their purposes are more mundane than training to one day battle Russians in the shopping malls and suburban sidestreets of America.

The prototype for all American right-wing guerrilla groups is the Minutemen, organized in 1960. Nobody before Bob DePugh had ever urged the right to buy guns and prepare to fight Communists in America. The Minutemen get full treatment in the next chapter; their effect on the Radical Right was, literally, revolutionary. That makes DePugh at least the tactical father of present-day guerrillas, and his observations carry some weight.

"I'm not sure that it's possible to organize a really workable underground organization in this country in peacetime," he said in a recent interview. "The American people are not psychologically in tune with such a thing. Such success as anybody is going to have will have to be very low-key, hidden away and limited to those people that feel it's the thing to do."

And what of groups that advertise their military training?

"My big complaint with that kind of activity now is that it's generally not being used for the purpose that the participants are told that it's for," DePugh said. "In my opinion, those people are not training for a militia, they are going through a little show for the publicity purposes of a leader of the organization, and I don't know of any place where it's being done openly for any other purpose."

That acknowledges a fact of both journalistic and radical life: The press is utterly fascinated by people toting guns, and most leaders on the Radical Right are convinced that they need national media coverage to swell their membership lists. When Bill Wilkinson appears at a press conference in a pinstripe business suit, he is not a figure to set the TV cameras whirring and the strobe flashes winking, dapper though he may be. But let him don the satin robes, and let him be flanked by a half-dozen scowling Klansmen, some of them hefting shotguns and others with their hands wrapped around the tommy guns for which the Invisible Empire somehow obtained federal licenses . . . not only is that a picture for the wire services and the local evening news, but somehow even Wilkinson's words sound more convincing.

It is a matter of image, in part. The various Klan factions have for several years been competing for members and contributions, and the Invisible Empire isn't one bit hurt if it is known among its prospective members as the Klan with the submachine guns.

I broached the subject of the guns as a publicity tool during an interview with Wilkinson. He bristled.

"Those machine guns weren't brought out for the media's benefit," he said. "We've been attacked many times, but we've never been attacked when we've had our guns out. It's a deterrent to those that would attack us, and it works like a champ. There's not many fools that's going to attack a bunch of people that's got a slew of guns."

Point of fact: Wilkinson himself, later in the interview, related the story of an incident in Tupelo, Mississippi, in which a carload of blacks shot at a group of gun-carrying Klansmen, who returned fire and destroyed the automobiles; nobody was seriously wounded. Aside from their value as a practical deterrent, the truth is that guns do rivet the attention of the media, otherwise hard to rouse; and a number of organizations on the Radical Right, including Wilkinson's Klan, seek just that attention for their own purposes.

The Invisible Empire's recent enterprise in guerrilla training shows some different wrinkles when seen in that light.

In September 1980—just a few days before a black man was to go on trial for the shooting of a Klansman in Decatur, Alabama—state Grand Dragon Roger Handley invited three reporters to tour what he said was a training camp for a Klan special forces elite near Cullman, Alabama. The reporters were blindfolded, and put into the bed of a pickup truck, and driven to the campsite. When the blindfolds were removed, the reporters saw about ten men and one woman dressed in combat fatigues and armed with "what appeared to be automatic weapons." The commandos practiced at a firing range and demonstrated their skill over an obstacle course with a rope bridge and a barbed-wire crawl. The camp, the reporters were told, was named My Lai, after the Vietnamese village, and was moved every three months "to avoid detection by the Federal Bureau of Investigation or other law enforcement authorities."

The quotations, and all the other details, are from an article in the September 28, 1980, Sunday *New York Times*. The first two paragraphs suggest that the excursion had its full effect.

CULLMAN, Ala., Sept. 26—Hidden in the hills of northern Alabama, a small contingent of Ku Klux Klansmen, and a woman, are training to become commandos prepared to provide security at Klan rallies and to kill black people in "the race war that's coming," their leader says.

They consider themselves to be an elite cadre and call themselves the

Klan special forces. Rogert Handley, Alabama's Grand Dragon of the Invisible Empire, Knights of the Ku Klux Klan, said they were also ready to insure that places like Birmingham and Decatur, Ala., "don't become another Miami."

The photograph accompanying the articles shows six men and a woman, all in camouflage fatigues, crouched around a campfire in a forest clearing; several of them look distinctly uncomfortable. In the background are two pup tents, a larger open tent over some folding chairs, two kerosene lanterns, and a Confederate Stars and Bars hanging so stiffly that it seems to be starched. Five of the commandos are holding what seem to be semiautomatic rifles. One in the middle of the group is displaying what looks very much like—you guessed it—a submachine gun.

To a reporter who had been blindfolded, driven in the bed of a pickup truck, and jounced into a lonely section of Alabama woods, it was surely impressive stuff. Too impressive, maybe, for the Invisible Empire's purposes, since the Klanwatch project of the Southern Poverty Law Center reprinted the *Times* article and used it in a fund-raising mail campaign the next year. The image of an armed and dangerous Klan commando group lent a certain urgency to Klanwatch's plea for money. In all, an interesting exercise: One group creates what may well be a paper army, and its opposition seizes the image and brandishes it to prove just how significant are its own efforts.

The sarcasm is not meant to imply that the would-be Green Berets in the forest—or Klanwatch, for that matter—are anything but earnest in what they're doing. But any resistance movement that publicizes its own existence is probably a contradiction of itself. True commando training is a most difficult and arduous process that requires more time than the one weekend per month that the Klansmen were reported to devote to it. And the Klan "special forces" apparently are too few to be of much significance in a military operation. None of these facts seems to diminish the commandos' news value, however.

This should not obscure the fact that the various Klans, especially the Invisible Empire, have for years been building what amounts to a virtual standing army with their general memberships. These men own guns, they know how to use guns with deadly effect, and in many cases they need little provocation to flick off the safety—assertions all compellingly supported by the 1980 shoot-out in Greensboro, North Carolina, in which five members of the Communist Workers Party died during an exchange of gunfire with a group of American Nazis and splinter-group Klansmen. The eleven Nazis and Klansmen charged in the case were acquitted when they argued that they were returning fire from the victims.

The lesson in all of this is that Bill Wilkinson and Bob Shelton have within their ranks hundreds of men who can shoot guns, and will. It is an army that neither man is anxious to claim, for it is an army without discipline, without training, without organization. Those inclined to worry about the armed threat from the Klan would be well advised to focus not so much on the army that it claims as on the one that has been silently, informally swelling for years within the klaverns.

Then there is the curious phenomenon of the Christian-Patriots Defense League. It is a paradox, being the pure product of a deftly manipulated press but a legitimate point of convergence on the Radical Right, nonetheless. The group has tried to appeal to a range from basic conservatives to segregationists to Chicken Little doomsayers, and somewhere within that spectrum fall those who choose weekly target practice as a mode of political expression. The Defense League trains what it calls a "militia." It counts two former U.S. Army colonels among its training staff, and once or twice a year it holds exercises open to public and press. Again, there's a real question about the ultimate purpose of this training.

Like every other Radical Right group of any consequence, the C-PDL is the creation and the responsibility of one man: in this case, John R. Harrell, a onetime salesman of mausoleums and real estate who turned to conservative politics and fundamental religion after what he claims was a miraculous recovery from lymph cancer in 1959. (In a booklet that he publishes privately, Harrell relates in detail how a physical manifestation of the Holy Spirit extracted cancerous tissue from his body while he lay dying in a hospital bed.) From that moment, Harrell says, he dedicated his life to the service of God and country. He ran for the U.S. Senate from Illinois in 1960 and was decisively defeated. A few months later, he gave refuge to a young Marine deserter on the grounds of his twenty-five-acre estate in Louisville, Illinois, in the south-central part of the state. The deserter told Harrell he was fleeing the immorality and debauchery he had found in the corps. Harrell refused to allow federal officers on the property to question the man.

By then, Harrell already had founded the Christian Conservative Church, which would become the financial anchor for a series of right-wing groups. He also had a small band of followers living with him in outbuildings on the estate grounds, and fifteen of those supporters, as well as Harrell and his thirteen-year-old son, were arrested and charged with harboring the deserter after more than a hundred agents surrounded the grounds and rammed a gate with a half-track personnel carrier.

In 1963, with IRS troubles and an indictment for harboring a fugitive hovering over him, Harrell disappeared with his family. He was himself a fugitive for a year and a half before being arrested in Arkansas. He served four years in federal penitentiaries in Terre Haute and Leavenworth, and he boasts today that he still owes over $500,000 in unpaid taxes, and that the FBI turned over more than 3,000 pages under his name when he requested his files through the Freedom of Information Act.

When his probation ended in 1976, Harrell formed in short order the Christian-Patriots Defense League, the Citizens Emergency Defense System, the Paul Revere Club, and the Save America Gun Club. The point of this variety is uncertain, since membership in any one of the organizations qualifies someone for membership in all of the others. Membership in all the groups is open, anyway; only the Paul Revere Club demands even minimal dues, $5 per month.

Surely there is a legal rationale for the jumble of names. By all appearances, it is the Christian Conservative Church that channels money to the other operations, while the political linchpin of Harrell's organization is the Christian-Patriots Defense League. The hyphen, Harrell says, is deliberate. He wanted to make clear when he formed the group that he was casting out his message not only to Christian patriots but to those who might be only Christian or only patriotic. The group's message (and Harrell's): The nation is sliding to perdition on greased tracks, its downward momentum so great that we can only prepare for the inevitable crash.

Once or twice a year since 1977, Harrell's groups have sponsored a four-day "freedom festival" on the church grounds in Louisville, Illinois. The 1981 gathering brought to the estate about 1,500 people, many families, with political persuasions that evidently included survivalists, supporters of a gold standard, tax-strikers, Klansmen, National Socialists, white racists, and a heavy representation of Identity Christians. (Harrell recently abandoned his own fundamentalist beliefs in favor of a version of Identity doctrine.) Admission is open to anyone who applies, as long as anyone is white; Harrell is a complete and unrepentant segregationist. He says that freedom festivals for other races are held elsewhere, in undisclosed locations.

With that exception, however, admission is open to anyone, including the press. Harrell and his group have been the subject of at least six articles in major newspapers in the last two years. *Time* magazine covered the festival in autumn of 1979, and ABC News featured the group extensively in a 1981 story about the militant right. Harrell knows public relations. He makes the job of TV news crews easy, liberally dispensing short, colorful quotes that can be inserted into a ninety-second film story.

"We work with the media," he told a gathering last summer. "We give 'em coffee to drink—we haven't put anything that's harmful in it yet—we wish them well, and then when they write a bad story, we tell them they ought to be ashamed of themselves, call them on the telephone, write them a letter, and then get ready for the next round."

Harrell wants names on his membership lists. To get them, he does some advertising (his classified ads sometimes run in the back pages of *Soldier of Fortune* magazine, between offerings of bulletproof vests and mercenaries), but he relies mostly on exposure in the media. His theory is that multitudes of Americans will be attracted to his group if they can only learn that it exists; therefore, mention of the group in any context is valuable, and the only bad press is no press at all.

"This is one of hundreds of recently published accounts of our activities," a C-PDL broadsheet noted of the *Time* article. "Although few publications present the issues and dangers in the proper light and understanding, nevertheless, it spreads the word to the extent that concerned and interested American patriots can know of our effort. Therefore, any article that has even a tendency to alert citizens is valuable, for patriots are now beginning to read between the lines of any report. This reprint has been considered by many to be quite beneficial, especially in the contact of those who are more liberal-minded, as many of them will rally to the nation's standard when they see that all they have is about to be destroyed forever."

The Defense League gets special attention—in this chapter, in *Time* magazine, and elsewhere—because it claims to be raising and training a militia composed of its members. It lists as its two principal military advisers Colonel B. F. von Stahl (U.S. Army, retired), and Colonel Gordon "Jack" Mohr (U.S. Army, retired), the onetime member of the John Birch Society's lecture staff. The two lend at least a faint military air to an operation that otherwise looks decidedly slapdash. The turnout for the Defense League military exercises in the summer of 1981 seemed to be less than 200 volunteers, the majority of them men apparently in their late forties and older. Most had a novice's uncomfortable look, which seemed to support the common belief elsewhere on the Radical Right that Harrell's groups experience an unusually high turnover rate, even for this movement with its chronically dissatisfied and peripatetic membership.

Again, the military realities: Training once or twice a year does not produce a commando group, not even a militia. Harrell's public training serves him well when the TV cameras roll, but it would seem to be of little value otherwise.

Still, should Harrell's apocalypse ever come to pass, he and his followers won't go undefended. Harrell, as a convicted felon, can't own a gun, but it is almost certain that his groups and supporters do have guns and ammunition in some quantity. Harrell's church and the Defense League have developed several survival centers in the Midwest, and they would be unusual survivalists if they were unable to defend themselves against marauders. But their armaments would be cached where one day they might be needed; they would not be distributed to an erstwhile volunteer militia that faithfully performs for the media.

Harrell is also affiliated with a Christian Identity survival community in rural Missouri called the Covenant, the Sword, the Arm of the Lord (CSA). The group operates a school for survival and paramilitary techniques. CSA members provided the security force for the Defense League's freedom festivals, and several also were instructors in self-defense and weaponry. They were men in their twenties and thirties. Many claimed to be military veterans. They gave every appearance of knowing what they were doing and why.

By Bob DePugh's definition, the perfect underground army of the right is one that we don't know about. The Posse Comitatus is not far from that description. The organization is no secret. Nor is it a secret that Posse members buy and use guns, and defend jealously their right to do so. But unanswered is the question of whether Posse members are training as a militia-style group. There are reports that in at least one state they are doing exactly that. Furthermore, unlike the Invisible Empire or the C-PDL, they are wary of attracting attention. This all makes the angry defiance of Posse rhetoric especially disturbing. The renegade urge runs strong here.

"The majority of the 'laws' passed by Congress have no Constitutional authority and thus are null and void. For example: Interstate Commerce Commission, Federal Reserve, Social Security, FTC, FAA, FCC, FDA, OSHA, FEA, CPSC, NEA, LEAA, and gun legislation," wrote one Posse member in a letter that he distributed to state and county officials in California several years ago. "As long as we are burdened with these unconstitutional agencies we will never be a free country, but will continue to degenerate into tyranny, where revolution will be the ONLY SOLUTION."

The letter suggests remedies, among them: "(1) Understand that you do NOT represent the people, but the UNITED STATES CONSTITUTION. (2) Read the Constitution and realize that it is a DOCUMENT OF FREEDOM, not slavery. . . . (3) THINKING must be re-oriented to limited government and FREE PEOPLE. (4) Understand that MORALS, CHARACTER, and RESPONSIBILITY cannot be legislated. (5) GOVERNMENT cannot keep people from making mistakes. . . ."

And finally, the meat of the matter. Under "ACTIONS WE WILL

TAKE," the letter lists: "(1) We will obey no unconstitutional statute. (2) We will discontinue paying income and social security taxes. (3) We will remain armed regardless of laws initiated in congress to repeal our second amendment rights."

That is the Posse, stubbornly demanding every right, every freedom that can be squeezed and cajoled out of the Constitution, the Magna Carta, and the Articles of Confederation. It would be a good deal easier to dismiss them as crackpots if their independence and their hardheaded insistence were not so much a part of our revolutionary history. Even today, this is not a nation in which to argue against an excess of freedom, or even to suggest that such an excess could exist.

But the Posse's defiance has a way of slipping into sheer belligerence. Their tactics seem less valiant than mean-spirited, a nastiness that we don't associate with Jefferson or Patrick Henry. And what usually begins as a suspicion of all government has a way of turning into a hostility toward this government in particular.

In Wisconsin, where the Posse seems strongest (local organizers claim 2,000 members in thirteen counties there), its leaders have filed common-law nuisance liens totaling millions of dollars against state officials.[1] Such suits freeze the respondents' personal assets until the claims are dismissed. Some other Posse activity smacks of juvenile pranksterism: The Posse in Wisconsin, and elsewhere, for example, has sold for 50¢ a "universal sportsman's license," which is supposed to grant the holder unlimited hunting and fishing privileges on public land.[2] The Posse claims that states have no right to regulate the use of public lands. To back up their claim, they occasionally park their camper trucks and claim squatters' rights on property controlled by the state or the federal government.[3]

Often, Posse activities go from foolish to demonstrably dangerous. In the San Joaquin valley of California, Posse members have worn sheriff-style badges and have affixed ersatz police insignia to their cars and trucks.[4] They also have been known to covet the power of police. The San Joaquin Posse once placed a full-page ad in a Stockton newspaper, claiming that it could make arrests of errant county officials, and then tried to prove the claim by attempting citizens' arrests of the sheriff and the San Joaquin County district attorney.[5] The sheriff retaliated with a $198-million suit against Posse officials, demanding that they put away their badges and insignia, and charging that sheriff's officers had received "intimidating" messages from Posse members.

In Stanfield, Oregon, seven Posse members seized a potato-packing shed during a land dispute in 1976. They were charged with burglary and inciting to riot.[6]

In 1974, Wisconsin Posse members assaulted and briefly held prisoner an IRS agent.[7] They photographed him, interrogated him, and demanded that he sign a "public servants' questionnaire"—a thirty-three-item document asking for a variety of personal and official information, including the name and address of anyone who has been paid to furnish information about the taxpayer. Thomas Stockheimer, Posse chairman in Wisconsin, was convicted of assault in that case and served ninety days in jail.

In Wisconsin, Posse members have been arrested for illegal possession of weapons and for impersonating police officers. And judges in that state at times receive letters of complaint under the letterhead of the Committee to Save Judges from Hanging Even Though They Deserve It.

Again in Wisconsin, where Posse activity seems strongest, a Posse member who had been stopped for questioning by a state highway patrolman radioed for assistance by citizens' band radio; six other members arrived (some armed with semiautomatic rifles) and overpowered the policeman. The driver is now serving a seven-year sentence for assault.

Behind all this is a certain arrogance, a conviction that justice is ill-served by the present system and that the Posse's members have a better way. Indignation runs strong through the renegades on the right. From their perspective, the gap to insurrection and disobedience looks narrow and easily crossed. For the Posse, that step would take the form of vigilante action, justice swiftly and unflinchingly delivered by citizens without legal rights or restrictions. The step is one that Posse members seem to discuss constantly.

Guns make thuggery especially ominous, and the Posse does have guns. Its members often carry guns strapped to their hips or within easy reach in car or truck. In California and Wisconsin, at least, the Posse is thought to have conducted weapons training in secluded rural areas. Some Posse members do so only at great risk. Those who are convicted felons can neither vote nor—perhaps more important to them—possess a firearm. And because they have persistently, almost pathologically, bucked the established legal order, the most committed Posse members often find themselves convicted of serious crimes and thus legally prohibited from ever again putting their hands on their favored tool of social change. Felons in the Posse who succumb to the lure of gunmetal and burnt powder do so at considerable peril, and usually only in the most private circumstances, a condition that may help to explain those dire warnings to trespassing police with which Posse members sometimes post their property.

It is a convenience to use the singular term "the Posse," but any implications of concerted force or nationally unified action are misleading. The Posse Comitatus is unified only in general principle. It is, at its most cohesive, a loose confederation of a relative few zealots who tend to form in clusters of six or eight or a dozen close acquaintances. Men who join the Posse bring with them a fundamental abhorrence of regimentation and cooperation. To follow orders en masse would violate every natural precept by which they live.

The group known collectively as "the Posse," then, consists mainly of men free-lancing a private idea of justice. For all but a minuscule number, the main commitment is less to the organization than to the principles it holds. They are Posse members only as long as being in the Posse and wearing that badge suit them. They are likely to belong to other groups as well, especially organizations of tax protesters and national gun-control opponents. The clusters of eight or ten or a dozen men are capable of erratic, illegal, even violent acts, but it is worth remembering that whenever they act, they do so on their own, without direction or assistance.

The Radical Right's taste in guns is revealing. The most popular models aren't sporting rifles or double-barreled trapshooter's shotguns, but military weapons or their closest legal equivalent.

For at least ten years, the right's gun-toters have favored civilian versions of the U.S. Army's M-14 and M-16 rifles. The Colt AR-15 is one: light, with an indestructible military-style stock, not the sort of rifle most hunters would take into a forest when stalking deer. The Ruger Mini-14 is one of the most popular rifles on the Radical Right, compact, light, purposeful. Cartridges for both guns are available in bulk quantities of military surplus for just pennies per shell—an important consideration for someone who may fire several hundred rounds in a weekend of training. The mechanisms of both guns can be fitted with a pistol-grip "paratrooper" stock made of nylon and plastic, and with a series of accessories that include "flash suppressors" that can be screwed to the end of the barrel, a clip-on telescopic sight, and a so-called assault bipod to support the end of the barrel when the shooter is firing from the prostrate position.

The AR-15, when fully outfitted with all the appurtenances, can fetch $700 or more, and is almost indistinguishable from a military weapon. However, there is one important difference. Military rifles offer selective fire, either semiautomatic (one shot fired each time the trigger is pulled) or fully automatic (firing rapidly and continuously as long as the trigger is depressed). Automatic weapons are illegal by federal law, except when the owner holds a special tax permit that is rarely granted. Consequently, there is a lively trade in trigger sear pieces that can be installed in less than an hour.

In the summer of 1981, the hot topic among the Radical Right's gun fanciers was a proposed new weapon, the Atchisson Assault-12 "streetsweeper" shotgun that was to be introduced late in the year. Manufactured with a stock similar to the AR-15's, the AA-12 was planned in both semiautomatic and automatic versions. It was to fire twenty 12-gauge shotgun shells from an optional circular magazine and was available with a bayonet. The introductory price of $500 was not expensive for a new modern weapon, though operating expenses were potentially high, since an automatic shotgun could burn several dollars' worth of ammunition in a few seconds. When loaded with buckshot and set for automatic firing, the AA-12 could be the most devastating weapon ever put into private hands, the *ne plus ultra* to which militant Klansmen, Posse members, and survivalists aspire.

The well-equipped commando doesn't stop with a shoulder arm, however. Pistols are considered backup insurance. Revolvers, even in the magnum calibers, are thought to be a second choice despite their reputation for reliability. Instead, paramilitarists usually prefer the semiautomatic handguns; the military .45 is the standard. Having invested perhaps $1,500 or more (sometimes *much* more) for the right firearms, few quasicommandos will fail to complete their armory with a knife or two: one double-bladed fighting knife for the belt; another—maybe a pencil-thin stiletto—for hiding in a boot scabbard. Crossbows, throwing knives, garrots, and eight-bladed martial arts "throwing stars," while held to be slightly esoteric, nevertheless are respected as emergency weapons that may be called upon when the situation demands stealth and silence.

All except cartridge-type firearms are available by mail from numerous companies that supply survivalists and paramilitarists. Their catalogs are amazing collections of surplus fatigues, combat boots, knives and bayonets, C-rations, gas masks, bulletproof clothing, telescopic sights, electronic bugging sensors, tear-gas guns, and flare guns. The existence of such mail-order houses suggests that *somebody* is buying this stuff.

Joseph Kerska's tastes in guns are relatively pedestrian. He owns a shotgun, a revolver, a hunting rifle—the sort of weapons to be found in most sporting-goods stores. His most exotic gun is an Italian replica of a Colt .44 navy revolver that shoots a black-powder charge. Still, Kerska would defend the right of the Posse Comitatus to buy all it wants of customized AR-15s and twenty-shot streetsweeper shotguns. Snub-nosed Magnums, cheap .38 specials, 12-gauge pumps with barrels cut SWAT-style—Kerska stands by them all. They are as dear to him as an uncensored press is to a newspaper publisher, and for the same reason: Guns are our expressly granted constitutional privilege, he holds, and they are not to be trifled with.

So strongly does he believe this that he formed his own organization to

do the job that the National Rifle Association and the National Pistol and
Rifle Association and the National Alliance to Keep and Bear Arms and the
Second Amendment Committee—to name just four among many—seem
to be doing admirably. No matter. With two of his sons and three friends,
Kerska founded the Sons of Liberty in August of 1977. He intended at first
to use the group to generally support constitutional freedoms, he says, but
the threat to the Second Amendment appeared so great that the battle
began to occupy most of his time.

I came across Kerska when I was looking for a typically fervent opponent of gun control. Not a difficult search; there are dozens of groups
similar to his and thousands of individuals who share Kerska's passion for
preserving Americans' rights to buy, keep, and sell guns without impedi-
ment. His politics tend toward intransigent conservatism, so in most matters he probably falls short of the arbitrarily defined Radical Right. But the
vehemence with which Kerska defends his interpretation of the Second
Amendment is typical of the movement.

It is an argument from the heart, something that puzzles people on the
other side of the issue. They see world leaders assassinated, children killed
with guns they pluck from dresser drawers, mugging victims blown away
by $30 handguns. And they cannot comprehend why others write letters
and badger congressmen and contribute fortunes for the right to own the
homely little hunks of metal that cause all this destruction.

I went to Kerska looking for an answer to that. It happened that we
spoke just three days after a young man with a gun had nearly killed
Ronald Reagan, whom Kerska would call "our greatest president since
Abraham Lincoln." I wanted to know if that attempted assassination had
convinced him that the potential of the handgun was too awful to
defend.

Kerska is sixty-three years old, a former private investigator, now a
commercial photographer in Brisbane, California, the first municipality
south of San Francisco. He speaks in a slow, measured manner, and his
words carry the tone of total conviction. He is insistent. He will not be
budged.

"I belong to all the gun organizations," he said. "NRA, APRA, the California Rifle and Pistol Association, and some others I can't think of right
away. I contribute to them, what I can scrape up after paying for the
operation of the Sons of Liberty, which only generates about half its own
income through contributions. It's a losing proposition, but that's okay, it
gives me another soapbox."

He uses Sons of Liberty stationery to fire off furious letters to newspapers, television stations, politicians. And when letters seem insufficient, he

sometimes just shouts. For more than ten years, the more liberal of his elected representatives have found him a general pain in the nether parts.

"I got interested in politics when I was living in San Francisco and they tried to bus my children," Kerska said. "My children were attending a school three blocks from our home and the school board wanted to bus them to schools far away. When the busing controversy started, I was one of the loudest speakers. Before that, I was interested only in business, making a living. But the busing started me. I joined the American Independent party and I voted for George Wallace because I liked what he was saying. He was for states' rights, he was for freedom. I ended up running for Congress on the American Independent ticket, but I didn't have a chance.

"Some of these politicians, you can't seem to get through to them. Like McCloskey [Paul McCloskey, a liberal Republican who served several terms in the House of Representatives from a district adjacent to the one where Kerska lives]. McCloskey was on TV the other night, arguing about guns. He thinks terrible things about pistols—pistols are awful, they're just for killing people, but rifles and shotguns are okay. Fine. If he were to abolish handguns, which is an impossibility, a total impossibility, but if he could, give me half an hour and a hacksaw and I'll make a pistol out of my rifle and my shotgun. His argument is utterly disastrous. I can make a concealable weapon out of a shotgun, which is a much more formidable weapon than the pistol, because you can miss with a pistol. You can't miss with a sawed-off shotgun, even in the dark."

For years, Kerska's own representative in the House was Leo Ryan, a Democrat whose liberal politics were typical of the San Francisco Bay Area. Ryan was the congressman gunned down on a landing strip in Guyana after visiting the Jonestown settlement.

"I had a terrible argument with Ryan over pistols," Kerska said. "He was campaigning in San Mateo, a meet-the-public sort of thing. It started when I hit him with his gun bill when he was making a speech." (Nothing physical. It is Kerska's style to "hit" TV commentators with letters, to "hit" school board members with complaints, to "hit" his representative with a gun bill.) "He denied that he had ever sponsored a gun bill calling for confiscation of weapons, so I pulled out his bill and flashed it at him. Later on I cornered him and we had a terrible argument. I called him a traitor, and he didn't like that at all. A month after our argument about guns, he goes down to South America and gets himself shot."

Kerska's tone here was not unsympathetic; the irony did not elude him, but it did not disturb his convictions, either.

His opponents on the pistol issue might be surprised to learn that Kerska is not a gun nut. That is, he does not spend thousands of dollars on an elaborate collection, does not rhapsodize about muzzle velocity and flat trajectory and foot/pounds of kinetic energy. He does own several handguns, and he talks about them in the same dispassionate manner in which a weekend handyman might discuss his circular saw.

"I own a rifle and a shotgun, but I don't hunt anymore," he said. "I hunt with a camera. The gun is for one thing only, self-defense. And really, the pistol's the thing for that."

For this Joseph Kerska strikes out with fusillades of letters, baits his congressman, and nurtures a nonprofit organization that pays only half its own expenses? For a tool?

Not just a tool, he says.

"What we're talking about is a constitutional right, and the Second Amendment is the only constitutional right that's in constant jeopardy. The handgun is the American symbol of freedom. You have to keep fighting, keep fighting for it. You can win battle after battle, but you haven't won the war, because they continue coming out of the woodwork, like termites they keep coming. If the day comes that they take away the handgun, the rifle and the shotgun will go soon, and after that all we'll have is crossbows, arrows, and knives."

If that happened, the termites might ask, would that be so bad? Sportsmen say yes, for their own reasons. Constitutionalists like Kerska read in the Second Amendment an implicit mandate for an armed American population. We need our guns to defend ourselves, Kerska says, not only against felons but against those who would overwhelm us from outside.

"The world now is a jungle. If you can't defend yourself against the animals, they'll eat you up. We are at war with Russia. Maybe not shooting, but in every other way. They're trying to capture as much of the world as possible. When they capture a country through what they call their 'wars of liberation'—liberation, hell, it's wars of captivity—the people come over here. The time will eventually come when there's so little land left in the free world, and so many people, that there's got to be some battle, unless communism falls of its own weight."

We talked for a while about politics, about his photography business, about pollsters, whom he's convinced produce unreliable results in their gun-control polls because they're predisposed against guns. We got on the subject of Ronald Reagan.

"It's an achievement that this country has elected such a man," he said. "Politicians promise all kinds of things, but here's a man who is doing the things he's promised to do, or at least he's trying. I've written to our representatives and urged them to give him wholehearted support. He appears to be the best president since Lincoln."

Then, I said, what a tragedy it would have been for a single man with an easily acquired handgun to have deprived the nation of its president. Had the grim possibility made him reconsider his stand, just for a moment?

No, he said. And the arguments came spilling out again.

"You can't stop a nut from getting a gun," he said. "It's an impossibility. Even if you were to confiscate all the guns in the U.S., the nuts and the criminals would make their own. Take guns away from the honest people and you'd have a booming black market in pistols. The Mafia would go into the business of making guns. Anybody can make a gun. It's a very simple thing. I've got a muzzle-loader that shoots one shot, black powder. Very simple. All you need is a lathe to make that gun. Because it shoots black powder, the metal doesn't have to be perfect, because the pressures aren't that great. Want to ban powder? Anybody with a home chemistry set can make it. It's composed of readily available chemicals. You can make lead bullets from lead fishing sinkers."

Before I left, Kerska showed me a plaque bearing words attributed to Thomas Jefferson. "Let your gun be your constant companion on your walks," it read. "This gives exercise to the body and independence to the mind. No free man shall be debarred the use of arms."

"My hero," Kerska said.

The quotation from Jefferson, I learned later, is popular among the Second Amendment's champions on the right. There is another one that can be seen even more often, usually on bumper stickers and T-shirts, where it is commonly used with the scowling face of a man who holds a large pistol. It says:

WANT MY GUN? COME AND GET IT.

WITNESSING

Guerrillas

(The following is excerpted from an article by Robert C. Miles in the May-June, 1981 issue of his newsletter, *From the Mountain*. Miles is a former leader of a Michigan Klan.)

Consider the Klan guerrilla training camps. These are misnomers. They were intended to be self-defense training centers, akin to survivalist camps. One Klan even invited the U.S. Justice Department to inspect their camps!

Naturally the redfeds were delighted to put a stamp of approval on such. It then served as an identification magnet for their agent provocateurs. Most klans delighted in having reporters attend their sessions. . . . The spate of press sensationalism was used effectively by the Klan to warn the reds, the Jews and the blacks that the Klan was armed and ready.

. . . Let us rid the self-defense forces of the label of guerrilla. Let it be the name of the theatrical function of one phase of the Resistance. For, there is no guerrilla training program possible in a land controlled by your foe. The foe permits none to exist. . . . If one wants real guerrilla training, let them enter the armed forces, keeping their racial beliefs covered, and thus acquire such skill. . . . Note that the ADL rarely attacks the guerrilla camps. The JDL emulates them. The FBI delights in them. They make keeping track of militant klansmen even more simple. If you need rifle practice, why not join some local sporting club and sharpen your skill in such innocent company? If you need practice in surviving in the wilderness, why not obtain it through outdoor sport and hiking associations? Penetrate these. Join accepted clubs and camps. Keep your racial attitudes concealed while building your skills for the day we all know lies ahead. . . .

Soldiers must be rewarded, traitors punished. Can you pay such a price now? Can you support one soldier in the terror army? It takes $15,000 a year to support one in Italy, according to the Red Brigades. Are you able to really support armed action today? The first requirement for action is the ability of a group to pay its soldiers. No one fights for free. No matter what our propaganda leads you to believe. If you can't pay your soldiers, then you aren't ready to fight.

Can you build your chain of safe houses across this land before you move? Are there fifty such families who can be trusted and who have never subscribed to any racialist paper or publication, never been on any list or attended any local racialist meetings?

How many lawyers are there who are eager to defend your cause in court? Can your group arrange a war chest of $1,000,000 to serve as a retainer for such a nationwide group of legal defenders? It had better have these before armed action begins, for if it tries to gain it after such action begins, it is doomed to failure.

. . . Do you have the doctors and nurses recruited, with medical facilities set up either in homes or inside actual hospitals used as covers? Your soldiers will need fifty such medical facilities. Not just for wounds, but for the regular daily illnesses which strike anyone. Only these patients cannot be seen at regular clinics by medical personnel not sympathetic to the cause. Have you even started to recruit one in your group? . . .

Where do your soldiers go for rest, once the armed action begins? To which nation can your hunted ones flee when the heat is too much to stand for them in their own land? Where indeed is a sanctuary for a white racist?

It is folly . . . nay, it is treason, for any leader to enter into an armed action until the preparatory work has been done. . . . Everything has to have its time and its season. Do the work which is required of you in this season. Prepare for the work ahead. Know that the hour of the harvest comes. In the right time, more than just the moon shall rise.

8

Our nation has reached a point of no return—a point beyond which the American people can no longer defend their freedom by the traditional means of politics and public opinion.

Robert B. DePugh,
Blueprint for Victory,
Fifth Edition, 1978

. . . having banished from our land that religious intolerance under which mankind has so long bled and suffered, we have yet gained little if we countenance a political intolerance as despotic, as wicked, and capable of as bitter and bloody persecutions. . . . If there be any among us who would wish to dissolve this Union or to change its republican form, let them stand undisturbed as monuments of the safety with which error of opinion may be tolerated, where reason is left free to combat it.

Thomas Jefferson,
First Inaugural Address
March 4, 1801

The Administration should take steps to end the Minutemen . . . they . . . represent a dangerous precedent in our democracy.

Walter Reuther and Victor Reuther,
"The Reuther Memorandum"
December 19, 1961

If it is a question of identifying heroes and villains, Good Guys and Bad Guys, then there is no sure answer. Who is wrong here? Bob DePugh, who

113

on and off has talked for twenty years about circumventing government, whose illegal weapons gave his talk a very grim substance? Or a generation of liberals who feared DePugh for his words and his ideas long before there was proof that he had broken a law? Is DePugh's "freedom" half as tolerant as Jefferson's, or would he, given the chance, countenance his own bitter and bloody persecutions in the name of principle?

The questions get thorny and troublesome when an open mind lingers too long on the Radical Right. The political extremities are littered with the carcasses of those who have stood up to the bustling express of the established order, and who have been swept aside. They can't forever be ignored, and, once faced, they pose a very difficult decision. How are we supposed to feel about someone who shouts "liberty forever" with a gun in his hand? Is such a man inevitably a fraud?

The Radical Right is rife with those eager to leap the fences of good sense, fairness, and accepted values. They detest limits; it seems their natural inclination to take ideology and political action as far as they will travel. Almost always they leave behind the multitudes, and they often cross the legal boundaries when they do. It is a long, lonely ride to the last stop on the line, but Bob DePugh was willing to pay full fare and travel as far as the ticket would take him.

Even for that reason alone, as an example of the type, he is worth careful examination. He served four years in federal prisons for a variety of firearms offenses that included possession of a .50-caliber machine gun, a murderous weapon made to do nothing but kill the enemy in a battle. Yet there are those who consider DePugh to have been a political prisoner—and in the loosest sense, he was, for if he had not flaunted his surly, petulant politics, he might without much jeopardy have acquired all the guns he wished. But DePugh took it all to the limit, and past. He could not merely proclaim that legal government was a failure; he had to buy guns to fortify his contention. And then he could not be satisfied with prosaic pistol and rifle; his guns had to include the most lethal, the most flagrantly illegal.

DePugh is an almost uniquely fascinating character in his sphere. Even granting the constant, pervasive influence of Robert Welch, DePugh may well be the most important figure on the Radical Right since he formed the Minutemen in 1960. To discern his motives and his political morality is no simple undertaking, for he is a complex man and so much of the truth about him is buried in simplistic rhetoric—some from his enemies, some of his own making. But understanding DePugh has its rewards, for it may be a great step toward seeing the Radical Right for what it really is and how it really operates.

That is not to say, however, that DePugh is typical of the entire Radical Right. He is unique in some respects. He is a thinker, a theoretician, of the sort usually associated with the intellectual left. Nobody else has set down so clearly the philosophy of the right-wing movement—its ideals, its goals, its place in the national life. For one who proclaims that "words won't win—action will" (the slogan of the Minutemen), he is a remarkably effective and prolific writer. He attempts logical sequences of thought and a historical perspective. (This will seem like slighting praise only to those unfamiliar with the turgid literature of the Radical Right, where logic is tortured into strange configurations, and perspective usually extends no further than the last newsletter.)

In *Blueprint for Victory,* DePugh examines some subjects—like the work ethic, the nature of revolution, and the implications of illegal resistance—that don't seem to occur to other right-wing leaders, many of whom seem befuddled by capitalism and how it affects the right. Within the movement, there is an instinctive mistrust of big business (or, for that matter, of any institution that represents power and clout); it is a rare figure on the Radical Right who is confident enough to wrestle with the question. DePugh, though, is unfazed: Wealth produced by the capitalist system, he writes, has given the freedom of a private home, freedom from hunger, and an unprecedented mobility that is essential to personal freedom. And he argues that private capital alone, not labor, creates wealth. *Blueprint for Victory* may not be in a league with *Das Kapital,* but its intentions alone are enough to make DePugh an impressive oddity on the right wing with its here-and-now obsession.

DePugh's stature within the movement may be judged by the reactions he inspired among his natural foes—leftists and liberals. In this respect, DePugh was unequaled for at least ten years, during the Sixties. Liberals regarded most right-wing figures of that period—George Wallace, Robert Welch, Billy James Hargis most prominent among them—with varying degrees of contempt, derision, or confusion. But DePugh was something else: not an orator, not a politician, not a sponsor of radio shows, not a preacher. DePugh took up arms. The Minutemen were dread figures in the shadows, out there somewhere with bazookas and tommy guns, unpredictable, erratic, totally beyond the ken of most of us. They seemed sprung from the darkest recesses of the national psyche, a scary portent of what might await. *Better sign all your antiwar petitions and keep up your ADA dues, or the Minutemen gonna come get you.* This was a specter that DePugh carefully cultivated, but few knew that then, and the knowledge that he was so calculating probably would have been little comfort anyway.

In all, an intriguing study. He is a formidable man, intelligent and self-assured, by no means a pitiable misfit, apparently capable of much besides political extremism. But because he could not resist buying the ticket to the end of the line, he became a political reckoning point by which right-wing radicalism may be charted. There is much to be gained from a close look at Bob DePugh's strange, strange odyssey beyond the limits of our national forbearance.

"We all get started down a certain road," said Bob DePugh last year, "and the further along you get, the harder it is to turn back."

Bob DePugh, as nearly as he will say or anyone can determine, took his critical first steps in 1960. There are a couple of versions of how it came about. One of them is in *A Short History of the Minutemen,* a leaflet that DePugh published in the mid-Sixties. It all began, this tale goes, with DePugh and nine friends building duckblinds on a lakeshore in Missouri. One of the ten mentioned the dismal condition of international politics, and another joked, "Well, if the Russians invade us, we can come up here and fight on as a guerrilla band." A week later, the story claims, one of the group, who had taken Special Forces training in the military, brought some instructional manuals to the duckblinds.

"Most books on guerrilla warfare have been written by persons with deep political convictions," the leaflet states, "and we found that as we studied strategy and tactics we also became increasingly concerned with the world political situation."

In this way, the leaflet claims, a counterrevolutionary cadre was formed from a nucleus of "ten average Americans"—a category into which DePugh has rarely been placed and to which he probably has never aspired.

DePugh told it a little differently twenty-one years later, when he described himself as a politically naïve businessman, thirty-seven years old before he took much notice of current politics. He had been busy making a living and caring for his family, but by 1959, he said, he had made a small fortune from his company, BioLab, a pharmaceutical research firm in Norborne, Missouri, that specialized in canine food supplements called Fidomins. (This version of his financial success is plausible, for the family and the corporation both survived years of expensive court battles and DePugh's years in jail and as a fugitive.) With financial success in the late Fifties, DePugh said, came the leisure to look at the world around him, and the realization that he now had a good deal at stake in the ideological stability of the nation. So he joined the John Birch Society, and he became aroused—not an atypical reaction of a newcomer in the JBS. He decided to devote time and money to the right-wing cause. But not haphazardly.

"I made a list of the most influential, the most important patriotic leaders in the country at that time," he said, "and I went to visit each one of them. There must have been at least twenty. I wanted to talk to them and to find out what kind of people they were and which one of them would be the most effective. It was quite an undertaking."

He made the rounds. And he was, as he told it last year, disappointed in almost every one of them. He found them lacking either personally or philosophically. Only one, a conservative minister from Aurora, Colorado, named Ken Goff, appealed to him as a man. And while DePugh had doubts at first about Goff's politics—Goff having for several years been a member of the Communist party—he eventually became convinced that Goff was as steadfast a patriot as he could hope to find.

Goff aside, he had been shocked by the state of the nation's right-wing leadership. Was this the last line of the nation's defense, its conservative conscience, its guard on the watchtower? DePugh, previously aroused, now became thoroughly alarmed. Somebody had to do something and Bob DePugh would leave the job to nobody else. In 1960, he conceived and began an armed resistance group to combat what he considered an entrenched revolution. By drawing on close acquaintances (some of whom actually did belong to a duck-hunting club), he circumvented the right-wing establishment. His troops, he decided, would use guerrilla cunning, guerrilla tactics, guerrilla secrecy. He called them the Minutemen; he made Independence, Missouri, their headquarters; and he adopted as their symbol the crossed hairs of a telescopic rifle sight.

DePugh decided early to seek attention through publicity. Having advertised in the classified sections of several newspapers during the summer of 1961 ("Help put real strength into civilian defense. Pledge yourself and your rifle to a free America. For full details write 'Minutemen' . . ."), DePugh was able to muster more than twenty members for a weekend exercise in Shiloh, Illinois, during October of that year. The group notified reporters, so the press was there at Shiloh as the Minutemen heard lectures on guerrilla warfare and examined an arms display that included antitank guns, a recoilless rifle, and a Browning automatic rifle. The press was there, too, when deputy sheriffs arrested one of the Minutemen for possession of illegal weapons, charges that later were dropped. And several reporters were there the next morning when about a dozen of the Minutemen in combat uniforms, including a thirty-eight-year-old pharmaceuticals manufacturer named Robert DePugh, went through two hours of combat maneuvers.

The Associated Press carried reports of the exercises, the arsenal, the arrest. So did the *Kansas City Star* and the *St. Louis Globe-Democrat*. *The Nation, Time,* and *Newsweek* all noticed the Minutemen in the next few weeks. In fact, the Minutemen were hard to miss. A leadership dispute within the California branch of the Minutemen, and disclosure of a morals conviction against one of the disputants, kept the group in the news there during November of 1961. The Minutemen's literature, much of it marked by DePugh's direct, purposeful writing style and his knack for epic indignation, was sometimes newsworthy in itself. Newsletters from the Radical Right are usually mailed straight into oblivion, but *On Target* uniquely created shock waves beyond its list of sympathetic subscribers. An example is the issue of March 15, 1963, following a congressional challenge of the House Un-American Activities Committee. Above the names of twenty congressmen who had voted against the committee was the legend "In Memoriam" and a statement that read, in part:

> We have studied your Communist Smersh, Mao, Che, Bucharin. We have learned your lessons well and have added a few home-grown Yankee tricks of our own. Before you start your next smear campaign, before you murder again, before you railroad another patriot into a mental institution . . . better think it over.
>
> See the old man at the corner where you buy your paper? He may have a silencer-equipped pistol under his coat. That extra fountain pen in the pocket of the insurance salesman that calls on you may be a cyanide-gas gun. What about your milkman? Arsenic works slow but sure. Your auto mechanic may stay up nights studying booby traps.
>
> These patriots are not going to let you take their freedom away from them. They have learned the silent knife, the strangler's cord, the target rifle that hits sparrows at 200 yards. Only their leaders restrain them. Traitors, beware! Even now the cross hairs are on the back of your necks. . . .

One of the twenty congressmen, Henry Gonzalez of Texas, cited that passage several months later when he demanded a Justice Department investigation of the Minutemen. Later, the passage was adapted for use as a gummed sticker, which the Minutemen received in quantity with their newsletters. The uses to which an imaginative counterrevolutionary might put the gummed labels did not require suggestion.

By 1963, the reaction of Gonzalez had become typical. DePugh outraged officialdom so consistently that his actions now seem carefully calculated. And once he had provoked outrage, he knew how to make capital of it. The Minutemen became renowned for the stature and the wrath of their opponents. In 1961 alone, the group was denounced by Governors Otto Kerner of Illinois and Edmund "Pat" Brown of California, both of whom ordered investigations of the group within their respective states; by New York senator Jacob Javits; by California attorney general Stanley Mosk; by California congressman John Shelley; and even in backhanded reference by President John Kennedy, who, during a November 18 speech in which he excoriated the extreme right, mentioned "armed bands of civilian guerrillas that are more likely to supply local vigilantes than national vigilance."

But nobody boosted the Minutemen's prestige more than Walter Reuther, then president of the United Auto Workers, and his brother, Victor, who headed the union's international-affairs section. Shortly after Kennedy's sharp notice of the right, Attorney General Robert Kennedy asked the Reuthers to draft suggestions for dealing with right-wing elements in the country. The Reuthers replied on December 19, 1961, with a memorandum that was supposed to have remained confidential, but which somehow was leaked to the press shortly afterward.

The document is not one of the nobler legacies of the Kennedy administration. It is, in effect, a suggested agenda for using presidential influence to destroy nettlesome political opponents,* and it is disturbingly similar in approach to the "enemies list" that would be drafted in the Nixon White House a decade later.

In its first paragraph, the memorandum states that it "may have some value in focusing attention upon possible Administration policies and programs to combat the radical right," and it goes on to state that "as the radical right cannot be wished away or ignored, likewise its demise is not something that can be readily accomplished." It suggests, among other tactics, the revocation of tax-exempt status for some right-wing groups; IRS scrutiny of right-wingers' tax returns and of contributions by businesses to the offending organizations; use of the Federal Communications Commission to discourage the free time being given to right-wing speakers; and FBI infiltration of right-wing groups.

After a general discussion of the state of the right and of the obstacles that it posed to administration policy, the Reuthers devoted the second half of the memo to five suggestions for action. One can only imagine the glee with which DePugh read the fourth of the five subheadings in the section:

---

* After the Minutemen, the groups and personalities most prominently mentioned were Billy James Hargis, Fred Schwartz's Christian Anti-Communist Crusade, the John Birch Society, and the "Life Line" radio series that was sponsored for years by the late oil billionaire H. L. Hunt. While all were extremely conservative and adamantly opposed to the Kennedy presidency, they advocated political stability and change through the system. Though they at times dealt in misleading or exaggerated statements—and could even have been accused of inflammatory bombast without much chance of contradiction—none was ever charged with a violent or subversive political act. In 1961, actually, the same could even have been said of the Minutemen.

1. The radical right inside the armed services presents an immediate and special problem requiring immediate and special measures.
2. The radical right and the Attorney General's subversive list.
3. The flow of big money to the radical right should be dammed to the extent possible.
4. The Administration should take steps to end the Minutemen.
5. The domestic Communist problem should be put in proper perspective for the American people, thus exposing the basic fallacy of the radical right.

Once again, DePugh had demonstrated his talent for antagonizing authority and irritating liberals, and this time the results were spectacular. The Minutemen now were certifiably dangerous, worthy of the most stringent measures that the attorney general could bring to bear against them. For DePugh in his world, the memorandum became the equivalent of a purple cloak fringed with ermine. It had been barely two years from duckblind to the Reuthers' high dudgeon.

The fifth edition of *Blueprint for Victory* contains a paragraph that isn't to be found in the earliest versions. At the end of a chapter discussing the "grey area" of effective action—the area in which one can be effective and still be safely within the law—DePugh writes, almost ruefully: "But be forewarned—these are not safe and easy pursuits. To stay within the effective zone without straying over the danger line requires close attention to business, a lesson I learned the hard way."

DePugh and the Minutemen had gained much from twitting irritable authority. Within two years they had gone from total obscurity to national notoriety. They had clamored for the spotlight, and they had gotten it, but with it came a scrutiny that they could not withstand. The sudden glare made them obvious to every sheriff's office, every police department, every federal enforcement agent.

Rich Laughli, who had been arrested during the breakthrough demonstration at Shiloh in 1961, left the group a year later but was arrested in 1964 and later convicted of selling more than 100 submachine guns to an agent of the Treasury Department's Alcohol and Tobacco Tax unit. He attempted, but was unable to make good, a defense of entrapment.

Through 1963 and 1964, several men tied in some way to the Minutemen were arrested on firearms violations. Usually the arrests included confiscation of an amazing quantity and variety of exotic weapons. A gunshop owner in Glendale, California, whom the state attorney general's office identified as a member of the Minutemen, got a one-to-ten-year sentence in 1965 when he was convicted of possessing more than half a ton of stolen explosives.

DePugh's first clash with the law came in 1965, when he was charged with kidnapping after two young women, ages sixteen and twenty-one, told police in Independence that DePugh had had them held against their will for a week while trying to recruit them as spies for the Minutemen. There were such serious discrepancies in the story that a grand jury refused to return an indictment, but the case received extensive publicity, which DePugh claims still dogs him.* It also signaled the beginning of a period when his legal difficulties began to consume increasing amounts of DePugh's time and money—and his grip on the organization apparently began to loosen.

His troubles multiplied. Officers attempting to arrest DePugh on the kidnap charges found a cache of weapons that included dynamite, hand grenades, land mines, and rocket launchers. DePugh for a year faced bomb charges that were later dismissed. Around this same time, DePugh also risked a contempt citation when he failed to comply with a grand jury's subpoena of the Minutemen's membership rolls and financial records.

Even so, DePugh and the Minutemen did not spend all their time in court. Through most of the Sixties, they continued their training exercises (mostly in secret now, after the initial splurge of publicity), continued to stockpile their incredible collections of armaments, and pursued what DePugh termed "psychological warfare," which ranged from name-calling to petty mischief to clever stunts to dangerous and illegal harassment.

Laird Wilcox, a sociology major and a student radical at the University of Kansas in Lawrence—about forty miles from the Minutemen's home base in Independence, Missouri—became involved in a series of entanglements with DePugh and the Minutemen during that period. Alternately amusing and frightening, they give something of the flavor of the Minutemen, and their rather unusual approach to political action.

In July 1964, while announcing that the Minutemen would sponsor a summer training program for college students, DePugh took the customary whacks at leftists on American college campuses. As an example of the type, DePugh mentioned Wilcox, who had been a founder of the Student Peace Union at KU. Wilcox, said DePugh, was a "professional . . . leftist

* "It was the most blatant frame-up you ever heard of," DePugh said in an interview, "but it got publicity to the point that if I try to hire a secretary today, I'm still liable to have the girl go home and say, 'I started working for Bob DePugh today,' and her mother will say, 'I remember him, he's a kidnapper,' and I'll have to go out and find another secretary."

agitator" who had registered at the university for the purpose of organizing students for Communist causes. His notice of Wilcox was especially interesting since, two months earlier, an alternative newspaper that Wilcox edited had been the victim of a creditable fake edition that, according to Wilcox, had made the paper appear far more radical than it actually was.

Wilcox had his revenge. In 1966, he managed to locate a former four-year member of the Minutemen named Jerry Brooks, who had been subpoenaed to appear before a federal grand jury to discuss the organization. Brooks was gifted with total recall, and, while taping a series of interviews with Wilcox, he named several dozen Minutemen in the Kansas City area, with their addresses and telephone numbers. Wilcox remembers that one night he and another KU student radical, using DePugh's code identification, Number 551, ordered all the Minutemen by telephone to an emergency dawn meeting at DePugh's home in Norborne. Later they watched several of the Minutemen leaving their homes in the middle of the night with gun cases slung over their shoulders as they began the two-hour drive from Kansas City. At that point, Wilcox says, he telephoned the state police with an anonymous tip that armed Ku Klux Klansmen were converging on Norborne for a cross-burning.

In time, partly on the strength of information that Brooks had given in the interviews, Wilcox became known as a local expert on the mysterious Minutemen and even was deputized to aid in a Shawnee County investigation of the Minutemen in 1966. It was during this time, Wilcox says, that the windshield of his pickup truck was shot out as it sat parked one night. Another time, he says, he found the lug nuts loosened on one wheel of his wife's car. So when he discovered two of the local Minutemen cruising outside his apartment one night, Wilcox and a friend grabbed a pistol and a shotgun and began to chase the men through Lawrence.

Maybe the most remarkable part of all this is that Wilcox is now an amiable acquaintance of DePugh and relates this series of events almost as a sort of escalating campaign of practical jokes. Still, there were times, he admits, when "they [the Minutemen] made my life miserable. They were a little crazy, but no crazier than any SDS member, and in some ways a hell of a lot more sane."

The lesson, probably, is that even fun and games had a grim aspect with the Minutemen. And by the fall of 1966, the grimness was almost unrelieved. Partly on the strength of testimony by Jerry Brooks, DePugh had stood accused and convicted of a series of firearms violations. Also convicted were Walter Peyson, who was thought to be DePugh's second-in-command, and Troy Houghton, West Coast coordinator for the Minutemen. DePugh was sentenced to four years in prison, Houghton three years, and Peyson two years. All were released on bond pending appeal.

There was more. In 1967, DePugh pleaded *nolo contendere* to a charge of transporting a .38 revolver while under a felony indictment. He received a year's sentence but again he made bond.

In October 1967, police arrested nineteen Minutemen in raids around New York City and charged them with plotting to bomb three leftist-oriented youth camps in New York State, Connecticut, and New Jersey. (Sixteen were indicted and later convicted, and the partial list of weapons seized in the raids included ten pipe bombs, five mortars, twelve .30-caliber automatic weapons, 125 rifles, one bazooka, three grenade launchers, fifty 80-millimeter mortar shells, six hand grenades, and one million rounds of ammunition.) *On Target* acknowledged that the accused were affiliated with the national Minutemen group, though DePugh maintained that the plans for the attack were drawn up solely as a training exercise, and that he knew nothing of the operation in any case.

On August 23, 1968, four members of the Minutemen were arrested in the Bronx for trying to kill Communist leader Herbert Aptheker with a bomb. That same year, while DePugh was free on bond awaiting appeal of the federal conviction, he was indicted for complicity in an alleged bank-robbery plot near Seattle, Washington. The plot involved blowing up a power station to create a diversion for three bank holdups. Though DePugh later was cleared in the case, at that point he faced many years in prison. He slipped his surveillance in Missouri, traveled to California to meet with lawyers in the Redmond case, and then simply disappeared. He was a fugitive for nearly two years before federal agents captured him near Truth or Consequences, New Mexico.

Why did DePugh choose to form the Minutemen? His motives and purposes could provide an infinite source for argument. He does seem to consider himself a leader, and the idea of commanding a secret band of committed men surely had its appeal. But that alone can't explain the chances he took long after leadership must have lost its luster. The most charitable and credible explanation is his own: that he was jolted into awareness and that he saw to his own satisfaction the need for an armed resistance movement. That few other Americans perceived such a need does not rule out his sincerity, for the principle of solitary enlightenment is well established and thoroughly respected on the Radical Right. The movement is full of solitary Gnostics who consider themselves validated when nobody else shares their insights. Thus, it is not at all incredible that

Bob DePugh and a few of his friends should have unquestioningly accepted a private vision.

Certainly time, travail, and his persistence have precluded all possibility that DePugh was in it for the money. There is in fact no evidence to dispute his claim that his political activities have cost him far more than they ever earned him through dues and contributions, yet he has remained active, both with the Minutemen on a reduced scale and with the Committee of Ten Million, long after a profiteer would have junked both.

Thus, the most tenable theory is that DePugh believed in what he was doing when he formed the Minutemen in 1960, but that the enterprise was not without its psychological attraction.

There is another, separate set of questions. What did DePugh intend? Were the Minutemen the malignant growth they've been portrayed to be? His writings aren't much help here. They are colorful but contradictory. In the November 1964 issue of the Minutemen's newsletter, *On Target,* he laments Lyndon Johnson's sweeping victory over Barry Goldwater in the presidential race and repeats a portion of *A Short History of the Minutemen:* "We also decided that a pro-American government could no longer be established by normal political means [and that] any further effort, time or money spent in trying to save our country by political means would be wasted. . . ." Yet one page later he states: "We are not proposing violent action. We are not proposing that anyone grab his gun and head for the hills. We have never made such proposals."

The two stands aren't totally contradictory, perhaps, but the line between them is surely so fine as to be almost nonexistent, and there's a real question of how many of the Minutemen or their sympathizers would bother to make the distinction.

The most truthful measure is to compare what the group threatened to do with what it actually did.

First, the threats. DePugh and the followers closest to him spoke often of launching a counterrevolt against what they claimed was a revolution soon to come. In his fine book *The Minutemen* (Doubleday, 1968), Harry J. Jones relates a conversation he had had with DePugh in 1964, in which DePugh stated that the Minutemen had considered assassinating twenty-five to thirty members of what he called "the hidden government" of the Communists. This would not take place, DePugh said, until after the Communists had actually taken over the government. The Minutemen, he said, had determined the identities of those in this "hidden government" and would act when those people had been installed in office. Some of the Minutemen would infiltrate leftist organizations, in order to gather intelligence and to identify traitors.

The record shows that much of this never got beyond the stage of threat, and there is reason to believe that DePugh never intended otherwise.

The Minutemen did train as an armed militia, and did study guerrilla tactics—neither of which was necessarily illegal. The national office distributed information on high explosives, booby traps, and the manufacture of pistol silencers. Members of the group, either individually or as Minutemen, bought implements of war like bazookas, mortars, and the automatic weapons that eventually brought jail sentences for DePugh and Minutemen Walter Peyson and Troy Houghton.

Members also infiltrated some leftist and liberal groups. Again, maybe only DePugh, if anyone, knows how many and with what results. Wilcox, when he was an antiwar activist in 1965, did expose a member of the University of Kansas SDS chapter as an informant for the Minutemen.

There is also evidence, cited in Harry Jones's *The Minutemen,* that members of the group harassed their suspected adversaries with telephone calls, threats, and even violence, though none was ever convicted on these accounts.

This may, in fact, have been the original purpose of the Minutemen: to upset, to misinform and mislead, and generally to intimidate those whom DePugh saw as the enemy. He must have known that organized military action by civilians is pointless and suicidal as long as elected government exists here. That left the alternative of psychological warfare, which actually does manage to wedge itself into the minute cleft between "spurning wasteful political means" and advocating outright violence.

His "cross hairs on the back of the neck" was patent psychological bullying. So, in a larger sense, were the open training sessions, the constantly implied promise of violence, even the dramatic weaponry. Moreover, while DePugh stressed internal security and secrecy, he was often available to the press, and much of what we now know about the organization and its supposedly violent contingencies has come from statements Depugh made openly during the Sixties, at the peak of the controversies that boiled around the organization.

All of this suggests that the Minutemen's image as the bad boys of the right was very much as DePugh wanted it to be, and that he wanted the image honed to a fine edge and broadcast as far as possible. And not without a purpose. Accept the premise that DePugh truly saw liberalism leading the nation into the hands of the commissars—a belief that is one of the few accepted constants on the Radical Right, however skeptically it may be received elsewhere—and it is not so difficult to imagine that at some point he simply hoped to scare liberals off their chosen course.

"Psychological warfare against the enemy must be merciless" is the way a Minutemen booklet on guerrilla warfare puts it. "To the general population he must always be 'the outsider.' He must know that he is always looked down upon. He is held in silent contempt. The enemy must never be allowed to feel at home. He must be made lonely, afraid, uncomfortable. He must never eat a bite of food without wondering if it is poisoned. He must never close his eyes at night without wondering if some cold blade will find his heart while he is sleeping."

Very likely, DePugh would have considered his mission accomplished if he could have produced any such sensations in some select leftists.

Finally, there is the record of the group's first several years, when DePugh's authority and his attention were undivided by legal problems. During that time, the Minutemen agitated mightily but never once followed through on its threats of violence. During those years, until about 1965, for all the heralded training, all the thousands of rounds that the group must have fired, all the bombastic talk, there is no record that the national leadership once ordered any military operation against this country's government, its officials, or any of its people. This was a time of unprecedented violence by the Radical Right—the Sixties saw dozens of bombings of black churches, numerous beatings, and at least four murders of civil-rights workers in the South. Yet there is little in those five years beyond the rhetoric and the sensational speculation to suggest that official policy in Norborne was as provocative and criminal as has been supposed.

This isn't to suggest that the Minutemen's training was anything less than earnest, that DePugh and most of his followers did not truly expect to one day do battle against invaders. They surely did; many probably still do. But DePugh is far too canny to have escaped the conclusion that a civilian militia is foredoomed in this country unless it observes some strict rules. When reality rules out violent action, the threat of violence becomes the next best alternative, and the Minutemen maintained that threat convincingly.

DePugh is far from blameless. The constitutional umbrella doesn't cover the personal intimidation that was part of his variety of "psychological warfare." Moreover, it seems obvious that he played a most reckless hand when he urged his followers to action. The Minutemen's rhetoric was incendiary, however much it may have been accompanied by cautions and qualifiers and disclaimers. DePugh is capable of semantic nimbleness and careful scrutiny of words and ideas, to a degree beyond that of most other members of the Minutemen—or of almost anyone else. He urged his followers to buy guns and to practice their fighting techniques at the same time that he bemoaned the nation's rapid deterioration. It was a complex and ambiguous call to arms, and DePugh issued it knowing that one day he might have no direct control over his subordinates' actions.

Consider the nature of the group's structure. During the mid-Sixties, the Minutemen were thought to have organized groups numbering 200 or more each, divided into smaller bands or teams, in New York, California, Missouri, and Illinois alone. And while DePugh long claimed that the Minutemen's policies were dictated by an anonymous ten-member council, there is no indication that anyone except DePugh ever made a national policy decision. (Even DePugh has admitted that the group became dormant when he was a fugitive.)

In the group's early years, when its membership was smaller and he was able to give full attention to administration, he may have been able to exercise direct control, to hold in check the precipitous impulses that he provoked with his words. Later, as the group grew and DePugh found himself in legal jeopardy, it is likely that he would have been unable to review the specific exercises for each of the dozens of bands. Thus, he might have encouraged quiet individual initiative, partly for reasons of security and partly because to carry on business otherwise was impractical. But to do so meant trusting the wisdom, the patience, and the judgment of some who—to put it mildly—had been known to become agitated by the actions of a government that they viewed with such a jaundiced and vigilant eye.

The arrests in New York and Washington suggest that the emotions DePugh had once deftly manipulated were now out of hand. They weren't what he had planned at all, and matters began to unravel. Maybe pranks and infiltration began to bore the more anxious elements of the group. Maybe the more militant units around the country viewed the legal action against their leader as a sign that restraint was outdated, that the revolution was finally under way. In the frantic months of 1968, the Minutemen—in fragments, if not wholly—finally lived up to their reputation as an explosive menace.

WITNESSING

DePugh and the Minutemen

We guarantee that all law suits filed against this news letter will be settled out of court.

Declaration on early copies of *On Target*

Words won't win—action will.

Motto of the Minutemen

BUT WHAT KIND OF ACTION?

Twenty-one citizens of the state of Mississippi have recently been arrested on criminal charges resulting from the deaths last June of Andrew Goodman, Michael Schwerner and James Chaney.

These three "civil rights workers" had traveled into a community foreign from their own and were attempting to cause dissention and civil disobedience. A careful investigation would probably prove that they were financed, at least in part, by the communist party and they were certainly promoting the "divide and conquer" tactics that the communists have used so well.

Personally, I feel nothing but contempt for these three men and am almost tempted to agree with those who say, "They got what they deserved." I have no idea as to whether or not those who have been arrested did or did not commit these crimes. That is something for the courts to decide.

Of one thing, I am absolutely certain—the persons who did commit these crimes did not help themselves, did not help their state, and certainly did not help the cause of freedom.

For so long as the constitutional government can be preserved, for so long as the integrity of the state courts can be maintained and so long as a citizen can obtain a fair trial by jury, then the laws of this land must be respected.

Bob DePugh, in December 1, 1964, issue of *On Target*

NOW, LET'S GET BUSY

The hopes of millions of Americans that the communist tide could be stopped with ballots instead of bullets have turned to dust.

Of Lyndon Johnson's closest friends, one has been publicly identified as a thief, another as a sex pervert, and the third as a communist-fronter. Yet, this man has just been elected to the Presidency by a land-slide vote. What more is needed as proof of the basic premise on which the Minutemen were organized—*"The time is past when the American people might have saved themselves by traditional political processes."*

Among the weak-kneed conservatives many will be shaking their heads sadly and saying "We simply must win in 1968." I hope the readers of this newsletter are not so naive. We are not going to have a free election in 1968. The last election which could possibly be called free was 1960. . . .

In all the conservative movement you cannot find another organization that worked harder than the Minutemen have to elect Barry Goldwater. Literally millions of pieces of campaign literature were distributed by our members. Our members worked as volunteers in many local Republican headquarters.

The Minutemen organization worked for Goldwater not because we thought he would win but in spite of the fact that we knew he would lose. . . .

From November 4, 1964, issue of *On Target*

If the situation is so far gone that Americans can no longer regain representative government through the normal channels of public opinion and political activity, then the question still remains, "What can we do that will really be effective?" . . .

We have tried to study the present situation calmly and objectively. There are only a few courses of action which we can see that actually will contribute to ultimate victory. . . .

First, we must learn all that we can about the enemy. It is useless to talk about them in general terms. We must know our enemies by name, address, and phone number. Their leaders must be subjected to special scrutiny. We must know their habits, their likes, their weak and strong points. We must have a complete physical description of them. We must know the license number of their cars and where they are apt to hide in time of danger.

Secondly, we must infiltrate the enemy organizations. We must misdirect their plans and confuse their programs just as they continuously do in anti-communist organizations. We must cause suspicion between them and increase their natural jealousies and intrigues.

Third, we must bring every pressure to bear against the army of fellow travelers, dupes, and starry-eyed intellectuals which surround the communists and do their work for them. . . . We must show the left-wing professor and the pro-communist minister that liberalism is not always a bed of roses. There are penalties which they too must pay for selling their country out to the enemy.

Fourth, we must upset the enemies' timetable. We must seize the initiative from them and make them react at times and places that are to our own advantage.

Fifth, we must personally realize that if we are to be saved from communist enslavement, then we will have to do it ourselves. If we do not act quickly then we are selling our children into slavery for generations to come. What greater crime can you think of?

From February 1, 1964, issue of *On Target*

9

The Radical Right doesn't like to talk numbers. Not votes, not dollars, not names on a membership list. That's because the numbers are embarrassing. They betray the movement by revealing it as the truly slight collection that it is. Even if it were a united political force—which it is by no means— the Radical Right would still be just a minor component of the real-world political system. In its current—and seemingly perpetual—state of fragmentation, it is negligible in immediate political power.

The real numbers are elusive. There is no reliable source for membership figures of Radical Right groups. There is no wholly accurate list even of the groups alone. Thus, absolute accuracy is impossible. The best that can be hoped for is a reasonable synthesis of previously published estimates, hearsay evidence gleaned from interviews, and personal observation.

The best start is to collect reasonable estimates of membership figures throughout the movement. The John Birch Society, which may once have approached 80,000 members at its mid-Sixties peak, probably is down to about one-third that number. Willis Carto's Liberty Lobby seems to be overtaking the JBS in overall influence and popularity; actual membership in Liberty Lobby may be close to 30,000. With its $5 lifetime membership, the Committee of Ten Million may have attracted as many as 35,000 members in the last five years. The Christian-Patriots Defense League and its affiliated groups, which charge nothing for membership, may carry an additional 40,000 names on the rolls. The General Accounting Office says that the IRS identified more than 20,000 tax protesters from returns in 1980; while not all were necessarily inspired by the right-wing tax-revolt movement, that figure still makes possible a rough estimate of total membership of tax-fighting groups—say 60,000, on the assumption that for every protestor the IRS identified, there were perhaps two sympathizers who filed properly to avoid prosecution.

Beyond that, the numbers drop off sharply. Membership in the various Ku Klux Klans may number 10,000 together. Other white-racist or racial-nationalist groups may be good for 5,000 total, by generous measure. The Posse Comitatus may carry 5,000 names. The Nazis may add another 500 at the most.

Some observations about these numbers.

First, they don't include conservative Christians as a group. They don't include organizations commonly identified with the New Right, such as antiabortion forces. The point has been made already that while individuals in such conservative groups may sympathize with some aspects of Radical Right philosophy, the organizations themselves, and most of their members, don't belong in that company.

Second, while many of the preceding figures are speculative, there is a consistent suggestion of a limit that even the most ambitious and accessible groups fail to exceed. That number appears to be under 100,000, and, except for the John Birch Society's recruiting successes in the Sixties, the limit seems more like about 50,000.

Third, as this phenomenon suggests, there is a great deal of overlapping in memberships. Gun advocates, tax rebels, militant anticommunists, and generic right-wingers can drift comfortably among Liberty Lobby, the JBS, the Committee of Ten Million, the Christian-Patriots Defense League, and the various single-issue groups, even though the leaders of those groups tend to have implacable differences. These differences often are more personal than ideological.

Fourth, membership size alone does not determine the strength of a group. Bill Wilkinson's Invisible Empire KKK has a psychological impact beyond the group's actual size. And while the John Birch Society and the Christian-Patriots Defense League seem to have roughly the same number of names on their membership lists, the JBS has much more influence because its members generally are more active and involved than those of the Defense League, which requires—and often receives—nothing of its members.

Fifth, there are signs that the Radical Right can sporadically find support beyond its membership. The performances of white racists Tom Metzger,

Harold Covington, and Gerald Carlson in 1980 primary elections suggests
that the movement can reach beyond its boundaries.

All this means that the combined membership of all Radical Right
groups, a figure somewhere around 220,000, needs a good deal more
examination and analysis. Eliminate redundant names from that total,
take into account the apparently inflexible 50,000-member barrier, and
try for size a raw total of perhaps 100,000 people who have joined one or
more Radical Right groups in the past several years. The figure does not
strain credulity. Remember that that number is dispersed among a population of more than 210 million and the Radical Right's siege mentality is
not so difficult to understand. This really is an embattled minority.

Even more clarification is in order, because that 100,000 figure is misleading in a couple of ways.

Of that number, there are relatively few true activists who devote significant amounts of time and money to the cause. Most attendance estimates for the Christian-Patriots Defense League's "freedom festivals" run
around 1,500 to 2,000 people for a weekend—probably less than 10 percent of the group's nominal membership, though the festivals are the
group's only important activity. Most leaders in the movement concede
that their membership rolls are heavy with those who join, pay dues, and
contribute little else, so it is not unreasonable to assume that fewer than
one of five average members is a reliable source of money or time. It is
conceivable that about 20,000 zealots sustain the Radical Right.

But there also is evidence that the movement has a pool of potential
supporters who are on no membership lists. If that were not so, then no
Klansman would ever win a major-party nomination for Congress as Tom
Metzger did, or as self-described ex-Klansman Gerald Carlson did in
Michigan with $180 in reported campaign expenses. The Radical Right has
always claimed sympathizers in the millions, but has rarely tried to tap
that resource. In the last twenty years there have been three different
attempts to extend the traditionally constricted boundaries of the Radical
Right. They are important enough to be considered separately.

The Duck Book

When Robert White decided to save America in the summer of 1980, he
sat down before a typewriter and produced a huge hero sandwich of a
patriotic magazine, a slapdash concoction of tax-fighting advice, unornamented angry words about the Trilateral Commission and the Council on
Foreign Relations, reprints from doomsday financial reports and survivalist newsletters, ads from coin dealers and hard-money brokers, and
(whimsically enough) cartoons of a comical duck defending the Panama

Canal, piloting a B-1 bomber, sassing the Russian bear. Its grim message was standard fare these days on the Radical Right—something on the order of *The country's in ruins; cover your ass*—but its rough-edged amateurishness and Bob White's sputtering indignation, and, yes, that duck, somehow made the new magazine piquant and even endearing where others were only dreary. Something else set it apart as well. With that issue, and with the thirteen that followed it through December of 1981, White was sounding for the depths of that silent and usually invisible support that the Radical Right has always claimed to have.

His come-on was hard to resist. He wanted $10 for a lifetime subscription—not the subscriber's life, he stressed, but his own, which was endangered by cancer. This was a pyramid scam, he admitted, a Ponzi scheme with a patriotic point. From the June 1981 issue:

> By the time you folks receive this long-winded letter, we will have passed the 100,000 subscriber mark. THAT'S THE NUCLEUS TO GO FOR A MILLION. If each of you will only pass this letter on to your neighbor and tell him or her to let the moths out of their checkbook and send me ten bucks for a subscription, we will double in one month. . . . We should with your help pass the quarter of a million mark in 60 days. And my big July issue plus all of the Duck Clubs in operation should easily double that to half a million by September. We pass the million before Christmas for sure. . . . THEN WE LOWER THE BOOM COME 1982. FACT: In the last off year for congressional elections only 35.1 percent of those eligible turned out to vote. Now, hopefully, you can see that just a million or two conservative-minded patriotic Americans can save our free enterprise system and send Rockefeller and his socialist one-world government pimps packing like you would a pack of egg-sucking curs which have taken over the hen house—like they have taken over our government.

White tried. He begged and finagled and bartered for mailing lists of all possible supporters, and promptly dispatched to every name a current copy of the magazine and a subscription pitch. He urged subscribers to buy lifetime subscriptions for others. He claims to have printed at least one press run of 500,000 copies, most sent free to potential subscribers. He tried to encourage supporters to form local "Duck Clubs"—many did—and he published directories of volunteers who were willing to organize *Duck Book* subscribers into a political force. After nearly a year of steady growth, that goal of one million subscribers by Christmas '81 seemed far-fetched but not impossible. He was losing money, but if the numbers multiplied as he hoped, he would be able to raise ad rates and the magazine would be self-supporting.

It all ended that June. His earliest subscribers were still enthusiastic, but the second and third tiers—latecomers who had received subscriptions and the merely curious who had spent the $10 because it seemed like a good deal—had failed to show much enthusiasm for political activity.

In November 1981 White sent all subscribers a letter notifying them that his cancer was cured, that he was losing money, and that he had printed the last issue under the lifetime offer. *The Duck Book* was finished.

White estimated that word of his enterprise had reached twenty million people through articles in *Esquire*, both Dallas dailies, the Chicago *Tribune,* the Miami *Herald,* the *Wall Street Journal*, the Knight-Ridder and Gannett chains, more than 41 radio and TV talk shows, 200 small local papers, and 165 financial newsletters. It was phenomenal coverage, most of it concentrated in spring and summer of '81 as White began his big push for one million by Christmas. Yet his momentum had evaporated. Paid circulation had hit 100,000 in June and had not budged beyond that.

The letter that announced the demise of *The Duck Book* also announced *Duck Book II,* which was being offered at an introductory price of $20 annually, soon to become the *Duck Book Digest*, costing $30 a year. This was more than a change in sales tactics. It meant a whole new strategy.

> The fact is [White wrote] that I'm sending *Duck Books* to over 50,000 people whose subscriptions were paid for by a friend. . . . I'm just wasting postage on them since less than three per cent of those who received *The Duck Book* for free have shown any interest in the "Duck Movement" by buying one of their friends a subscription or by attending a seminar. It's the same old story—when people receive something for nothing, they don't appreciate it. So now comes the new *Duck Book II,* to separate the wheat from the chaff, so I can concentrate on those who care about their country and freedom and want to do something about it.

I talked to White in early January 1982.

"The apathy in this country is simply unbelievable," he said from his office in Cocoa, Florida. "I lost eight hundred thousand dollars this past year. My accountant just brought me the statement. I couldn't afford to throw another million into it."

(White made a fortune, large but obviously not limitless, by selling airstrip-maintenance machines.)

"The new book is going to have a five-buck price on the cover," he said. "That'll make it the most expensive financial magazine in the world. People will read it instead of throwing it away. That's the way it is: People associate quality with price. They assume they're getting something valuable if they have to pay for it."

GODS, GUTS, AND GUNS

And how had his subscribers reacted to the change?

"I have to say, better than my expectations. My hard core, about ten thousand people who bought subscriptions for other people or who attended a *Duck Book* seminar, almost eighty percent of them paid the twenty within the first couple of weeks. The others, I'm getting about eight percent response from them. I'm going to keep hitting away at 'em. Eventually I'll get fifty percent of 'em back. Support is deep, it's really deep. You can't believe how much mail I get. I've got six thousand letters here I haven't even got time to answer. People are mad."

And was he still expecting to chase out the rascals in the off-year elections?

"You bet your sweet ass."

But it seemed improbable. In one year, Bob White had scratched harder and deeper for right-wing support than anyone had ever scratched before. He had created a phenomenon of some note. For a few weeks, the Radical Right had gone public, with a buy-in as cheap as anybody could have asked. It would never get a better chance to prove its strength.

And in the end, he had not found enough supporters in the entire nation to carry even a gubernatorial election in some of the larger states.

Liberty Lobby

The numbers haven't been as harsh for Willis Carto as they have been elsewhere on the Radical Right. Unlike White, Carto seems to have avoided publicity. His approach has been a cautious mustering of support. He has quietly (sometimes anonymously) sponsored a myriad of right-wing groups that have provided him with strong, reliable mailing lists.* If anyone has isolated and identified the committed core of the Radical Right, that person is Willis Carto. Nobody can reach the active right-wingers as easily as he.

The centerpiece of Carto's operation is Liberty Lobby, a nonprofit organization founded in 1955 with offices at 300 Independence Avenue, SE, in Washington, D.C., several blocks from the U.S. Capitol. That address is the nominal headquarters of many of Carto's enterprises, but the real headquarters is probably wherever Carto happens to be, for there

---

* Among the groups and publications with which Carto has been connected are Americans for National Security; Save Our Schools; *American Mercury; Liberty Letter; Washington Observer;* Congress of Freedom; We, the People; United Congressional Appeal; Liberty and Property; Friends of Rhodesian Independence; Noontide Press; *Liberty Lowdown;* Legion for the Survival of Freedom; Committee for Religious Development; Government Educational Foundation; Youth for Wallace, et al.

is reason to believe that he reserves to himself the final decision in matters large and minute.

Liberty Lobby's literature describes the group's philosophy as "nationalist" and "populist." If that sounds vague, it may not be accidental. Because Liberty Lobby espouses a general patriotism and adopts some broad conservative stances, right-wingers find the group easy to like. A partial list of Liberty Lobby's published positions:

FOR	*AGAINST*
Free enterprise	Foreign aid
Less government spending	Pornography
Lower taxes	Tax-supported housing
Disenfranchising welfare recipients	Forced racial busing
Constitutional money	Wage and price controls
End to illegal immigration	Metric system

There are few shocks in that collection. Ostensibly, Liberty Lobby's positions are determined by the votes of its members. However, a highly critical study of Carto and his groups in the September 10, 1971, *National Review* claimed that the ballots of the members are "forever being mailed back to the Liberty Building, where they are never counted."

Liberty Lobby's real power is in its weekly newspaper, the *Spotlight*. Its latest annual statement filed with the Post Office claims an average paid weekly circulation of 315,102, which makes the *Spotlight* by far the best-selling periodical produced by the Radical Right.

Imagine a scandal tabloid like the *National Enquirer* devoted to right-wing politics instead of horoscopes and Hollywood capers and you've got the *Spotlight*. The sensational headlines are there: "Certain Terrorists Have License to Kill at Will," "Campaign of Terror is Aimed at 'Right-Wing' Dissidents," "Must the World Face a Nuclear Holocaust?" and "Court Ruling Would Cancel Free Speech."

Inside, the weekly offerings are almost invariable: articles about gold or silver as investments; an article or two about government failing to work or harassing citizens (stories of heavy-handed IRS tactics are favorites); advertisements for nostrums, tear-gas revolvers, vitamins, and gadgets; and occasional pieces about those organizations that Carto controls (most frequently the Institute for Historical Review, which attempts to disprove the Holocaust of World War II) and those groups or publications that are currently in his graces.

But the real staple is a strong anti-Zionist tilt. Articles in the *Spotlight* have accused Israel of joining Libya in a terror campaign in the United

States; have accused Israel of helping to assassinate Egyptian President Anwar Sadat; have claimed that U.S. foreign policy is dictated by the Begin government; declared that the Israeli secret service, the Mossad, operates without restriction in the United States. The phrase "dual loyalists" is a common one on the newspaper's pages. It refers to Jews, who are by implication, as committed to the nation of Israel as they are to the United States.

All this has helped to give Liberty Lobby and the *Spotlight* a reputation for anti-Semitism, and has kept the group confined to the Radical Right, however much Carto would like to extend its influence into the conservative wing. When the Reagan administration proposed Warren Richardson as assistant secretary of the Department of Health and Human Services, his nomination was challenged in the House because he had worked as Liberty Lobby's general counsel from 1969 through 1973.

Whether Liberty Lobby and the *Spotlight* are anti-Semitic depends on the definition of the term. If absolute anti-Zionism is anti-Semitic, then Liberty Lobby and the *Spotlight* are manifestly anti-Semitic. Accept a more restricted definition and the group probably doesn't meet the criteria. In general, it does not play on racial stereotypes or resort to vulgar racist terms, though infrequent references to "culture distorters" seem to have anti-Semitic implications. While it criticizes a power-hungry elite in pages that adjoin its anti-Zionist diatribes, it stops just short of connecting the two and claiming a Zionist one-world conspiracy: a deft job of picking a path through a minefield. The casual reader gets the distinct impression that the *Spotlight* is talking in a sort of shorthand that the paper's editors and its regular readers both understand perfectly, but which does away with the messy business of outright hatemongering.

John Birch Society
There is no better-known entity on the Radical Right. Funded in 1958 by former candymaker Robert Welch, the JBS was an attempt to create a network of affiliated organizations, modeled on what he took to be the Communist system of "front" groups answering to Moscow alone. He hoped to bring conservatives, right-wingers, and fundamentalists together in politically powerful pressure groups anonymously influenced by the JBS. But the low-profile approach became impossible in 1960 with the revelation that Welch, in a book-length manuscript distributed to hundreds of supporters, had denounced Presidents Eisenhower, Truman, and Roosevelt as Communist conspirators. Eisenhower's secretary of state, John Foster Dulles, was called "a Communist agent," and Eisenhower's brother, Milton, was probably "Dwight Eisenhower's superior and boss

within the Communist Party." Of Dwight Eisenhower, Welch wrote: "There is only one possible word to describe his purpose and actions. That word is 'treason.' " In a phrase that would become his albatross, Welch called Eisenhower a "dedicated, conscious agent of the Communist conspiracy."

Welch later explained that the document was personal, and not an official publication of his group, but since Welch is the JBS's ultimate and abiding authority, that disclaimer had little effect.

Still, a Gallup poll in February 1962, just after Welch and the JBS had been scored by press and politicians, showed surprising support for the organization. Gallup found that a million Americans had heard of the John Birch Society, and that 8 percent of those were favorably inclined, 43 percent were unfavorable to the group, and nearly half had no opinion. That meant a potential 4.5 million supporters for Welch's group when the results were projected over the entire national population.

No other Radical Right group has ever been subjected to such intense public criticism as the JBS was in the early Sixties. And until *The Duck Book*, none ever received such serendipitous attention. The flap was a boon for Welch and his new group, for it exposed them to sympathizers they might never have reached. The public controversy helped the Society to break out of the insulated vacuum within which the Radical Right so often struggles.

By 1962, the JBS had a working fund of $1.6 million annually, with income from publishing, dues, and large donations. Today on the Radical Right, only Willis Carto's combined enterprises appear to match that total in a 1982 equivalent.

The product of that money is obvious. No other group on the Radical Right has churned out so many words in books, periodicals, newsletters, and assorted ephemera. No other group has sponsored so many lecturers speaking to such large audiences. And none other has shown such a fetish for internal organization.

The JBS publishes a weekly magazine (*Review of the News*), a monthly (*American Opinion*), and a John Birch Society *Bulletin,* also monthly, often written by Welch himself. It has a book-publishing arm (Western Island Press), a speakers' bureau, and a staff of researchers. Most large American cities have a Birch-owned American Opinion bookstore. Millions of Americans have read JBS literature, sometimes without even knowing its source, for the Society's acronymic front groups also produce their own material. Best-known among such groups are: MOTOREDE (Movement to Restore Decency), TRIM (Tax Reform Immediately), TRAIN (To Restore American Independence Now), and SYLP (Support Your Local Police). The proliferation of single-issue groups is supposed to attract support from sympathizers who might not be inclined to join the JBS itself, but former JBS members have claimed that the groups rarely reach beyond the Society's own membership.

That is a minor one of the several controversies that have attached themselves to the JBS over the years, though most have flared only within the tight and exclusive little circle of the Radical Right. For all their heat and incandescence, they were only dimly observed outside.

One former Birch researcher, Nicholas Bove, charged in a book, *The Belmont Brotherhood* (Get US Out Committee, Minneapolis, 1974), that Welch and charter members of the JBS were members of a Masonic conspiracy trying to subvert the right wing. Considerably less fanciful are repeated complaints by JBS members and staffers that the Society's high command is really only an autocracy, that Welch alone makes important decisions, and that the Birch Council has only a weak advisory role. Former Birch staffer Bill Murray claimed in his self-published *Belmont Syndrome* (1978) that Welch and others in the JBS headquarters refused to use modern methods of direct-mail and marketing to reach untapped sympathizers, and that the group was slowly atrophying because of an archaic, inflexible approach.

Within the right the most persistent criticism of the JBS comes from those who are outraged by Welch's color-blind, nonracist stance. Not merely does he refuse to cast the Great Conspiracy in racial terms, but the JBS also admits nonwhite members and employs blacks and Jews as speakers and staff organizers. Racial rhetoric is discouraged at Birch meetings.

"If we found a Klan member, a Nazi or a Communist in our ranks, he would be removed," Birch organizer Scott Thompson said in a newspaper interview in 1979. "If somebody joins our organization and starts raising a huff about Jews being behind the country's economic problems, and saying that all blacks should be shipped to Africa, we try to educate the man. If he persists in that line of thinking, he's removed from the organization."

That stance infuriates white racists. There has been tension for years between the JBS and the National States Rights party, and the question of racial emphasis seems to be the underlying cause. In March 1979, the NSRP's *Thunderbolt*, reporting on a JBS meeting in Atlanta, said:

> One way in which the Birch Society silences those who would dare to speak up for the PRESERVATION OF THE WHITE RACE is to have negro and Jew speakers at their larger meetings. They expect you to be polite and socialize with the blacks at such meetings and this, of course, constitutes

RACIAL INTEGRATION! . . . The main guest speaker was negro Charles Smith. . . . Everything he said about how bad Red China is was correct. BUT WHY DO WE HAVE TO HAVE A NEGRO LECTURE US ON THIS SUBJECT? Any White man could have said the same things more effectively.

This isn't to imply that there are no racists in the JBS. Surely they are there. FBI files from 1964 indicate that the Pine Bluff, Arkansas, chapter of the JBS was controlled by Ku Klux Klan members. But Welch, as a point of conviction, discourages racial overtones in any of his group's literature or activities, and racists are told that they must check their hate at the door. So even at the peak of the public denunciation of the JBS during the Sixties, there was no room for serious suggestion that Welch had fractured that ultimate taboo.

Thus, to become known as a "Birchite" might be a political injury, but it isn't necessarily fatal. Birchers have been elected to office. Former Connecticut governor Meldrim Thompson has belonged to the JBS. So have Rep. Larry McDonald (R-Georgia), Rep. John Rousselot (R-Calif.) and California assemblyman John Schmitz.*

That is a record which no other Radical Right group can match in the last thirty years. Since the end of the Klan revival in the Thirties, the Radical Right's performance in electoral politics has been dismal. The movement's racist predilections are one reason. Another is that the mechanics of fund raising, canvassing, and forming a political machine strike most militants as pedestrian and pointless. Finally, it is the very nature of extremism that its proponents find little sustained popular support. And truly significant national voting blocs are counted in the tens of millions, not in bare thousands.

Still, there are those who would say that the Radical Right has an indirect influence on the mood of the electorate; that by some inexplicable process of ideological osmosis, some of the Radical Right's basics somehow seep into the national consciousness.

The Invisible Empire's Bill Wilkinson endorsed Ronald Reagan for president in 1980; Reagan promptly rejected the endorsement, but Wilkinson didn't seem disappointed. "It was probably one of the most widely publicized endorsements," he said a year later. "I feel we garnered millions of votes for him. I really do. We weren't the decisive issue. But if it had been a close battle, we might have been able to say that we made the difference."

* The JBS removed Schmitz from its national council last year after he described women attending a committee hearing on abortion as "bull dykes" and "lesbians" with "hard, Jewish, and (arguably) female faces." One he called a "slick butch lawyeress."

Bob DePugh of the Minutemen expands the theory more convincingly. "I think we could pat ourselves on the back, tell ourselves we did a good job, that we got our man into office and we got the country turned around," he said in the summer of 1981. "People talk about the Reagan landslide. It wasn't that great. Every bit was important. Like Robert Welch. I think that man can honestly say that he elected Ronald Reagan. And there's some of the rest of us who can come awfully close to saying that we made the difference.

"The effect was a long time coming, but it was cumulative. A lot of people have said that our literature was extreme, but it did attract attention. And people ever so slowly considered the right wing and the rightist alternative. Ronald Reagan couldn't have been elected twenty years ago. Something had to happen to bring about the change in attitude, the atmosphere that made it possible. A lot of it was strictly word of mouth. You get back to the true meaning of the word 'propaganda,' to propagate. If I tell you something, it's not propaganda unless you pass it on to somebody else and it gets passed on from there, over and over again. If it develops into a rumor, or folklore, or a matter of common interest that's discussed on the street, then that's real propaganda.

"A lot of right-wing philosophy becomes true propaganda like that. A stranger may walk into a John Birch Society meeting and walk out staggering with all he's been told, probably thinking he wants to find some nice liberal who'll tell him that the world isn't really about to end after all. Maybe he never goes to another meeting. But when he gets over his shock and he sorts through what he's heard, he'll find something that doesn't sound so crazy after all. And the next day he'll say to his friends, 'I went to the doggonedest meeting last night, a real bunch of kooks, but one of them did have this to say that was kind of interesting,' and he'll pass that along. And when he's forgotten about the kooks, that's what he'll remember.

"Look at the tremendous effort at education that Bob Welch has done over the years, all the books and meetings, and not just him but a lot of the rest of us, too, and you can see how it would have an effect after a while."

The theory has some merit. It is, at least, one possible ingredient in the complex of political realities that helped to elect the most conservative American president in fifty years.

And is Reagan, as DePugh says, really the candidate of choice for the Radical Right? That depends on the pragmatism of whomever you're asking, and pragmatism isn't the commonest commodity in these parts. Generally, the more dogmatic extremists scorn him. An Identity Christian who believes that the nation is in the grip of Jewish Satanists isn't likely to expect much relief from any president. Those who see a National Socialist dictatorship as the nation's only hope for survival find little to like about Reagan. The Radical Right's pessimists have been crowing for years that the nation has deteriorated beyond repair. For them to say now that Reagan can make a difference would be out of character.

The Duck Book's Bob White, avid believer in a Trilateralist conspiracy:

> When are you "ducks" going to wake up and realize nothing has changed in Washington, except the puppets? Haig and Weinberger are giving you that same crap that Brzezinski and Brown gave you. They have Reagan boxed in even more than they had Carter. Don't you realize there's more of Rocky's Trilateralist pimps surrounding Reagan than Carter?

And Sheldon Emry, Identity pastor from Phoenix, writing to his national congregation:

> I think some who say they are trusting in God are really "hoping" in Ronald Reagan. I have been skeptical of Reagan for years. . . . Reagan has mouthed patriotic platitudes in public and then worked with both hands to get every liberal and left-wing program and individual advanced in government whenever he had the opportunity to do so. . . . Since becoming president, Reagan has appointed almost 100 per cent left-wing pro-communist people in top government positions. . . . I have never trusted him and I think he is proving my worst suspicions. He is an actor playing a part, NOT a patriot! Be prepared to find that out for yourself soon.

Others have at least some reserved praise for Reagan. Some on the Radical Right cheered the demise of the Bureau of Alcohol, Tobacco, and Firearms (BATF); others decried his plans to add more agents to the Internal Revenue Service for collection and auditing duties. There was praise for the administration when it studied a revival of the gold standard; criticism when that revival was abandoned. And Reagan brought first elation and then disappointment to racists and some conservative Christians when he first supported and then disavowed the granting of tax-exempt status to private schools that don't meet federal racial guidelines.

Specific issues aside, there are those on the Radical Right, like Bob DePugh, who simply like Reagan's tone and approach. They are heartened by his tough stand against world communism and they see in his words and actions at least a pale reflection of their own ideals. He may be flawed, according to their standards, but at least a few of them realize that he is more acceptable than any tiny, fragmented, powerless minority has a right to expect.

WITNESSING

Great Expectations

A COUP IS TAKING PLACE IN WASHINGTON!
Foreign agents have almost completed a total takeover of U.S. Government.
Dear Fellow American:

A coup is under way as I write these lines . . . right now . . . accompanied by physical and psychological terrorism of the most scientific kind. Unless you support the foreign policy of Israel you are targeted for this terrorism.

Like it or not, you must make up your mind—do you support the beggar nation of Israel which lives off your tax dollars to pursue its theft of other people's lands and its constant aggression against its neighbors? Or are you an American?

You had better face up to this fact: LIBERTY LOBBY, the bastion of pro-American action for the past 26 years, is under violent attack by gangs of bloodthirsty terrorists. Should we fall, the coup would be complete!

We stand alone in this struggle. Even the so-called "conservatives" are against us! . . .

For many years a gaggle of disgusting profiteers calling themselves "conservatives," thumping the Bible and waving the flag, have squeezed money out of American patriots to fatten their own pocketbooks. Well, they have shown their true colors in this crisis, and I assure you that their colors are the blue and white of Israel—and with plenty of yellow!—not the red, white and blue of Americans. . . .

Without us, we would already be in the midst of a NO-WIN war, cannon fodder and lickspittles of the insane leaders of Israel. At the least, this war would immediately plunge America into dictatorship as our imported oil would be totally cut off, resulting in anarchy. In all probability the war would quickly escalate into global nuclear holocaust and unimaginable devastation. The end of America. . . .

From a Liberty Lobby fund-raising letter

THE ULTIMATE SCAM

First I'll create the biggest magazine in America simply by corraling the brightest financial and survival editors in the world and nail subscribers at the bargain basement price of ten dollars for a lifetime subscription plus give them a thousand bucks worth of expensive newsletters in one, big fancy book. Then they will obviously tell their friends about the bargain of a lifetime and I'll add more "marks" to the computer who in turn will become my "pushers" to pull in more ten dollar "marks." . . . After the first million subscribers are on the computer which should be by January 1, 1982, we will form political cadres in each ZIP code area. . . . By the time the third or fourth meeting rolls around each ZIP code area group should be able to find a small businessman (no lawyers or politicians) to give up two years of his life to sit in the House of Representatives.

THEN WE WILL ELECT HIM. AS SLICK AS THE COON THAT GOT INTO THE HEN HOUSE WHILE ROVER WAS TAKING A NAP.

How? The same as the Republicans and Democrats do it—with money. Only we won't use the power brokers and their special interest money they corrupt honest men with. We will use 200 million dollars worth of "Duck" money. . . . When I reach twenty million circulation which should be in about ten months, if current figures hold the same I will put out another big supplemental economic and survival issue containing complete up to date newsletter reprints by my superstar financial editors at ten bucks a copy. Again the reading bargain of a lifetime. Twenty million times ten bucks and there is your 200 million. Simple, you bet your butt it is.

From a Duck Book advertising circular

10

This was the scorecard of fraternal cooperation on the Radical Right as of 1982.

Bob DePugh was still unhappy with John Harrell after the failure of the Patriots' Leadership Council.

Willis Carto was said to be still miffed with DePugh about the four-part series in *On Target,* which claimed at one point that "no person in the entire conservative movement has done more to foster dissension and disunity than Willis A. Carto."

DePugh still had strong ties with Bob Shelton, while Shelton remained locked in competition with Bill Wilkinson.

Edward Fields of the National States Rights party was thought not to have healed his rift of several years' standing with DePugh, but Fields's main target of the moment was—Shelton's rival, Bill Wilkinson. (Where this put Fields with Shelton was anybody's guess.)

Wilkinson was trying to downplay the news that he had supplied information to the FBI for seven years, but that disclosure was provoking indignant howls from almost everybody. Wilkinson, meanwhile, was refusing to discuss his feud with David Duke, which began when he split from Duke's Klan, not long after he agreed to cooperate with the FBI.

Harold Covington, who had mystified and shaken North Carolina's Republicans with his 43-percent showing in that party's attorney-general primary, was writing a series of bitter dispatches and planning a new white

145

nationalist organization, for he had been deposed as chairman of the National Socialist Party of America.

In all, a standard state of affairs within the movement. Rifts and alliances seem to form almost randomly. Whatever the superficial pattern, an abiding, organic distrust is constant. The right forms circular firing squads, Sam Potter said. He might also have added that its marksmanship is excellent.

To an outsider it all seems inexplicable craziness. Why are these people fighting? A Kennedy liberal, applying the standards of the mainstream, is not likely to discern much difference between Edward Fields and Bill Wilkinson. They would seem to be natural allies, mutually supportive. Racists, both. Implacable opponents of forced busing, Affirmative Action, the Voting Rights Act, equal-opportunity housing. They share a vision of a Utopia that has whites separated from other races at work, in schools and churches, in neighborhoods. One can easily imagine the two men meeting frequently to compare tactics, to exchange aid and advice, to discuss a strategy by which they can support each other in their mutual goal of an unblemished white America. Certainly, they would rally to one another's aid in time of crisis. Yet, there is no indication that Wilkinson's Invisible Empire has ever cooperated with the NSRP, even over so insignificant a matter as mailing lists. And when Wilkinson was being assailed as an informant, did Fields rush to his defense? Well, not exactly. Actually, he trumpeted the news of Wilkinson's FBI connection in a highly critical double-truck exposé, complete with screaming headlines in red ink.

The strange case of DePugh and Harrell is no more explicable. Their ideologies are indistinguishable to any but the most sensitive observer. Each has advocated arming his followers, despaired of American government's future course, condemned creeping collectivism in the strongest terms. Each has been a fugitive from a federal sentence. Each has served time in prison. While Harrell is perhaps more overtly religious, more explicitly segregationist, so little separates their beliefs that the deep division between the two men seems almost inconceivable. Yet it is real.

There are other examples, puzzling rivalries and bitterness in places where felicitous cooperation ought logically to be the rule. In fact, such cooperation is disdained among the Radical Right's leadership. Instead, jealousies have reduced the movement to an archipelago of isolated warring fiefdoms. There is no movement at all, except as individual groups coincidentally lurch in the same ideological direction. Movement in the sense of mutual planning simply does not exist.

Why should this be so? The Radical Right itself has several answers, and all have disturbing implications.

Maybe the most popular explanation is that the right does not attract those who willingly subordinate themselves to an abstract. *We are free men,* leaders of the Radical Right like to boast. *We choose our own ways.* The argument is true up to a point; the Radical Right is the last haven for idiosyncratic individualists. This may be one of the movement's strengths, and is certainly prominent among its arcane charms. But implicit in such an attitude is the belief held by each individual that his is the only correct way, and that anyone who fails to perceive this obvious fact is deluded and unworthy of consideration.

Other leaders declare that the movement is being subverted by scurrilous characters who must be purged before any progress is possible. This, they say, justifies their unbending attitude. Again, there is an element of truth here. A year's observation of the Radical Right compels the admission that the movement's leadership abounds in hucksters, con men, and self-interested buffoons. But some of those who bemoan the bankrupt leadership of the movement have themselves made an art of perfidy. There is good reason to question the motives of anyone who snipes heavily at his rivals.

A third explanation: The Radical Right is divided because it encompasses such a multitude of diverse ideas. Once more, true in a fashion: Reviving the gold standard and pulling this country out of the United Nations, for example, are two of the Radical Rights's favorite causes, yet they have little in common. But while the movement's causes are diverse, they are not incompatible. The Radical Right has a strong substructure of common values: a commitment to free enterprise, a yearning for smaller and simpler government, a reverence for religion and the family—the same philosophical foundation that supports the more moderate, conservative wing. It is instructive to note what the two groups have made of the same essentials.

Conservatives and conservative Christians have become a political force in ten years by seeking out that upon which they agree and by rallying behind a few visible figures: Paul Weyrich, Jerry Falwell, Phyllis Schlafly, Jesse Helms, Richard Viguerie, a few others. They melded a coalition that has been called the New Right. They have not always known accord on the minor issues, but they have chosen not to become distracted by their differences, and they have not thrashed their disagreements out in public. They have presented to the political machines what is by all appearances a seamless battle line. They seem to believe that results are impossible without a united front. So Schlafly's Eagle Forum may work with the Reverend Donald Wildmon's Coalition for Better Television in matters of their mutual concern, and the Moral Majority remains closely allied with the National Conservative Political Action Committee. They have chosen not to emphasize their differences, and their electoral successes of 1980 can only have affirmed that decision.

But what of the Radical Right? Infighting is still the rule. In a movement burdened by lack of money and manpower, leaders and would-be leaders are apt to squander as many of their resources on upbraiding their rivals as they spend presenting political ideas. They are purists of the most exacting sort; any departure from what are presumed to be acceptable positions (on which there never is a consensus, of course) is sufficient reason for the most thorough chastising.

Bob DePugh makes the case that a shortage of assets causes much of the competition within the Radical Right. With funds and followers so scarce—the movement having put a wide distance between itself and any source of real power—cooperation would seem to be doubly important, yet the movement's squabbling factions persist in duplicating and sometimes canceling each other's efforts. It is difficult to imagine how healthy bank accounts could change such self-destructive peevishness.

What does all this signify about the people of the Radical Right?

About the movement's followers, it means little, except that they have shown amazing tolerance for their leaders' foolishness. The distrust that is endemic among the leaders seems not to affect the movement's foot soldiers at all. At the local, personal level, they even show a certain inclination for compromise. Far from the reaches of organizational command, the followers form their own alliances of convenience. Klansmen and Nazis are supposed to be incompatible—so goes the line from Imperial Wizards, Grand Dragons, and their immediate retinue—but the followers find one another and cooperate informally. They know that they have much in common, even if their leaders deny it. Those who belong to one group on the Radical Right frequently belong to two or three others, which may all be officially tangled in complicated and meaningless feuds. The followers often read several different newsletters and bulletins. What they think of the charges and denials and countercharges that they read on those pages can only be imagined. They seem oblivious to the furious battling that rages above them. When they shift allegiances in great numbers, as they did several years ago in defecting from Shelton's United Klans to Wilkinson's Invisible Empire, it is because they sense a change in tactics and policies. The posturing and acrimonious debate among those who would give them direction seem not to influence them at all.

But the quarreling does reveal much about the leaders. There is no doubt that the constant infighting drains the movement's energies; still, the leaders battle on regardless. It is evident that they could find much in common if they wished; instead, they persist in searching out minor deviations in doctrine. The only possible conclusion is that they care more for their own interests than for the ultimate future of the ideology they claim to support, that they are more interested in dominating and profiting than in truly leading.

Probably they are not all so self-involved. But of those who sincerely put the cause above their own aggrandizement, there is another indictment, maybe even more serious. By spurning the methods of compromise, by wasting their resources, they make a tacit admission that they have given up on the normal political means that the New Right has used so well. This is an injustice to many of their followers, who still are convinced that their money and their time may one day pay off. And it is frightening to anyone else who realizes that when the Radical Right gives up on the accepted channels, it often turns to violence.

There have been efforts at reconciliation. Beginning in about 1976, DePugh tried to form a leadership council of important Radical Right figures. He tried to gather the major gun groups and tax-revolt groups with Harrell's Christian-Patriots Defense League, Shelton's UKA, and Carto's Liberty Lobby under the infinitely expansive umbrella of his own Committee of Ten Million. He claims to have achieved some measure of cooperation among the first four members of the council, but he apparently exceeded critical mass when he introduced eight new members in 1978. Six months later, the council was in fragments. An intriguing photograph shows the twelve council members, some of the most important men in the movement, gathered for a group photograph in an atmosphere of somewhat restrained conviviality. It was the first and probably the last time all twelve ever got together on anything.

Lately Harrell has been urging cooperation. He has borrowed Benjamin Franklin's admonition, "If we do not hang together, we most assuredly will hang separately." The phrase recurs in his speeches and in his group's publications. Harrell would like to have the quarreling factions of the Radical Right find a common ground, preferably in his own organization.

"It is truly annoying and disturbing to observe how many sincere and dedicated Patriots are estranged from one another over relatively minor differences of opinion and/or approach," a C-PDL policy statement says. "To remain so estranged is to be easily destroyed in crises."

But even a conciliatory leader on the Radical Right can't resist taking a shot or two before getting on with business. The statement continues: "However, we do not mean to include in this category the charlatan or the social or insincere Patriot, who is to be shunned, disdained, and separated from at every opportunity; but even then, always bearing in mind as a responsible family does, not to publicly air differences. . . . We know the day is near at hand when all must hang together and stand shoulder to shoulder . . . and in that hour, those with whom we may have violently disagreed on basically petty matters may now be required to stand side by side for survival. . . . Therefore, my Fellow-Patriots, may we all conduct ourselves wisely in these few moments remaining before the thunders of destruction roll across all of our horizons and galvanize us into a oneness heretofore unknown."

That bit of imagery is at least two years old. The leaders of the Radical Right remain ungalvanized—maybe the thunders of destruction haven't been rolling loudly enough. That oneness is still elusive, if only because nobody is trying very hard to find it.

There is a paradox in all of this: Those who carp on slight deviations from the presumed line of belief seem content to ignore the real philosophical division in the Radical Right. This is true of leaders and followers. All seem undisturbed by a conflict between authoritarian and libertarian impulses in their thinking. To anyone else, the clash of perspectives would be irreconcilable, but on the Radical Right, leaders and followers alike seem not even to recognize the inconsistency. Within this conundrum is the reason for the Libertarian party's failure to gain even a fingerhold among people with whom it ought, in theory, to own a comfortable niche.

The conflict is simple: While the Radical Right makes individual liberty through reduced government a cornerstone of its beliefs, it simultaneously embraces those who would burden us with more laws. Religion figures in the paradox. Except among some anti-Zionists and Identity converts, Jerry Falwell is respected on the Radical Right. Some of his staunchest admirers are men who rail against intrusive government's meddling, but they are not at all disturbed that the conservative Christians who look to Falwell for cues have supported laws that would restrict homosexual teachers, the public display of suggestive literature, even some sexual acts in private between consenting adults.

This forces the conclusion that their freedom is less free than they claim. But that doesn't entirely explain the contradiction. Sam Potter, the Posse member who went to jail for his adamant disobedience, gives every indication of being principled and sincere about personal freedom. He cherishes the idea. He is also enthusiastic about the Reverend Falwell. Argument is impossible; Sam just refuses to acknowledge the clash of ideals.

Falwell is a great American, his actions beyond reproach, Sam maintains.

The conflict has another facet, one apparent more often in Birch-style rightists, who usually conform to the popular image of law-and-order conservatism. The Birch philosophy, like much of right-wing thinking, favors maximum personal liberty. But Birchers also tend to support increased powers for police, including greater latitude for surveillance by law-enforcement authorities. Birchers at once demand lower taxes (a Libertarian tenet) and increased budgets for the military.

The Libertarians have not fared well in this schizophrenic atmosphere. Their ideology is at least consistent. All citizens, they hold, should be able to conduct their lives as they please without interference, so long as they do not endanger the lives or the freedoms of others. They envision a completely unrestrained society. Even slight regulation is excessive, they argue, for it upsets the natural equilibrium that a community or an economy will find if left totally to its own devices.

All the party's positions derive from that basic tenet. Given the opportunity, Libertarians would demolish the CIA and the FBI, and would end welfare payments, government subsidies, corporate regulations, laws against prostitution, drugs, and gambling. They would reduce the military to a minimum required to defend the nation's shores. They would begin immediately to dismantle all but the bare bones of government, starting with the Federal Trade Commission and the Securities and Exchange Commission. In a sense, their ideology is more extreme than any on the Radical Right. They would truly remake the world that we know.

Some of their positions betray the party's genealogy, which is heavy on right-wing influences. A 1969 convention of the Young Americans for Freedom helped to clarify the issues. Those Libertarian-minded YAF delegates, who were urging both a free economy and a tolerant society, wore buttons that read "Laissez-Faire." Other delegates ridiculed them as "laissez-fairies"—the Libertarian policy includes full freedom for all sexual choices—and the Libertarians walked out of the convention. In the next few years, they found allies in gay-rights organizations and sexual freedom leagues, in anarchistic leftists, and in legal reformers pushing for a liberalization of drug laws. Their most important connection was with free-market advocates who had previously found their friendliest audience in the conservative wing. (The party's most generous contributor has been oil executive Frederick Koch, a charter member of the Birch society.)

In 1976, the Libertarian party was on the presidential ballot in thirty-two states; candidate Roger MacBride won 175,000 votes. In 1978, Libertarian Ed Clark won more than 380,000 votes in California's gubernatorial campaign, and the Alaska state legislature has had at least one Libertarian in its midst since 1976;* one Libertarian study group, the Cato Institute, is regarded as an outstanding source of free-market economic research.

With their emphasis on limited government and hands-off economics, the Libertarians would seem to have enormous appeal on the right. But with few exceptions, they've been shunned. The Radical Right doesn't trust these new ideas; the concept of liberty taken to its ultimate conclusion seems to provoke a nervous response. For example, Joseph Kerska, who finds in the Libertarians a supporter in his battle against gun control, nevertheless says: "I'm a little suspicious of the Libertarians. What they espouse sounds good, but they may not be as freedom-loving as they'd like us to believe." And conservative Christians are repelled by the idea that mankind's evil impulses should go unchecked. Says Janine Hansen Triggs: "Some of them are anarchists. I do not believe in anarchy. Anarchy leads to a vacuum of power, which ultimately leads to tyranny. Someone comes in and fills the gap and then there is tyranny. I have a lot of agreement with their fiscal policies. But on the other side of the coin, some of their moral ideas are abhorrent to me."

What she perceives is politics without morality; the Libertarians start with a principle and leave the morality for others to take or reject, which may be an approach too radical even for the Radical Right. That may explain why the Libertarians are shunned in a place where they might have expected welcome, and there may even be a clue here to the right's philosophical paradox. Try this: For the Radical Right, politics is not so much a philosophical as a moral issue. And morality is always subjective. What seems a contradiction to an outsider can be perfectly consistent to one who sees politics through a filter of right and wrong.

WITNESSING

Fraternity

(David) Duke is the *darling* of the talk show circuit. Is there a reason? Yes. Is it (as he claims) because he is so articulate? No. Duke is the judas goat leading

---

* Libertarian pressure in the legislature was at least partially responsible for repeal of the state's income and sales taxes. One Libertarian legislator, Dick Randolph of Fairbanks, is among the state's best-known politicians. When the state was debating uses for its large budget surplus from oil revenues recently, Randolph suggested that the money be drawn in cash, placed into bundles, and then tossed from an airplane flying across the state's vast wilderness, where the bravest and hardiest fortune-seekers might find a suitable reward for their individual initiative. Some Alaskans still aren't entirely convinced that Randolph was only kidding.

the klan movement to slaughter. He has neutralized more good men than the communists could ever expect to accomplish by any other means. . . . It is for no other reason than that Duke's organization is a one-way dead-end street for patriots. . . .

As we were going to press, a news story released from the East Baton Rouge School Board Office has stated that David Duke has asked that his request for the use of a high school auditorium be withdrawn. This is astonishing since the ACLU, acting in Duke's behalf, filed suit in court after the school board denied him use of the auditorium. . . . The school board finally agreed to allow Duke use of the facility. DUKE KNEW THAT HE COULD NOT FILL THAT AUDITORIUM and thereby asked that his request be withdrawn. Another humuliation for the White race!

From "The Truth About David Duke," a pamphlet published in 1978 by an organization calling itself "The Truth Forum"

It is with great reluctance that we present the following information. We realize that some sincere and well-intentioned patriots subscribe to *The Spotlight*. We are also aware that some conservatives are connected with Liberty Lobby. Frankly we would prefer not to lay it out as straight as we have. But we believe the time has come to do so. . . .

. . . (As) part of its program for pushing populism, *Spotlight* came out in favor of leftist Senator Birch Bayh's putative constitutional amendment for further democratizing our Republic by abolishing the Electoral College. . . . Even more incredible than this support of leftist sponsored and supported legislation is the praise and assistance given to the Leninist-Communist revolutionaries at the United States Labor Party. . . . *The Spotlight* offers for sale the publications of these violently anti-American terrorists. This assistance has lent support to the current media campaign to identify the USLP in the public mind as being a conservative organization. . . .

The U.S. Labor Party, however, is not the only Communist supported group to receive praise and support from *The Spotlight*. Literally feet of newsprint have been devoted to defending the Communist terrorists from the Palestine Liberation Organization. . . . *The Spotlight* has heaped much praise on Muammar el-Qaddafi, the dictator who runs the Soviet client state of Libya. . . . One more disturbing practice by *The Spotlight* crowd is . . . the practice of attacking members of the Staff of the John Birch Society as being Zionist agents. No definition ever is presented of what is meant by "Zionist" in this context. Nor does *The Spotlight* ever bother with anything as mundane as proof. Rather these strange patriots prefer to utilize leftist techniques of innuendo and veiled reference. . . .

For all of the reasons cited above and many others which would take far too long to document at present, we cannot but warn our members and friends of the unreliable, misleading, and slanted nature of much that is found in the sensationalist publication known as *The Spotlight*.

From "Memorandum on *The Spotlight*" issued in April 1980 by the John Birch Society

THE BATTLE AGAINST OUR OWN CORRUPTION AND INCOMPE-
TENCE IS THE MOST IMPORTANT FIGHT OF ALL, MORE IMPORTANT
THAN ANY ACTIONS WE MAY TAKE AGAINST THE RACIAL ENE-
MY . . .

Why? Simple. It is because *we are our own worst enemies.* And until we have
defeated the enemy within we must not even try to take on the racial enemy
on any major scale.

I ought to know. . . . I violated this precept in North Carolina and the
whole thing blew up in my face at the critical moment. I was squared off
with the enemy and ready to light into him when I went down for the count,
bludgeoned from behind by my most trusted "comrades." I warn you all:
we must never engage the enemy until we know for an absolute certainty
that our back is covered and there is no danger of treachery from within.

From "Circular Letter No. 2" by white nationalist Harold Covington, written in September 1981, after he had been deposed from his leadership position with the National Socialist Party of America

11

In July 1976, a nightmare in a manila envelope arrived in the mailboxes of Radical Right leaders and contributors. Within was a fifty-four-page typewritten document titled "Deguello," purportedly written by a group of international intelligence officers sympathetic to the cause. After some preliminary rehashing of socialist history and conspiracy theory, "Deguello" proceeded to accuse virtually every notable on the Radical Right of being either a Jew, a secret collectivist, or a closet homosexual. One well-known leader of a white racist group was termed an "intellectual Jewish socialist homosexual." On the Radical Right, that covers all the bases—there is no harsher condemnation. There was enough recognizable truth, added to just enough current innuendo, for the charges to carry at least a hint of realism.

But this wasn't aimless slander. The paper named more than thirty leading conservative and right-wing figures as infiltrators who were deliberately destroying the movement. That was the nightmare: the fear nonpareil on the Radical Right that the enemy is everywhere, and that nobody can be trusted. In a way, that is implicit in the Radical Right's rampant squabbling, but nobody had ever said it so flatly before. Nobody had ever put into words the paranoia underlying so much of what the Radical Right is about.

That "Deguello" struck a nerve was unquestionable. The document became a source of controversy: accusation, denials, charges, and speculation about who could have written the paper. The author clearly knew the Radical Right, knew personal histories and popular slander and whispered weaknesses. The topic was hot enough that, nearly a year after the document appeared, anonymously authored bulletins under the letterhead "American Defense Group" set off a controversy of their own when they named the U.S. Labor Party as the source of "Deguello."

That has never been proved. Other names have been mentioned as possible authors. Some even suspect that "Deguello" and the American Defense Group bulletins were written by the same person. Except within the movement, the question is inconsequential. "Deguello" is interesting for the reaction it provoked, the indication it gave that the Radical Right is pricklishly sensitive to the possibility that it has been subverted. In some quarters, that is not so much a concern as a preoccupation.

Those on the Radical Right feel vulnerable in several ways. They fear that communists have set up dummy organizations to compile names of patriotic Americans. The mailing lists of those name-gathering groups, they feel, would then serve as directories of potential resisters if the nation were ever conquered. Most of us do not plan for such an event, but the Radical Right wants to be ready. Sometimes the apprehension isn't so tightly focused. It may simply be a wariness about who has the names of right-wingers, and what might be done with them.

The contention that infiltrators, with their outlandish actions, have discredited patriots is common on the Radical Right: By using extreme rhetoric and ridiculous tactics, some feel, infiltrators masquerading as patriots have cast a shadow on the whole movement. This is a dubious premise, mainly because such enormous quantities of nonsense issue forth monthly from the Radical Right. There is a surfeit of sincere believers who need no assistance in discrediting the movement with their earnest foolishness.

Finally, the Radical Right fears infiltration by *agents provocateurs* who would incite violence among its more unstable sympathizers.

The movement's leaders claim their groups are the targets of infiltration by domestic leftists, by foreign intelligence services, and by police. The record shows that they are right about at least one of the three: Police agents—especially those from the federal Justice and Treasury departments—have moved through the more militant sectors of the Radical Right since at least the early 1960s. The FBI's COINTELPRO included systematic infiltration of the various Klans and the National States Rights party, and there is more recent evidence that the FBI and state and local police continue to collect firsthand intelligence about the Radical Right. They do this sometimes with paid informants who are not sworn officers, and sometimes with regular agents who go under deep cover to get close

to the workings of the group they're studying. At times they get so close
that the possibility of entrapment becomes very much an issue—close
enough, at least, that some of loudest protests from the Radical Right in
recent days come from convicted conspirators.

May 1981: Federal agents and Baltimore County police arrest eight
members of an alleged conspiracy to bomb the Maryland headquarters of
the NAACP. The reported plot, which police say involved the leadership of
the Adamic Knights of the Ku Klux Klan, is discovered by an agent of the
Bureau of Alcohol, Tobacco, and Firearms who has infiltrated a New England Klan group. According to police reports, one undercover agent was
given an incendiary bomb for use against the NAACP building.[1]

July 1980: A BATF agent is discovered to have infiltrated the white
nationalists involved in the November 3, 1979, shoot-out with members of
the Communist Workers party in Greensboro, North Carolina. Reporters
for a Greensboro newspaper learn that the agent took part in planning the
motorcade by Klansmen and Nazis that ended with the fatal shootings.[2]

November 1981: Two members of a maverick Klan group and a member of a National Socialist group are convicted in Nashville of plotting to
blow up a synagogue, a television tower, and Jewish-owned businesses.
The defendants, including a fifty-year-old grandmother, are convicted
after testimony by a BATF agent who tape-recorded conversations about
the plot.[3]

December 1979: Two brothers, organizers of a tiny racist group called
the American White Nationalist party, are convicted and later sentenced
to six years each for conspiring to bomb an elementary school in Columbus, Ohio. A man they had known for two years as an opponent of forced
busing—before whom they discussed the plot—is revealed to have been a
paid infiltrator working for the Columbus Police Department. No bomb
was ever made.[4] The infiltrator tells a Columbus newspaper: "In ten years
as an undercover operative I've never set anyone up. I've never framed
anyone. I wouldn't entrap anyone. I know the entrapment laws, and I
know how to get around them." His only regret, he says, is that his infiltration of the group "is ended, and I can't mess them up anymore." He
says that although he has been exposed, he expects to continue a career as
an undercover agent that has included jobs for the FBI and the BATF.
"I've got many faces and many names," he says.[5]

All such is stale news, though, for a movement that had its direst suspicions confirmed in the mid-1970s with disclosure of the FBI's counterintelligence program against extremist political groups, left and right.

"Counterintelligence" is a tepid term, actually, for a variety of tactics to harass, disrupt, confuse, and impede the bureau's targets. Acts against left-wing groups—principally the Communist party U.S.A. and the Socialist Workers Party—comprised roughly 85 percent of COINTELPRO, according to FBI statistics. Those activities have been well publicized. The remaining 15 percent, against what the FBI termed "white hate groups," have received less attention. A brief review of COINTELPRO as it was used against the Radical Right is worthwhile here, if only to help explain some of the movement's wholesale paranoia.

"A fair, accurate and comprehensive understanding of the various COINTELPRO activities undertaken by the FBI is possible only in light of the context and climate in which the programs were established," says a bureau statement released with the COINTELPRO papers. The program against the right, the statement says, "grew out of the disruptive and harassing activities of these groups in their attempt to subvert the civil rights movement. The activities of these groups were characterized by lynching, burnings, bombings, and the like—a climate of violence and lawlessness which society and its law enforcement mechanisms seemed incapable of countering."

Beginning in 1964, FBI headquarters or field offices proposed 404 different programs of action against 17 Klan groups and 9 white racist groups then under active investigation by the bureau. Of the 404 proposals, 289 were actually approved and used. Many were legal—like a series of interview programs to show Klan members that their affiliation was not secret. Some were petty disruptions—like mailing 850 copies of a faked letter, apparently from the national office of the Minutemen, requesting that members of the group withhold their dues and contributions because of a security leak. Some were of questionable legality and of even more questionable morality—like a smear campaign against the UKA's Bob Shelton. Some were startling in their efficiency and directness—like the use of informants to vote out violent leadership in the Knoxville klavern of the UKA. (For the seven years of COINTELPRO, field reports indicate, the Knoxville klavern was docile and almost dormant.) And some—like commissioning staff artists to produce a cartoon jokebook called *The United Klowns of America, Inc.,* which was anonymously printed and distributed— seem in retrospect nothing more than exercises in silliness.

Released files on acts against the Radical Right alone number in the thousands of pages. They give an indication of just how vulnerable the movement can be to opponents with manpower, money, imagination, and a purpose.

Beginning early in the campaign, the counterintelligence unit sought information on right-wing leaders, especially Shelton and George Lincoln

Rockwell (until he was assassinated in 1967). "A special summary of all background data, especially names of relatives and ancestors, is needed," stated a 1966 directive from J. Edgar Hoover to the Birmingham, Alabama, field office, concerning Shelton. The suggestion is strong that the Bureau would very much have liked to have found evidence of miscegenation in an Imperial Wizard's bloodlines.

"In addition," the memorandum continues, "the Bureau desires a summary of information concerning Shelton's close associates, likes and dislikes, drinking habits and social habits. For example, include any information concerning Shelton's relationship with his wife, and other females or males, any unusual behavior patterns and general Klan talk concerning his use or misuse of Klan funds, what motivates him, etc.

"The reason for this information is to begin the planning of a 'Rockwell Report' put out by George Lincoln Rockwell of the American Nazi Party, 'exposing' some information about Shelton which would tend to discredit him."*

Three days after the memorandum left Hoover's office, the special agent in charge of the Birmingham office Teletyped a report that Shelton "doesn't drink, dislikes people who do, chainsmokes Pall Malls and dislikes grits."

But reports from informants often were not so trivial. Potentially harmful information could be used—and was—in anonymous mailings to employers, neighbors, and family. It might be leaked to sympathetic members of the press. A 1964 advisory states that Ralph McGill, then publisher of the *Atlanta Constitution,* could be used to pass harmful material about the Klan to a reporter on his staff who was preparing an article for the *Saturday Evening Post.* The advisory notes that McGill had published a column favorable to the bureau and "in this proposed counter-intelligence operation of furnishing Klan material . . . McGill would not betray our confidence."

A report that a speaker for the National States Rights party was driving with a revoked license was passed on to local police where he lived. The discovery that a klavern leader in the UKA had failed to file an income-tax return was shared with the IRS. The FBI alerted Cook County commissioners when informants revealed that the American Nazi party, after expending considerable time and money to open a chapter office in Chicago, still had failed to meet some requirements of the local building code.

---

* The inference that Rockwell actually was cooperating with the FBI has never been substantiated. Another possibility is that the Bureau was planning to issue a bogus "Rockwell Report."

"Great expense and time were expended by the Nazi Party in defending these actions," says a memorandum from October 1967, "and several arrests were made of ANP members for violations of the building code. The Chicago Office has just advised us that the City of Chicago has successfully closed the ANP headquarters once and for all. ANP records and furniture are stored in various locations and as of now the members have no place to meet."

Clearly, much of this was insiders' information. It seems to show just how thoroughly the Justice Department had infiltrated its target groups. In Knoxville, the FBI had accumulated enough members to swing a klavern election. A September 2, 1965, letter from the FBI to a White House assistant mentioned "nearly two thousand of our informants and sources . . . being operated to obtain up-to-date intelligence data concerning racial matters which we disseminate on a continuing basis." The letter continued: "Particularly significant has been the high-level penetration we have achieved of Klan organizations. At the present time, there are 14 Klan groups in existence. We have penetrated every one of them through informants and currently are operating informants in top-level positions of leadership in seven of them."

Those Klan groups found themselves facing a new rival in 1965, when a right-wing organization called the National Committee for Domestic Tranquility bombarded Klan members and sympathizers with anti-Klan newsletters that had a traditional patriotic flavor. The group, claiming chapters in eleven states, was headed by one Harmon Blennerhassett, an apparent recluse who was new on the conservative scene. Though Blennerhassett did challenge Bob Shelton to a debate, he made his presence known mostly by his signature beneath a series of messages which argued that Klan leaders, by disrupting national peace, actually were aiding the cause of the enemy—inevitably referred to as "the anti-Christ, the atheistic communist."

Put away your robes, Blennerhassett urged Klansmen in one especially stirring epistle. "It is to you, the misled and betrayed Klan members, that I humbly address myself," the letter read. "In the name of God, and in the name of our fathers, husbands, and sons who have made the supreme sacrifice in defense of their country, take a firm position now. Discard your Klan robes, disavow your Klan leaders, replace the black oath with a simple prayer, seek out and support your duly elected representatives, take your personal and political opinions to the ballot box, and let domestic tranquility reign. . . ."

Not for years did Klansmen learn positively that the National Committee for Domestic Tranquility was a dummy organization set up and administered by the FBI, one of the most ambitious programs in COINTELPRO. Harmon Blennerhassett did not exist; the original memorandum outlining the program noted that a Harmon Blennerhassett had been a financial supporter of Aaron Burr.

It was an elaborate hoax. The Bureau's exhibits section designed a letterhead, and agents in more than a dozen cities discreetly rented post-office boxes. Regularly, new chapters were added to the letterhead to demonstrate the organization's rapid growth. All the touches were right: the fulsome writing style of the newsletter, its religious tone and frequent references to "the anti-Christ," even its bumper-sticker-style slogan— "Quit the Klan and Back Our Boys in Vietnam." Using information developed by infiltrators, the FBI tried to target the committee's mailings to specific Klansmen who were considered receptive to its patriotic appeal. The Dallas field office suggested a refinement: By urging Klansmen to respond, the Bureau might build up a list of sympathetic Klan members who might be developed as new informants. The committee never held a public rally, never even called a meeting, but that wasn't considered unusual; many small right-wing groups have their headquarters in post-office boxes.

Other campaigns were not so subtle.

"Our experience has indicated that klansmen are not intellectuals," read an FBI memo of early 1966; ". . . their activities are prompted by their emotions, and a lengthy article, no matter how well written, fails to impress those who are members."

More effective, the memo suggested, would be a series of postcards printed with mimeographed Klan-baiting slogans, which would be sent to secret Klansmen identified by informants. "Which Klan leader is spending your money tonight?" was one message. Others: "Klansman—Trying to hide your identity behind a sheet? You received this—somebody knows who you are!" and "Is your job safe after everyone finds out you're a Klansman?" Besides the emotional impact of the messages, the memo suggested, the postcards would have several effects. Because the message was not in an envelope, several people might read it before it was delivered. Widespread mailing would cause concern about Klan security and secrecy. Wives and families might be disturbed by the messages. And cards sent to work addresses, as well as to homes, could cause additional problems for secret Klansmen.

A follow-up memo indicated that the cards had caused "severe consternation" when they arrived at the homes of Klansmen who had considered their identities secure. Several Klan leaders copied the cards and sent them randomly around their areas, hoping that this would neutralize their effect. But the FBI countered this tactic by sending more cards so uncomplimentary to the hierarchy that they would never be copied.

COINTELPRO files record literally dozens of similar actions, from forging Shelton's signature stamp and letterhead to anonymously ordering that 20,000 copies of the *Thunderbolt* be sent collect to an address in New York City that happened to be the headquarters of the Communist Party U.S.A. With the help of its informants and infiltrators, the bureau noted signs of distrust, dissent, and unease, and exploited them. It aggravated, agitated, and frustrated. It pandered to the paranoia of some very nervous people.

Its effects are undeniable. FBI memos recount how one campaign triggered angry confrontations between Klansmen over finances. One unhappy Klansman, convinced that his klavern leader was pocketing dues money, drew a gun so that his complaint would be heard. (It was.) And there are numerous accounts of dwindling memberships attributable to COINTELPRO. The Charlotte, North Carolina, field office reported a 70-percent drop in UKA enrollment from 1966 to 1968. One klavern in Lincoln County, Misssissippi, destroyed all its records after an FBI interview campaign.

There was one side effect not noted in any bureau memo. Those on the Radical Right who had always suspected that they were targets of infiltrators had their suspicions eternally confirmed with the release of the memos. Now extremists take for granted that the Justice Department is watching them, and infiltrating when it can. There are also many who suspect that their other enemies, both foreign and homegrown, are doing exactly the same.

Behind that conviction is a certain arrogance. The theory presumes that the Radical Right is regarded by its adversaries as such a threat that it must be neutralized. There is real doubt whether the movement really poses any such threat; with its incessant internal warfare, it really is a house many times divided against itself, rarely able to muster more than a perfunctory challenge. But the question is one of perception, not reality; and since there sometimes is no accounting for perceptions, the possibility that someone out there is out to get the Radical Right can't immediately be dismissed. Still, it is worth remembering through the next few pages that not everyone would consider the Radical Right worthy of any great risk.

Among racial extremists, there is an almost universal belief that the Anti-Defamation League of B'nai B'rith (ADL) operates a network of paid informants on the Radical Right. Besides monitoring the nation for signs of anti-Semitism, the ADL also provides news media with information about racist groups and about trends on the anti-Jewish right. The information is generally accurate, though some reporters and students of the right consider some of the membership figures released by the ADL to be a bit inflated. Occasionally, the ADL will release information that appears to have been developed by an insider (like a 1978 advance report of a cross-burning in New Jersey). As a rule, however, much of the ADL's material could have been deduced from a careful reading of several dozen right-wing newsletters a month—which, in its way, is not an entirely worthless method of doing deep research on the Radical Right, once all the players and their shifting allegiances have been identified. The ADL, at any rate, doesn't disclose how it gathers the material it supplies.

There is also periodic speculation in the movement that American Jews help to finance the most radical racist groups. Such extremists serve Jewish purposes, according to this reasoning, by keeping alive the specter of unfettered anti-Semitism, thus evoking sympathy from non-Jews while posing no actual threat. The matter is examined more closely in Chapter 13; the bare truth for the moment is that the allegation is all guess, no proof. It has survived this lack of evidence only because it seems to explain the otherwise inexplicable existence of the improbable Nazis.

The possibility that foreign governments would try to subvert the Radical Right suffers from the same lack of documentation. It is all postulating, theorizing, playing long hunches. Would the Soviet Union really go to the trouble of undermining a small, divided group of American ultrapatriots? Probably not. But nobody knows what the Kremlin sees when it looks at Bob DePugh or the Christian-Patriots Defense League. If, indeed, the Kremlin looks in that direction at all.

It is, however, a fact that the Soviet Union and its allies spend many millions of dollars every year on espionage and "disinformation"—the disseminating of unreliable information for propaganda. Conservative intelligence analysts, like author Arnaud de Borchgrave, have claimed that we would be foolish to believe that a disinformation apparatus well established in Europe would not have found at least tentative footing here.

Another fact: Soviet agents have encouraged and goaded some extreme European rightists. In *KGB: The Secret Work of Soviet Secret Agents,* author John Barron describes how Czech intelligence agents under KGB direction invented a neo-Nazi group in West Germany and mailed hate literature through Europe and into the United States in 1956. Several months later, Barron says, four Czech agents mailed a bomb to the home of a French government official; it killed a maid when it exploded, and KGB-inspired reports in the European press soon were blaming the nonexistent Nazis for the explosion. Three years later, anti-Jewish desecrations suddenly blossomed across Europe, in America, even in Australia. German Jews received threatening telephone calls. Swastikas appeared on synagogue walls. West German officials counted more than 800 anti-Jewish acts in seven weeks. Then, in mid-February 1960, the campaign suddenly ended. Years later, a KGB defector told Western intelligence sources that the operation had been carried out by KGB agents around the world. Its purpose was to encourage spontaneous anti-Semitism on the right, and also to turn world opinion against West Germany by making the country appear to be harboring a Nazi revival.

In 1978, CZAS (the *Times*), a Polish-language weekly published in Winnipeg, Manitoba, claimed that it had been victimized by a forgery calculated to discredit it with its readers. The paper has a strong anti-Communist bent. The alleged forgery, which the paper claimed was the work of Communist disinformation specialists, was published when the staff took a two-week summer vacation.[6]

There is also good reason to believe that Poland's Communist regime engineered an anti-Semitic campaign to discredit the labor union, Solidarity, a few days after martial law was thrust on that country in December of 1981. Polish national radio broadcast an interview on December 15, two days after the crackdown, in which a professor charged that Jews had misled Poland and had turned the popular union "into an anti-national body." Among the claims in the interview were that Jewish groups had taken control of 80 percent of Polish industry and that "the chauvinist Jewish international"—a phrase that could have come straight out of a dozen American Radical Right newspapers and newsletters—was trying to take power in Poland.

Unsigned leaflets at Solidarity's summer congress had raised questions about Jewish influence in the union.[7] Columnist Jack Anderson quoted confidential diplomatic dispatches saying that the major source of much anti-Semitic material was the "Grunwald Group," an ostensible neo-Nazi band that actually was set up with government approval. Leaflets printed by the Grunwald Group, Anderson said, had been mailed out of the country with a postmark from Gdansk, where Solidarity was formed.[8]

That is far from proof of a continuing, long-range Soviet operation with right-wing credentials. For a foreign intelligence service to create, sustain, and operate a major group for years on the American Radical Right would be difficult and risky. It seems improbable.

Nevertheless, many on the Radical Right continue to insist that it has been done, and there is no shaking them. This is not the only instance in which the people of this movement have clung desperately to unsupported articles of faith.

WITNESSING

Infiltrations

(Extracts from the "Deguello Communication." Identifications of the living have been altered.)

You have been identified as a person whose integrity is highly regarded among patriotic Nationalists of the United States. For this reason we are sending you this material free of charge and without obligation on your part.

We can describe ourselves to you only to this extent: All members of Deguello are either present or past employees of government Intelligence Services from a number of different nations in the so-called free world. . . . Working together, and in strictest secrecy, we pool our efforts and resources in a purely personal effort to fight back against those forces that would destroy all free nations of the world, supplanting them with a one world government.

Freedom loving peoples throughout the entire world look to the United States in their hope for salvation. What a feeble hope that is! . . . Of all Nationalist movements to be found within the major nations of the world, the Nationalist movement within the United States is the most heavily infiltrated by those whom they seek to defend themselves against.

We can say it this way: Communism has three faces. These are socialism, Judaism, and homosexualism. Each of these faces represents a vast and semi-independent conspiratorial apparatus. . . . It may be said that the Socialist conspiracy is the most direct, forceful, and aggressive. The Jewish conspiracy is perhaps the most persistent, clever, and conniving. The homosexual conspiracy is most apt to have surprising, subtle, and unexpected effects. . . .

The real and actual infiltrators into United States Nationalist organizations are always helped by an even greater number of profiteers and charlatans who will do anything to make money or boost their own ego, even at the expense of their nation's freedom. . . . Some of these charlatans give reasonable stories and others tell stories so ridiculous as to be pathetic. It is a poor testimonial regarding the gullibility of United States Nationalists that they fall so easily for these things.

Dale J., founder of [a conservative group], was for many years a member of the League for Industrial Democracy and is, to this day, a member of the Fabian Society. [Conservative group] has become a major instrument for the confusion of American Nationalists.

The first and foremost objectives of all Jewish propaganda is to convince their own people that non-Jews are always against them and thus insure cohesiveness within their own community. To help do this they have set up anti-Jewish organizations and printed much anti-Jewish propaganda. Although the exact origin of the "Protocols of the Learned Elders of Zion" is in doubt, there is proof that Jewish conspirators have revived the popularity of this book and have financed the distribution of hundreds of thousands of copies because it serves these purposes for them. . . .

In spite of the Jewish emphasis on strong family units within their own race, Jews have always had a high propensity toward homosexuality. . . . Michael C., leader of [a white nationalist group], has been an especially destructive Jew infiltrator into the United States Nationalist movement. His specialty is running for office so as to gain public exposure where he spews forth a stream of such venomous hatred toward the negro race as to convince most fair-minded Americans that the typical leader of an American Nationalist organization must be totally insane. Michael C. is also a homosexual. . . . The now aging homosexual James M. has for about thirty years led a small neo-Nazi organization called [white racist group]. Located in New York City, M. has always been financed by wealthy Jews. . . . The purpose which M. serves for his financial angels is to help keep alive the threat of "Nazism" in the public mind.

(From a newsletter distributed by the National Committee for Domestic Tranquility, an FBI front group; an internal memo notes that the message and the NCDT membership card enclosed with it "may appeal to those Klansmen who are deeply mystic.")

My fellow Americans:

The recent response to the National Committee for Domestic Tranquility evidenced by the mass exodus from the United Klans of America in the great State of Virginia has revitalized our belief that present day Klan leaders are, in general, in league with the anti-Christ.

The belief that the anti-Christ seeks to destroy the Christian world was recently demonstrated by the Grand Dragon of the United Klans of America in Virginia, when he publicly attacked, insulted, and damned the Baptist church that had introduced him to Christ. The public rejection of Christ by a leading Klan official demands sincere meditation and reflection.

The Eternal Book of Life shall bear the inscription of the faithful who stood in the face of adversity and publicly pronounced their commitment to Christ. . . .

Knowing full well that the conduct of our personal affairs will warrant us an eternal life, be it heaven or be it Hell, is it not fitting that we, the faithful, urgently offer a commitment to Christ so as to avoid the damnable fire of Hell that will separate the fallen souls from the Almighty? . . .

We, former Klansmen all, who bear witness in the light of day, urgently beseech you to embrace our public commitment to Christ, and disavow the path of the anti-Christ, delivered to you, the misdirected souls, on the sugary, forked tongues of deceitful Klan leaders.

For you who seek Christ and reject the Klan, we have enclosed a membership card announcing your commitment to Christ.

To join with us, merely display this card in your home which will demonstrate to those who are really concerned about you that "A Klansman I Was, A Christian I Am."

Harmon Blennerhasset
Executive Director

(Letter that an FBI field office proposed be written anonymously and be sent to the wife of a UKA Grand Dragon. The proposal added that the letter should be "typed on plain paper in an amateurish fashion.")

My Dear Mrs. [deleted]:

I write this letter to you only after a long period of praying to God. I must cleanse my soul of these thoughts. I certainly do not want to create problems inside a family but I owe my duty to the klans and its principles as well as to my own menfolk who have cast their divine lot with the klans. . . .

Your husband has been committing the greatest of the sins of our Lord for many years. He has taken the flesh of another unto himself.

Yes, Mrs. [deleted], he has been committing adultery. My menfolk say they don't believe this but I think they do. I feel like crying. I saw her with my own eyes. They call her Ruby. Her last name is something like [deleted]. I know this, I saw her strut around at a rally with her lust-filled eyes and smart aleck figure.

I cannot stand for this. I will not let my husband and two brothers stand side by side with your husband and this woman in the glorious robes of the klan. . . .

I am a loyal klanswoman and a good churchgoer. I feel this problem affects the future of our great country. I hope I do not cause you harm by this and if you believe in the Good Book as I do, you may soon receive your husband back into the fold. I pray for you and your beautiful little children and only wish I could tell you who I am. I will soon, but I am afraid my own men would be harmed if I do.

"A God-fearing klanswoman"

(Robert Miles, convicted of a bus-bombing in 1971 after testimony by informants, comments in a January–February issue of *From the Mountain* on the case of two brothers in Columbus, Ohio, who were similarly convicted.)

The Gerhardts erred. Despite the experiences of other racist leaders and spokesmen, the Gerhardts permitted discussions of illegal acts in their own presence. No lie detector test would have helped avoid this error. Sure, the depth of investigation of members might have uncovered the testimony of one fink . . . who obviously is regularly used as a moonlighting fink for various political and a-political purposes down that way. . . . But, that is not the point. The point is that no racist leader or spokesman can suffer talk, discussions or even mention of illegal acts in his presence. Those who talk, seldom act; those who act, seldom talk. The talkers should be suspect from the git!

Our fight, at this stage of the game, is psychological in nature. We are the Johnny Appleseeds, broadcasting the seed. The seeds must be given priority. The Hour for the Armed Party will come. As surely as the nuclear fire comes. When the central government implodes from its own corruption and decadence, then the original Ku Klux Klan will rise again. It will be the Posse Comitatus. It will be the law and the order in vacuums which the burning away of the Cesspool creates. The hour is not now. We prepare for it. We teach of its inevitability. Yet, our tasks lie within the legal boundaries to which we are restricted by today's conditions.

You, as a leader, must shut off the talking about illegal acts. Every word and discussion must be well considered. We are at war. Yet, we are in a strange phase of the war. We are open, identified, and no wishful thinking can change that fact. . . . You who form the elements of these arms of the Resistance must conform to the existing laws, like them or not.

12

This much, anyway, for the Ku Klux Klan in its many fragments: At least it is not so hard to understand. No complicated religious revisionism here, and not much question of foreign taint, either. The Klan is direct—a minor distinction, but a small favor for which a mind benumbed by the bizarre ambiguities of the Radical Right can be grateful. Its message has never been very complicated; its structure and its leadership and even its internal disputes have been ever straightforward and comprehensible. The Klan, to be blunt but probably not unfair, is nothing more or less than a bunch of American bigots being themselves.

The Klan is an American institution, though most of us would not class it with baseball (which it predates) or Fourth of July picnics (a few of which it has been known to sponsor). It is an institution of intolerance, one that has shown amazing tenacity, having endured changes in the political climate, wars, glaring scrutiny by the Justice Department, an often hostile body politic, and that vast social restructuring that we call the "civil-rights movement." As some desert flora will during a drought, the Klan has sometimes shriveled into a hard little kernel to survive unfavorable conditions, but it has always been there to grow and send out its tendrils when the hard times pass. Its chosen symbols—the hooded robes, the burning cross—are known and understood throughout the land, and are as capable as the swastika of evoking fear, revulsion, enmity, and (in at least a few) belligerent pride.

The Klan has also been a major character, favorably portrayed, in two of the most highly praised and popular films America has ever produced. In D. W. Griffith's *Birth of a Nation,* Klansmen are hooded knights making right the injustices of Reconstruction. In *Gone With the Wind,* the male leads go riding in the night to smite Reconstruction's evil residue. Though producer David O. Selznick decided to dispense with the robes and soft-pedal the Klan connection, Ashley and Rhett and the others clearly are not just chivalrous gents out for a romp when they go riding to clean out that black shantytown in the film's second half.* They represent the very first Klansmen, and the moral justification that both of those landmark movies present—something like, It's a Dirty, Glorious Job, and We're Glad We Have to Do It—has been part of the Klan tradition, for this is a classically reactionary organization that gains strength and momentum when it is spurred by circumstances. Bill Wilkinson, when he deplores forced busing and racial quotas, is no less aggrieved than Nathan Bedford Forrest must have been when he revolted against Reconstruction.

In the Twenties, the Klan elected governors and sent its candidates to Congress. It will never again know such power, but it is healthier now than it was ten years ago, when many of its leaders were in jail and membership numbers had dropped to skeleton levels. Three men are responsible for the Klan's resurgence. None are on speaking terms. Without Bob Shelton, David Duke, and Bill Wilkinson, the Klan might not now be a significant influence on the Radical Right.

Each man has been important for a different reason.

Shelton's Klan ties go back more than twenty years. During the late Sixties, when the Klan contracted and nearly collapsed under the weight of federal pressure, Shelton continued to organize. He gathered the core of now-and-forever Klansmen within the United Klans of America. There were other Wizards and other Klans, but only Shelton and the UKA were klanning with any determination. He had to trim back, consolidate, shrink

---

* In the popular novel by Margaret Mitchell upon which the film is based, the Klan is clearly identified as such and is presented as a righteous defender of the Southern Way. This posed something of a problem for Selznick when he planned the script in 1936, for he was wary of seeming to promote intolerance at a time when the world was becoming aware of fascism's threat. His solution was to keep the righteousness but to dispense with the robes. "It would be difficult, if not impossible, to clarify for audiences the differences between the old Klan and the Klan of our times," Selznick wrote in a letter to playwright Sidney Howard. ". . . The revenge for the attempted attack can very easily be identical with what it is without their being members of the Klan." (From *Memo from David O. Selznick,* edited by Rudy Behlmer, Viking, 1972.) The resulting script became something of an apologia for Klansmen who act like Klansmen but who don't use the name or wear the robes.

into low profile, but he brought into the Seventies a thousand or more followers who still saw the KKK as a means of radical political expression.

By the mid-Seventies, David Duke was coaxing some new, flattering public light onto the Klan movement. After a decade during which the term "KKK" carried only pejorative connotations, Duke was making Klan membership at least marginally respectable. Duke was like no other Imperial Wizard ever: a graduate of Louisiana State University, confident before microphones, impeccably and stylishly groomed. He spoke well, and in places where the Klan had never before trod. He appeared on college campuses. He ventured north of the Mason-Dixon line, and seemed not at all uncomfortable about it. He showed a penchant for publicity stunts, like a "border patrol" that he organized with his California Grand Dragon, Tom Metzger, ostensibly to stop illegal immigrants from crossing 1,200 miles of desert abutting Mexico.

Duke became a staple on radio interview shows, a spokesman for white racists whenever the press needed one. He was approachable, cooperative, and somehow not half as threatening as everyone had expected a top Klansman to be. He was as likely to wear a sport shirt as a robe. His rhetoric was racist but not overbearing. Maybe liberal thinking had grown flabby after fifteen years of political and social victories; whatever the reason, Duke always seemed to have an answer to the standard objections and predictable arguments of his adversaries. He sounded reasonable when he said, in effect, that the Klan wasn't so bad after all, nothing more than a lobbying organization working on behalf of the white majority to correct legislative excesses. Duke sounded as close to benevolent as any Klansman ever could.

But he made no friends among Klan leaders. His first real opposition came from Shelton, who criticized Duke as a sham. Shelton's UKA newsletter printed an anti-Duke diatribe, accusing Duke of lying about his Klan's origins, of appropriating Klan funds for himself, of rigging an election for Grand Wizard so that only he had a chance of winning, and of ruining the career of female jockey Mary Bacon by publicizing her as a Klan member. The article also accused Duke of having pseudononymously written a book of lethal hand-combat instructions for militant blacks. The book, *Africa Atto,* with an author named Mohammad X, was advertised in black-oriented magazines.

This disclosure led to one of Duke's few truly discomfiting moments with the press. It came about when Duke agreed to an interview with Wayne King, a national correspondent for the *New York Times* who had covered the Klan movement with several unusually well-researched articles. The interview was filmed for use in a Public Broadcasting Service documentary on the Klan, *The New Klan: Heritage of Hate,* which featured Duke, Metzger, and James Venable.

When pressed, Duke admitted during the interview that Klansmen under his direction had written *Africa Atto,* but he said that they had done so only to collect the names of violence-prone blacks around the country. At another point, King produced a photograph of a young David Duke, circa 1970, marching in a protest picket line carrying a sign that says, "Gas the Chicago Seven." On his left arm, Duke is wearing a swastika armband.

The appearance of the photo seemed to startle Duke. He hesitated, stammered, stumbled when King questioned him about his Nazi affiliations and about some of the titles on his Klan's book list: *Mein Kampf, Hitler Was My Friend, Dr. Joseph Goebbels* among them. Duke, usually glib and smooth, appeared befuddled by the goings-on; his smoothness had deserted him.

The same issue of the UKA newsletter that excoriated Duke also carried a headline about another upstart Klan leader. It read: "Bill Wilkerson Pollutes North Alabama."

Bill Wilkinson, whose rivals seem to take a perverse pleasure in misrepresenting his name, is the third important figure in the Klan's revival. Originally one of Duke's lieutenants and editor of his newsletter, Wilkinson broke away to form his own group, the Invisible Empire, Knights of the KKK. Wilkinson must have noticed Duke's skill with the media. He may also have seen that some Klansmen were restless with Duke's strategy. Some members of the Knights wanted to do more than paste clippings.

Through Wilkinson, the Klan movement entered its third stage of metamorphosis, from the entrenched commitment of Shelton to its "New Klan" reputation under Duke, to Wilkinson's open militance, a policy that has made the Invisible Empire the largest and most important Klan.

Shelton had advocated a hard-nosed image. Duke had shed the robes to court the press. Wilkinson, for at least six years, managed to have it both ways. He is quick to remind interviewers that he has received every bit as much publicity as Duke ever did, but he also boasts that no Klan group can produce so many robed Klansmen at so many different rallies in so many different parts of the nation. And he is right about that. The public history of the Invisible Empire since 1975 is one of public confrontation, civil disobedience, and well-publicized conflicts with police and opponents. It resembles nothing more than the tactics used by civil-rights activists in the

South during the Sixties, and the resemblance is not by chance. Wilkinson has even adopted civil suits and complaints to district attorneys in order to gain marching rights around the country.

Wilkinson gives his Klansmen the action they seem to crave. In August 1979, he organized a march of Klansmen through Alabama, from Selma to Montgomery, on the same route used by Martin Luther King and civil-rights demonstrators for a famed march in 1965. The march was stopped when police blocked the Klansmen on the outskirts of Montgomery and searched their cars and belongings for weapons. Eleven were arrested for violating a law against carrying firearms within 1,000 feet of a demonstration. A day later, after Montgomery officials denied Wilkinson a permit to march inside the city limits, the Klansmen walked anyway and all 164, including Wilkinson, were arrested for parading without a permit.

A year later, Wilkinson traveled to a town about forty miles east of Hartford, Connecticut, for a cross-burning and rally at which he named a Grand Dragon for that state. The reported 350 at the rally (only thirty-five in robes) were opposed by counterdemonstrators, and there were several fights between the two groups, resulting in eight injuries and nine arrests. Wilkinson was arrested and later released.

In October of that year, Wilkinson was in Pennsylvania for a cross-burning and recruitment rally. Two weeks later, he was one of eleven Klansmen arrested in Columbia, Mississippi, for passing out Klan literature without a license.

All this has kept Wilkinson and the Invisible Empire very visible indeed. It has also brought him members, sometimes at the expense of his rivals. He has cut into Shelton's membership and he seems at least partly responsible for Duke's decision in 1980 to abandon his Klan. (In 1980, Wilkinson played for reporters a surreptitiously taped telephone conversation in which Duke offered to sell Wilkinson his list of contributors.)

Maybe the most impressive indication of Wilkinson's clout is the protracted clash in Decatur, Alabama, involving black demonstrators, city officials, and Invisible Empire Klansmen.

In May 1978, a mentally retarded black man, Tommy Lee Hines, was arrested in Decatur on charges of raping three white women. The Southern Christian Leadership Conference sent an organizer named R. B. Cottonreader to Decatur to demonstrate on behalf of Hines. The city government took no action when Cottonreader put up a tent community he called Justice City on the lawn in front of the City Hall, so Wilkinson and the Klan erected their own tent city and began counterdemonstrating. A crowd reported to number 5,000 attended his first rally. The trial was shifted to Cullman, Alabama, and when Cottonreader attempted to lead a march there, his group was stopped by a Klan-led crowd of whites estimated at 3,000.

When Decatur officials passed a gun-control ordinance around that time, at least 150 Klansmen rode through the streets of the city in pickup trucks, openly carrying rifles and shotguns. The city took no action.

After almost a year of clashes, there was real violence. On May 26, 1979, Klansmen and SCLC demonstrators faced off on Decatur's main street: Klansmen with ax handles and pipes trying to block the path of demonstrators marching in protest. A melee began; somebody fired a shot that struck a Klansmen. More shots: A second Klansman and two blacks were hit. (All recovered.) A few hours later, fire broke out in a white-owned grocery store in a black section of town, and a sniper fired on police and firemen who arrived at the scene.

That was the peak of violence in Decatur, but Wilkinson had made his point. He had proved that he could rally whites and Klansmen in forces large enough to stand against significant opposition, and he had also proved that he and his Klansmen would not be unwilling to engage in racial conflict.

As of the end of 1981, Wilkinson stood almost unopposed in Klan leadership. Shelton still remained as Imperial Wizard of the UKA, but there were signs that his group had shrunk dramatically; Shelton simply hasn't shown that he can produce the public force that Wilkinson did in Decatur. Duke still relies on publicity plays—at the height of national attention to the series of murders of black children in Atlanta, Duke made the wire services with his purported offer of $10,000 for the arrest and conviction of the killer—but his National Association for the Advancement of White People seems to exist mostly in its press releases and its NAAWP *News.* It is just one of scores of white racist pressure groups, and it has not distinguished itself in any way yet.

Still, at a time when he should have been savoring his domination over all he surveyed in Klandom, Wilkinson appeared to be sweating. If he wore his crown uneasily, it was because of the disclosure in midyear that he had cooperated with the FBI for seven years, beginning when he was a lieutenant in Duke's Knights of the KKK.

Klan policy, in every faction of the organization, has always dictated against cooperation with the FBI or police. But in July 1981, Wilkinson admitted in an interview at his headquarters in Denham Springs, Louisiana, that he had shared information about his plans with police. The revelation seemed startling at the time, but in August 1981, the Nashville *Tennessean* revealed that Wilkinson had met secretly with FBI agents many times since 1974, including several lengthy conferences.

An FBI memo from 1975 refers to an informant "not willing to testify in open court or before administrative hearing boards. He has no plans to write any books or articles or publicize his activities. New Orleans [field office] feels assured that this source will not take any action to embarrass the Bureau as he has always indicted a strong desire that his contact with the Bureau not come to the attention of his colleagues or anyone else and has sought assurances that this contact not be revealed in any way."

The *Tennessean* reported that Ed Fields of the National States Rights party began circulating copies of the memo. Wilkinson admitted that he was the informant mentioned in the memo, and he explained that he had told agents only what they could learn from the press. In an interview with the *Tennessean,* Wilkinson said that he felt the FBI was largely patriotic and necessary, and that he wanted to show good faith by cooperating. He said that he had never been paid for his information.

Still, the disclosure shook the Radical Right. Wilkinson's rivals have been indignant; the ultimate effect is still to be seen. Klansmen disenchanted by the news that they've been following an FBI informant really have no place else to go; though Shelton would certainly be willing to absorb any defectors, his influence may have waned too much to make the UKA an attractive alternative. Duke's appeal has always been limited. Tom Metzger has been forceful and effective in organizing the California Klan, but he is in the wrong part of the country to have much influence.

That would leave disillusioned members of the Invisible Empire to drift off into Klan splinter groups, Nazi factions, or simple apathy. The Klan's latest renovation was built on uncertain foundations, and if the shock of Wilkinson's secret role goes deep enough, what has seemed to be a new vitality could disappear even more quickly than it came into being.

The Invisible Empire's international headquarters is more humble than it sounds. It is housed in a concrete bunker that could have been plucked off the bluffs above Normandy and deposited beside a trailer court outside Denham Springs, Louisiana. The only difference is that even a bunker has gun slits. This is four walls of gray concrete, broken only by a thick, heavy metal door with a tiny peephole. It is the sort of place where Bill Wilkinson might seek shelter if the race war he is predicting ever comes to pass.

I visited the bunker in early July 1981. The revelation of Wilkinson's links with the FBI was still several weeks away, and he had agreed to an interview. His directions over the telephone had brought me through Denham Springs, about ten miles from the state capital of Baton Rouge, off the main highway, across some railroad tracks, and down a driveway to the concrete bunker. In the gravel parking lot were three cars, all of them with bumper stickers that said "Reagan for President." I rapped bare knuckles on the green metal door; a matronly woman let me inside. It was dark, no sunlight and a couple of bare bulbs. I caught glimpses of rifles in a corner as the woman led me to Wilkinson's office: wood paneling, bookshelves, an executive's desk. Propped beside the desk was a pump shotgun.

Wilkinson was forty years old, chipmunk-cheeked but not as round-faced as he appears in some photographs. He has the practiced smile and expansive manner of a entrepreneur whose business has enjoyed several good years in a row. And so it had. As he spoke, he leaned back in a chair, smoked a cigar, and sometimes propped his feet on the desk—in every way a man for whom life had been going very well. He spent the first few minutes talking about the Invisible Empire as if it were a national franchise with all the attendant concerns of quality control, product uniformity, and imitative competitors.

"Depending on the locality," he said, "we have a lot of different issues. We have never been a single-issue organization. We've had many interests, and we try to pursue as many of 'em as we can without overburdening ourselves. In some regards, yes, we're well established. We've had our ups and downs. Right now we're on the way up. Unquestionably, to be perfectly candid, our influence is much greater than our membership is right now. That's partly because of the nature of the organization, because we have so many supporters and sympathizers that would never get directly involved but that do give us aid and comfort, not to mention financial support, along the way.

"We also have some members who are invisible. Just last week, they [police] thought they uncovered some klaverns up in New Jersey. I can't confirm or deny it, because our people up in that area are quite underground. But it did shock [the authorities] because they found what was obviously an operational klavern with all the trappings in an affluent neighborhood."

I asked him about the ease with which an ambitious racist can become an Imperial Wizard, simply by declaring himself the leader of a new Klan group.

"Unfortunately, that's one of the drawbacks of our secrecy," he said. A shrug of the shoulders; a Klan leader's life is never easy. "The media has no way of differentiating between what is the Klan and what isn't. And they are prone, when somebody says they're the Klan, to take 'em at face value and go with it. That's the disadvantage—that we have a lot of what I call 'crazies' running around saying they're Klan when they're not. We personally investigate everyone that applies to us for membership. They have to be investigated, interviewed, and checked to make sure that they do come up to our standards. Admittedly, we do sometimes have a klavern or a Kleagle somewhere that will take in people that they shouldn't. But as it comes to our attention, we will deal with it and get the people out of the organization.

"That's the problem with any organization as you get bigger. It diminishes our direct control over our people. We're also at an awkward stage in our growth, where we don't have the facilities to send independent investigators or agents around to the various states to check on them. We do this on a piecemeal basis, but not actively. We are looking forward in the near future to where we will have men under the national office that will go around—"

"And keep up the standards?"

"Right. Our own little OSHA."

I tried to steer him toward the Klan as a political group, but somehow he ended up talking like a businessman again.

"I consider ourselves part of the overall Klan," he said. "Granted, we don't maintain close liaison with anyone. I tried hard once to work for the unity of all Klans, back in seventy-three, seventy-four, seventy-five, but I came to the conclusion that some of these so-called Klans were not Klans at all. They were not interested in unity. The membership was, but the leadership wanted to maintain the status quo. I came to the conclusion that the way to do it was to start with whatever you had and build and build. Totally disassociate yourself from all the problems, the squabbles and conflicts, just build yourself up and in so doing swallow up all the other organizations. Which is what we have done. We have built the most powerful organization, the one with the most logistical support. This office may seem small and insignificant, but believe me, a lot of stuff travels through here. I have a very good staff. They work hard, they work long hours, and we support our people."

We nibbled at the edge of some questions, about Duke (Wilkinson did not speak his name and refused abruptly to talk about him); about the Klan as a way of life ("We have our social functions, our political and our religious functions, so you get pretty tangled up with each other"); about immigration ("In my opinion, we should build a wall between us and Mexico, like they have between East and West Berlin, and it should be strictly enforced, to the point of whatever force is necessary").

That was as close as he had come so far to any racial rhetoric. Where was the Klan firebrand, the leader of an organization that has stood for racial segregation for more than 100 years? He was talking about the media.

"Go ask Teddy Kennedy if the media is important to him," he said. "Of course it is. It's important to anyone who's in politics, which we are to an extent, or involved in the building of a mass movement that wants to get a message out to the people. I do my utmost to maintain my credibility to the media. I will not stage anything. I don't try to fool the media, because I know there's a lot of intelligent people in there. I used to think that they were easy, but they're not. Sure, there's some crooked ones, but you have some sharp cookies, too, a lot of 'em. You try to fool 'em too many times, and they'll catch you, and you're through."

When the invective came, it was mild, and it slipped in there as if neither one of us were expecting it. But if the rhetoric was something less than inflammatory, the idea that it surrounded was frightening because it was plausible. It didn't tax the imagination; it was grounded in the reality of the moment, and when Wilkinson told it, it sounded as if it could happen.

It came out when Wilkinson was talking about tactics.

"I'm a firm believer in the old axiom that a squeaky wheel gets the grease," he said. "That's how the civil-rights movement was won, at least temporarily. The way they squeaked was by burning the cities. I don't advocate that. But I do believe that, down the line, white people are going to have to stand up in masses and physically demonstrate, because petitions and telegrams and letters and voter-registration drives—all these fall on deaf ears now. I can walk around the corridors of the Cannon Building and the Rayburn Building (congressional office buildings). I have many friends there, and others who are just acquaintances, and, sadly, they all agree that the only thing that really gets the attention is who raises the most Cain, who causes the most trouble.

"So my goal right now is to mobilize millions of people, and prepare them to demonstrate at the right time. I can't tell you what the proper time is. It's going to be something like when Martin Luther King was shot. That was their time, and they hit it. I believe our time will be a time of reaction, not action."

Here it began to get interesting. Ronald Reagan, he seemed to suggest, was eventually going to bring about a race war.

"The programs that the government was pushing," Wilkinson said, "Affirmative Action, forced busing, block-busting, preferential treatment to minorities in, like, SBA loans, just dozens of things, were gonna polarize the two races, until the white people would get together and they would bloc-vote.

"That's what happened in 1980. That *was* a racial vote, there was no question. It wasn't an economic vote, like a lot of people would like to say. It was a racial vote, in that white people were opposing these programs. And that's what the Republicans promised—that they would oppose Affir-

mative Action, forced busing. They were for states' rights. These were the
key planks that attracted the votes that they got. If you'll look, you'll see
that Carter got eighty-five percent of the black vote.

"There was a poll on CBS recently, asking voters about Reagan's popularity. Everyone—rich, poor, businessmen, workers—everyone agreed
that the country was coming up and getting better, except for one
group."

He paused.

"Blacks," Bill Wilkinson said, and he paused once more and said the
word again, distinctly. "Blacks. It's a racial thing. Because Reagan is
opposed to welfare for able-bodied people, social programs for able-bodied people, blacks are opposed to him. White people accept it. I've said
when we did get our white candidate in there—and we've got him—that
he would start putting an end to these programs, and, sure as shooting,
he's doing it. And I've said that when it got to some given point—nobody
can say what that point is—that when the blacks saw they were going to
have to work for what they got, that they were going to have to produce it
and earn it themselves, no more giveaways, that they would do the one
thing they know best. And that's that they'll start looting, rioting, burning,
and murdering. And just about two weeks ago, maybe three, Attorney
General Smith announced that he is establishing a crisis alert watch, or
something of that nature, in ten major cities to be on the alert for racial
violence stemming from budget cuts. He is saying right now what I've said
before. That they are gonna get out there and hit the streets."

All this would have seemed more improbable to someone who had not
seen the sky over Washington, D.C., lit orange from fires one night in
1968. Those were horrifying days, and since then urban riots have always
seemed something more than just distant speculation.

"The riots may be short-lived," said Wilkinson, "if the federal government and the Justice Department, the president himself, tell the police
departments they can do their jobs without getting civil-rights charges
filed against them. They need to say, 'If you have to use force, use it. Shoot
if you have to shoot. Kill 'em if you have to kill 'em. Don't go on a raiding
party, but don't just cordon off part of the city and let it burn, like they did
all over the country when King was killed.' But I'm very pessimistic that
even Reagan will do that."

And when that happened, he said, when all else failed, then whites
would rise in the millions against them.

"There's any number of scenarios that could occur," Wilkinson said.
"I'm trying to orchestrate some of 'em myself."

There it was, as plain as anyone could have wanted it. The Klan is waiting for a race war—encouraging it, supporting a conservative president in the belief that his stringent economics may force the issue—and when it comes about, they expect to surge to the fore.

So the question sounded silly a few minutes later when I found myself mentioning Wilkinson's arrests and asking whether the turmoil was difficult to live with.

"That's like asking the owner of a restaurant whether it's difficult to deal with the fact that your waitresses aren't going to show up sometimes, that you'll have to double up or pay overtime. It's all part of the job. I deal with it when I have to. I've always known when I'm going to have opposition."

There must have been times, I commented, when he knew that he would be arrested.

"Yeah, true."

That's difficult for most people, I told him.

"I'll grant you, I don't like it either. But I also know that it's the only way we're going to achieve our goals."

Then how are his relations with police?

"Good. With police everywhere, excellent. With departments, sometimes; chiefs, mayors, outwardly sometimes it's not so good. But privately, normally it's good. Ninety-nine times out of a hundred, I tell police what my plans are, even though sometimes they'll try to stop me. I got arrested in Huntsville that way."

That brought up the FBI, and what he had to say sounded even more interesting a few weeks later when the *Tennessean* broke its story.

"I don't give a dang how many informants they have, how many infiltrators they have. We pay almost no attention. The only attention we pay to 'em is to teach our people how to deal with provocateurs. I don't care if I have an FBI agent in every klavern. He can document everything he wants and send it to Washington, because we don't do anything illegal as an organization. Occasionally some of our members do, but in those instances, we appreciate getting 'em out of our organization for us. The attempts of the conspiracy to bomb the synagogues and television station in Nashville, we instigated the investigation with the police there and they turned it over to the BATF."

There is a postscript that is probably meaningless in the larger scheme, but it is offered here anyway for whatever it may be worth.

It was lunchtime when the interview ended. Before I left, I asked Wilkinson where to find the best barbecue in town. He gave me directions to a place outside Baton Rouge, and handed me his business card.

"Give this to the manager," he said, "and tell him I said to take good care of you. You won't find any better barbecue."

His directions led past a storefront barbecue joint with delicious odors wafting out through the pit vent pipe: hickory smoke and sauce and dripping meat. This looked like the logical stop. Wrong; this place had black people behind the counter and blacks at the tables. But the paper plates were laden with ribs and chicken and I saw what looked like home-baked sweet potato pie sitting on a shelf. A tough decision, but I traveled on.

Wilkinson's choice was down the road a few more miles. It looked all wrong. Inside, the place was spotless, and it was decorated like a California fern bar. But there wasn't a black face in the house.

I ordered from a menu laminated in plastic. The sauce came in cute little plastic bottles. The food came on plastic plates. I kept Wilkinson's card in my pocket. And the barbecue was lousy.

WITNESSING

Racists
(From a fund-raising letter signed by David Duke)

It is important to note that we of the NAAWP are not arguing in favor of any division of the white race. All white peoples are mixtures of Mediterranean, Alpine, and Nordic blood. It is true that everyone has a different selection of genes from these three branches of the white race, but all of us have the qualities of these types of Caucasian man. One branch in particular, the Nordic, is facing extinction, not only from the overriding onslaught of the Third World, but from low birthrates within their communities. The complete loss of Nordic genetic characteristics would be a severe blow to the aesthetic and intellectual qualities of the white race. Although most of us have only a small percentage of Nordic blood within us, we should certainly work to ensure the preservation of this vital part of the white race, as well as of the race as a whole. . . .

(From "A Brief Personality Profile" of Bill Wilkinson)

. . . He enlisted in the United States Navy and reported to San Diego, California, for training. From San Diego the new enlistee was stationed in San Francisco. It was in San Francisco that young Wilkinson first became a racist. It is the common belief of persons living outside the southern states that all White people living in the South are necessarily racist. Unfortunately, this is not the case. The Negroes living in or near Sugartown, Louisiana, were docile and lived within their own communities, attended their own churches and schools, and generally kept to themselves. When there was contact between the two races, it was on a friendly basis with each race recognizing the realities of white superiority. The Negroes in San Francisco were another matter. They could be seen along the waterfront hugging and caressing White girls and leering unadulterated hatred at White people who dared to walk the streets. Blood boiled in the veins of the transplanted southerner and more than once, his White fists smashed the faces of arrogant blacks who refused to defer to the presence of a racial superior.

13

The urge is strong to ignore completely those few who wear the jackboots and the swastika armband. Logic and emotion say that they deserve no more than passing mention. They are insignificant in numbers, even on the Radical Right, where a crowd of fifty can be considered a full-strength battalion. They are shot through with infiltrators, they are inconsequential, and they get far more attention than they merit already. Moreover, they have little in common with the rest of the Radical Right except their bitter racism. They don't share the right-wing ideals of free enterprise, smaller government, or pure patriotism.

But the Nazis aren't to be so easily dismissed. The press has given them such stature that anyone who intends to write about American racists has to deal with them at some point. And the Radical Right, despite its studied rejection of national socialism, can't seem to overlook them completely, either. Nazis are a predictable source of controversy within the movement, and they also serve as ideological reference points by which the rest of the Radical Right may map its own beliefs. They are the extremists' extremists.

There are actually a couple of interesting questions about American Nazism. One is the possibility, often raised on the Radical Right, of bogus Nazi groups being run by Jews, or else being financed by Jews and leftists for their own obscure purposes. The second is the topic of homosexuality among the Nazis; there are persistent rumors that a number of the dozen or so Nazi groups are cliques of homophiles.

First, some basic background. The neo-Nazi movement in this country began in 1959, when George Lincoln Rockwell formed the American Nazi party and installed its headquarters in a frame house in Arlington, Virginia. There his followers—he called them his "troopers"—subsisted on a meager diet, churned out hate literature, and made plans for their frequent marches and rallies. The troopers usually numbered between six and a dozen. In their book *One More Victim: The Life and Death of an American-Jewish Nazi* (New American Library, 1967), A. M. Rosenthal and Arthur Gelb portray the drab and insular existence of the troopers in the house. They tell about pointless demonstrations, ridiculous pranks, hours spent cultivating illusions of power.

"Life at the barracks centered on incidents like the Battle of the Pizza Parlor. It was an atmosphere in which reality and fantasy and wish-fulfillment merged until nobody could quite tell them apart, nor wished to. The boys would sit around talking about how one day they would run the whole damned country. In the meantime they played with their toys— 'training': reveille and uniform inspection and decoration awards, the cleaning of the guns, standing guard."

After venturing forth to do battle, wrote Gelb and Rosenthal, the troopers would return to the barracks to replay the action. "Once in a while, somebody would say, ah hell, it didn't amount to much, and the others would glare at him. He had interrupted the play, but for a moment only, until they could push what he had said out of their minds and once again warm themselves in the rich fantasy."

From those beginnings spring the current splinter groups—splinters off a nonexistent main body. These days, Rockwell and the original troopers have achieved a sort of mythical status, to judge from recent Nazi literature. The overwhelming probability is that life among the Nazis has changed very little in twenty-two years, and that the Nazis of the Eighties are very much like those in Arlington during the Sixties, a crop that included Daniel Burros, the subject of the Rosenthal-Gelb book, who committed suicide when the *New York Times* revealed that he was Jewish; Frank Collin, the convicted child molester; and John Patler, who shot and killed Rockwell.

Today, the number of swastika-wearing National Socialists in this country is probably less than 500. Of those, according to one who has watched the Nazis for several years, "one-third are just plain nutty, one third are queer and enjoy dressing up in those uniforms, and one-third are watching the others for the police or the ADL."

There is reason to believe at least part of that flippancy. No collection of right-wing extremists is watched more diligently than the Nazis. Few are as easily infiltrated, for one thing; the tiny groups are always eager for new members who will pay dues and devote time to the cause, so scrutiny of new recruits is usually nil. And the Nazis invite scrutiny with their harsh line of racism and counterdemonstrations in full regalia against leftist or liberal rallies. So it is probably true that every Nazi faction includes at least one member whose purposes and loyalties are not what they seem to be.

Just plain nutty? That is how most of the Radical Right assesses the Nazis. While nuttiness is relative, it must be said that the Nazis seem to attract a disproportionate number of disaffected, disturbed, and unhappy men who join for reasons that are as much personal as political.

Some—and not just the anonymous author of the "Deguello Communication"—say that many Nazis are drawn to the swastika because they see Nazism as a form of homosexual role-playing. One racist who shuns the Nazis puts the theory with unusual eloquence: "The two biggest stigmas in American society are being gay and wearing the swastika. Except in a few big cities in this country, identifiable homosexuals are outcasts. If you put that damn swastika on your arm, you can't walk anywhere without having everybody stare at you, spit at you, call you names. It's a masochistic thing to do. So maybe some of them are acting out their guilt about being gay. Maybe some of the others are just coming of the closet for the second time, thumbing their noses at society. And I have a feeling that a few of them just like the look of those high-topped boots and the uniforms, with the brutal and authoritarian image that goes along with it all."

In fact, one Nazi group is openly gay. The National Socialist League, an apparently minuscule group with branches in San Francisco and Los Angeles, issues literature that is clearly gay-directed, including reprints of articles in gay periodicals. The NSL publication *National Mobilizer* depicts chains-and-leather bikers as well as highly idealized, statuesque Nazis. One NSL flyer shows a shirtless boy with a swastika stitched to his skintight jeans. But the NSL isn't entirely sexual; its message is full of Nazi polemic, too.

None of the other Nazi groups is overtly sexual, and the preferences of their members are a matter for speculation. FBI COINTELPRO files do name a current Nazi figure as a homosexual; this tidbit is attributed to an informant, and was passed on from a field office to headquarters for reference and possible later use. (Names are supposed to be deleted from released files; this one, for whatever reason, survived the censor's black pencil.)

The matter of sexual choice or even of mental stability is important only because the Nazis are so difficult to understand. They invite easy explanations that have a way of crumbling under reality's pressure. Those outside the Radical Right are mystified, outraged, or merely bemused by the Nazis. But within the right, the Nazis most often are a source of pure frustration, so there seems a genuine urgency to understand and explain their existence. From that frustration grows the theory mentioned earlier, that the Nazis are financed by Jews because they keep before the public the image of unchecked anti-Semitism—thus eliciting sympathy for Jewish causes while posing no actual threat.

A variation of this belief is the contention that rich leftists support the most vulgar racist groups to discredit the entire right-wing movement. Of proof, there is none. Rockwell used to boast that he believed Jews were the source of some of his anonymous donations; this amounts to speculation from a most erratic source, with no corroborating evidence, yet it is almost the only material support for a theory that nonetheless has its adherents among those searching to explain some of the movement's more bizarre aspects.

Laird Wilcox addressed the question of left-financed front groups several years ago in a conversation with Bayliss Corbett, a longtime observer of the right who annually publishes an annotated index of rightist periodicals called *CENSORED: Hard to Locate Sources of Information on Current Affairs*.

WILCOX: It's not hard to see the function that the existence of the Nazi movement serves. It does not serve the interests of those who would like to examine and explore the issue of racist differences. It does not even serve the interests of those who firmly believe in the existence of such differences and who believe in such things as segregation of the races. It serves only the interests of those who would like to convert the dialogue into a caricature, a crude, stupid, parody.

CORBETT: You have to evaluate what's going on by asking who benefits. And the net effect of these perversions of truth and sanity, whether it's a Hollywood-style tinpot führer or somebody else spinning sophisticated fairy tales to a quivering audience, the net effect is to discredit the right wing in general. With the Nazis, it's immaterial whether they're sincere and independent. The fact remains that they serve to discredit anyone else who may want to suggest that there are racial issues worthy of thoughtful, factual, discussion.

Corbett had an admonition for those who would see calculated subversion behind every aberration of thought.

"Some things are just plain ridiculous on the face of them," he said.

"And some people are just plain nutty. It requires no further explanation. If you pursue the essentially unanswerable question of why people do things, you are getting dangerously enmeshed in the psychology of the paranoid."

Still, the question was worth asking at least once. Could America's first new Nazis have been financed by the same people they claimed to despise?

George Clifford is one person whose answer might have some authority. In 1960, Clifford was a twenty-five-year-old sportswriter for the *Washington* (D.C.) *Daily News* who infiltrated Rockwell's new group across the Potomac River in Arlington. Clifford, an aggressive journalist who later became an investigator for columnist Jack Anderson, remained in Rockwell's group for three months at the same time that he covered the Washington Senators baseball team as a beat reporter. His recollections are intriguing.

"The idea was that I was going to go inside the group while another reporter, Tom Kelly, covered them from outside. Kelly would ask Rockwell questions, and I'd ask him the same questions and we'd compare notes. Tom Kelly wrote one of the great newspaper leads of all time when he was doing the series. He noticed that Rockwell's office at the barracks was full of pictures of Hitler and all this Nazi crap and he wrote: 'George Lincoln Rockwell has his room fixed up neater than any kid on the block.'

"Rockwell was a charlatan. He was in it for the money, I'm convinced of it. He'd get these contributions, and the first priority was his child support. Most of the others, they were just a bunch of assholes. And not very smart. There were a couple of true believers among them, who knew what they were doing. One of them was a guy whose father had sent him to [German-American] bund summer camp before the war. But most of them were just screwed up. Dan Burros, he was the worst of all. He had blue eyes, and I guess he thought that proved he couldn't be Jewish, so that became his criterion for deciding whether anybody else was Jewish. He'd walk up to you in the barracks and stare at your eyes, and if you had brown eyes he would be very suspicious of you.

"Patler, there was another one. They had this mongrel dog named Gas Chamber that they used to keep at the barracks. One day Gas Chamber went up to the screen door and barked because somebody was walking by on the sidewalk, and Patler, very seriously, looked at Rockwell and said, 'Commander, this dog is getting vicious.' That's what it was like around there, all the time. Before I walked into the place every day I had to sit in the car for fifteen or twenty minutes and psyche myself up for it, just so I could get myself thinking the same crazy way everybody else in there did.

"Rockwell was different. Rockwell wasn't stupid. If he had gotten into the Birch Society or some other established right-wing group, he'd have been dangerous, because he was bright and clever and he knew how to get publicity. He took advantage of the troopers. They ate chicken backs all the time because there was never any money for food. But Rockwell used to go to a greasy spoon around the corner and eat beef stew, and he'd giggle about the others with their chicken backs. He was doing this just because he wanted to be governor, he wanted the publicity, and he thought this would be the way to get it."

And Jewish financing?

"Not likely," he said. "I never did get to see the books, but I really can't see it happening. About that time, the city's Jewish leaders got together and asked the newspapers not to cover Rockwell. There was an embargo on covering the Nazis for a while there. Kelly and I really had a tough time talking the *News* into letting us do what we did. No, it wouldn't make sense to me that they'd give the guy money and then try to get a blackout against him."

So the Nazis remain inexplicable. And if they were puzzling in 1960, they are a real mystery now, for they are persisting despite having lost dozens of young, serious white nationalists. In 1960, rabid racists might have turned to National Socialism because there was no alternative. Today, committed white nationalists are being drawn to the militant core of the Christian-Patriots Defense League, to small fringe Klans, or to those informal and pragmatic alliances like the one that brought nominal Klansmen and nominal Nazis together in Greensboro. In general, they eschew National Socialism's trappings (which they consider an unnecessary magnet for public animosity), but they embrace its philosophy. They are tough-minded and serious racists who, while they may once have belonged to a National Socialist group, show an attitude for practical organization that seems totally lacking in the Nazis. They would have had little patience with the grotesquely named mongrel dogs and the mindless fantasies of Rockwell's bunch.

One of the remarkable artifacts of the new white nationalists is a book, *Brave Words and Bloody Knuckles,* by an author named Duke McCoy, published in 1981 by Loompanics Limited, a press specializing in right-wing esoterica. It is a guide to forming a white nationalist party, and within its ninety-one logically organized pages is advice on leadership, recruitment, propaganda, and psychopolitics, as well as a "Problem Management

Guide" and a chapter titled "On Becoming a Realistic Revolutionary"—a topic never covered in any Nazi handbook. It is the work of a man who knows what he hates about the society around him, and who has a clear notion of how he will change it. That the books exists at all seems proof that Duke McCoy is not alone out there in being dead set on making the United States a nation of, by, and for white people. And it also seems to show that such an idea is the only thing that Duke McCoy's audience shares with the wearers of the swastika.

WITNESSING

On the Front Lines
(From a lecture on "street action" delivered by John Austin, an activist member of the Christian-Patriots Defense League who has picketed the United Nations Building and has participated in Ku Klux Klan rallies in Connecticut.)

"I have been Maced, I have been hit by rocks, and I have given back better than I got, but it gets pretty hot and heavy out there. You cannot always rely on police protection if you're going to have a patriotic demonstration. You have to be prepared. For instance, the Communists have a favorite tactic of getting heavy bolts that you can throw like a fastball. They're small and hard to see, and they can fracture somebody's skull. They also have been known to throw acid, water balloons full of ammonia, razor blades, you name it. So the point is, prepare yourself.

"If it's going to be a small demonstration, nine times out of ten you will not need protective people. But if you announce ahead of time that you're going to have a demonstration demanding deportation of illegal aliens, for example, and if the communists find out about it, they will go out and use funds from their treasury to hire old school buses and bring in two or three hundred people who are often absolutely vicious.

"First, you have to have the means to repel an assault if it occurs. Second, you've got to plan in advance. You need to get a security force, just to be there to see that your people do not get molested. They should have some kind of distinctive mark, like everybody could wear a red sweatband, so that you know who your people are and who the enemy is in a crowded, swirling street situation. Make sure that you have people who will stay away from the main body of your group, because the communists will always try to surround you in the middle, get on all sides and then start throwing rocks in or spraying people with Mace. So you deploy at least a third of your security force facing them. At the same time, the other element of your security force should be out of action behind the communists. Then, if the communists start doing their old tricks, these men can rush up behind them and take them out, and they won't know what happened to them.

"You won't want to carry any kind of defensive weapons. The police probably won't allow it and it looks bad. The Nazis come out with jackboots and helmets, the whole bit, and it looks silly. It's like, what are these guys afraid of? You know? But as the situation escalates, you've got to deal with it at each level. So if you can't carry your weapons, you want to have them near. So you get a car, park it about a block away, and you put baseball bats on the front seat with a blanket over them. They're always there. If things get hot and heavy, you can always cut out to the car, open it up, and then you've got something. If you don't have anything handy, and you're being menaced, the best thing to do is to run to a trash can. You'd be surprised what you can find: an old bottle you can break, or the leg of a table somebody's thrown out, or a piece of pipe. You can also use trash can covers as a shield if somebody is throwing rocks at you. If you really need to improvise, and you have absolutely nothing, you go over to a car parked nearby—I know it isn't nice, but if it's a desperate situation, you break off the antenna and you've got a stainless-steel whip in your hands. You hit somebody across the face with that and they'll know what hit 'em.

In New York we wear uniforms, everything has a purpose. The belt. You can't carry brass knuckles to defend yourself, but there's no law against a belt. You just take it off, you've got a belt buckle here that weighs a quarter of a pound. You wrap the belt around your wrist, with the buckle in your hand, it's like brass knuckles. You can also carry a roll of dimes, roll of quarters in your hand. That's the poor man's brass knuckles right there. Never wear a necktie. All somebody's got to do is pull you by that tie and you can't get away. Don't leave a belt on, either. You do, somebody's got something to grab at from behind. Personal protection, for men, go to a sporting-goods store and buy a supporter with an aluminum cup, save yourself lots of grief. They also sell shin guards for soccer players, little padded pieces of fiber glass that go right under your socks. It hurts to get kicked in the shins, but with these things you don't even know it. I've had many guys glad that they wore 'em.

"We're out there to deliver a message, either with a bullhorn or a microphone or with literature. With literature, it's all the difference in the way it's presented. If you have something in fine print with a lot of different ideas on it, it doesn't work. A person doesn't take time to digest it. Keep it simple, stick to one point. We've used leaflets that were so simple they could also be used as posters, too.

"To put posters up, all you've got to do is mix a little flour with a little water and put them up anywhere. The best places are where people flow in and out. Like a tollbooth. If you can sneak a poster up there at night, the next morning everybody has to slow down for the toll and they'll all see your poster. You'll be surprised how many like-minded people will contact you when you do this. We've gone out with three hundred posters and produced thirty-eight new members, which is not bad considering that thirty-eight posters cost about a buck and a half at the printer. When you put up posters, usually the liberals and communists will try to rip 'em down. Just put a little ground glass in the mixture when you're mixing the paste. When a communist tries to rip it down then, he's ripping off his own fingertips. You can take a couple of thousand posters, go up on a roof in the middle of the city, and then toss the posters down during rush hour. It comes down like confetti; people look up and see the sky full of leaflets and they'll pick 'em up and see what they're about. You can put a stack of leaflets on the roof of a truck or a bus. As it goes through town, the leaflets fly off. That's free advertising.

"Once we went to Yankee Stadium, we had eight men on the upper level. We waited until the seventh-inning stretch, and then each dumped about five thousand of these leaflets. It looked like millions and millions of these things falling down. Just from that, we got about two hundred applications, and about sixty good people. There's an old saying, 'It pays to advertise,' and it's really true."

14

Want to meet DePugh? The question came from Laird Wilcox, and the answer was an easy yes. It came at the end of a day that I had spent at the University of Kansas's Spencer Library, poking through the quarter-mile of shelving that holds the enormous collection of extremist political literature that Wilcox has gathered during the last twenty years. I had passed half a day alone with back numbers of *On Target* from the mid-Sixties, when the Minutemen's newsletters dwelt increasingly on the legal controversies that already were surrounding DePugh and his group. Some of the writing had the graceless quality of a man too shrilly proclaiming his injured innocence, but the best of it was forceful, effective, and occasionally even verged on eloquence. It was fascinating for someone who had known the fearsome reputation of DePugh and his group; this was the real thing, some of the same stuff that had helped to make the reputation. This was what all the fuss had been about. An hour's reading was enough to suggest that there was much more to this man than his critics had ever implied. It was also enough to make apparent the fact that this man, this Bob DePugh, had gone out of his way to flag down the sort of life-wrenching conflict that most of us desperately try to avoid.

So, did I want to meet Bob DePugh? It would be a valuable interview; curiosity was far more compelling than any lingering dread. And Wilcox was the man to make the introduction. After their years as adversaries, he and DePugh were amicable acquaintances now. DePugh had ordered a copy of one of Wilcox's directories in 1980 and had included a note suggesting that the two meet sometime. Wilcox, after some trepidation, had contacted DePugh, and the two had met to talk over coffee several times since.

According to Wilcox, DePugh had even been known lately to give a cordial hello to Jerry Brooks, the ex-Minuteman whose testimony had been crucial in the 1968 conviction.

Still, I noticed that Wilcox was respectful, almost deferential, when he telephoned DePugh that afternoon. And Wilcox is not one to defer to just anybody.

We drove to the printing shop that DePugh now owned near downtown Kansas City. DePugh could be friendly, Wilcox told me, but he might also be brusque or distant with a stranger. There was also indication from Harry Jones's *The Minutemen* that DePugh was capable of apparently objective self-criticism. This trait, if verified, would be an absolute first in my experience with Radical Right leaders.

DePugh met us at the locked front door. A big man, close to six feet tall, big-shouldered and with an ample girth at the belt. It was a summer evening, and DePugh was dressed for a midwestern summer, with a light short-sleeved shirt, open at the neck, loose cotton trousers, and crepe-soled fabric shoes. He had a jutting forehead and thick brows; his eyes were deep-set and they looked straight at my face when he shook my hand.

We spoke for a few minutes in the anteroom of the printshop, and then he suggested something to eat, so we drove in his big American sedan to a restaurant on the outskirts of town. As he moved the car through traffic, he asked me questions in a slightly nasal voice marked by that rural Missouri twang which seems a shortened and flattened version of a mid-south drawl. Was this my first book? Whom had I interviewed already? What kind of an approach was I planning to take? Was I a full-time writer or was this just an avocation?

These questions did not come in rapid sequence but were separated by pauses of a minute of more when DePugh said nothing, gave no indication that he had even heard my answer.

"I ordinarily don't do interviews anymore," he said at one point. "I used to think that any publicity was good publicity, but I don't feel that way now."

Finally, he wanted to know how I had chosen this subject, and I told him the theory that massive political change is sometimes brought about by the concerted efforts of a few radicals on the extremes. If a change was under way in the country, I said (and I thought it was), then I wanted to find out who those radicals were and what they really believed.

For the first time, he smiled, and his voice took on some animation. "I believe you're on to something there," he said. "I've had an idea along those lines myself." And he gave me a brief outline of a thesis I would later hear in much longer form: The proposition is that the Radical Right has gradually created an atmosphere which became conducive to the election of a conservative like Ronald Reagan.

He seemed genuinely pleased, more expansive, more talkative after that. Later, as we ate, we traded innocuous gossip about personalities in the movement. He talked about prison, about his family, about his indecision over whether to devote full time to politics or else ease out completely. Near the end of the meal, he said that he would like to help me, that he would consent to an interview.

We met again a few days later in the deserted printshop. (His business, he explained later, was less from walk-in trade than from large contract jobs—like printing human-figure silhouette targets for gun clubs.) He dusted off a chair and I turned on a tape recorder.

What follows is the greater portion of that interview, for the most part unedited. It was not our last conversation, but it surely was the most productive. His thoughts do not always develop immediately. He does not talk in bumper stickers, but he always gets to the point eventually, and the trip there is sometimes half the fun. He talks about subjects that occur through this book—like intramural warfare, and mainstream politics and right-wing paranoia—subjects that pose many questions but provide few unimpeachable answers. DePugh has his own answers, and they are offered here with the comment that, while DePugh clearly has his self-interests, I have found nobody else on the Radical Right who has considered these matters as carefully as he.

Why is the right so divided?
"I could give you some obvious reasons, like the fact that there's something about the movement that attracts prima donnas in the leadership positions. They all tend to have big egos, almost without exception. And the jealousy and the infighting has become worse, because over the last twenty years there's been a continual shift, a growth of the moderate Reaganite type of conservative and a shrinking of what traditionally has been called the Radical Right. So these organizations that would include themselves on the Radical Right have found themselves competing for a dwindling supply of members, contributors, and so forth. At the same

time, there has been this terrible splintering of the right. Every conservative seems to expect instant success from the organization he joins, and if he doesn't get that within sixty days, he joins another one; and after he's done that about three or four times, he goes home and starts one of his own. So you have an ever-increasing number of organizations competing for an ever-diminishing supply of dues-payers and contributors. I think that an awful lot of these people, with a certain degree of megalomania, honestly feel that if Bill Smith gives Tom Jones a ten-dollar contribution, it's wasted. If he would only give that to me, they think, I could do something worthwhile with it.

"I have tried. I started in with high hopes twenty years ago, to be able to unify at least a major part of the right wing. And I ran into this thing over and over again. I resigned from the Minutemen leadership three different times. I resigned once as chairman of the Committee of Ten Million, as a gesture of humility, if you would, to say to the other people, 'Okay, you lead, I'll follow.' And it didn't work, any time. Always, when you get four or five Patriots' leaders together—at one time we had twelve, verbally committed to the principle of working together—sure as shooting you begin to sense this little maneuvering, maneuvering for advantage. And the others realize that this guy is maneuvering, so they start maneuvering back again. And within a matter of a few months it was the same old dog-eat-dog situation. It's partly in the temperament and nature of people who gravitate to leadership positions within the far right and conservative movement. Partly it's the nature of the situation in which we find ourselves."

What about the individualistic personality of people in the movement?
"Individualism is what they say they cherish most. But there's two definitions of 'individualism.' The older dictionaries would give two definitions. And the first was, Those who believe in a social and economic system that allows maximum personal freedom of all those within that system. The second definition, if it was given at all, was individualism as a selfishness or a me-first attitude. Now that has been changed around, in a sort of Orwellian newspeak situation, so the dictionaries today say that 'individualism' is the tendency to put one's own interests above the interests of the group. This transition of meaning has been a matter of cause and effect, effect and cause on the right wing. I've tried to emphasize, remind right-wingers, that there is another definition.

"Did you ever hear of the National Indignation Conference? It was a fellow named Frank McGehee, it was 1962. His mother was a member of the John Birch Society, but he didn't take much interest in it. He was a

Korean veteran, a fighter pilot, a member of the Air Force Reserve. When he went out to the base one day, there were some foreign-speaking pilots there taking training, and when he asked who they were, he was told they were Yugoslavians, we were training them. He said, 'My God, Yugoslavia's a communist country.' He was really indignant. He called his mother. He said, 'See if you can rent the city auditorium, every night for the next ten nights. If you can get it tonight, we'll have a meeting, and I want you to call all your friends in the John Birch Society, have them there.'

"He ran a little auto-repair shop in Dallas. He got three or four of the mechanics who worked for him, who were also veterans. They painted picket signs and they went out to the base and started picketing. So he got on TV and that night there were a couple of hundred people who showed up at the meeting, mostly Birchers, I imagine. But the TV was there. Frank gave them what I'm told was a very short speech. He told them that this wasn't enough people to make a difference, so he sent them home and told them to tell everybody they could reach that there was going to be another meeting the next night.

"The next night there were about four hundred people, and the next night after that about twelve hundred, and the next night a couple of thousand. One of my friends down there told me to come on down, that he really had something going. I was a speaker on the eighth night. There were eleven thousand people in that auditorium. Frank was a dynamic speaker, only because he was putting his heart into it. When he was finished speaking, he said, 'Look, you people. We need money. We need phone lines, we need literature. Now come on, you people, give me some money, throw it down here.' And everybody went down into their pockets for money, and they threw it down on the floor. It got swept up with push brooms and put into garbage cans. And there was seventeen thousand dollars swept up from the floor that night. Today, you could take all the right-wing organizations put together, and if you gave them a year to organize all together they couldn't get eleven thousand people in one meeting room."

Why?

"There's been a drifting away. We have not recruited new people, younger people. The older people have burned out, got tired, resigned, given up, and the middle group in between have gone into the Republican party. Which may not be bad. I'm not real sure whether those of us in leadership positions now—and I kind of consider myself one of the younger members of the old guard—whether we should try to build a new movement with new strategy and tactics, or whether we should just pat ourselves on the back, tell ourselves we did a good job, we got our man into office, we turned the country around, now we're going to do some of the things we want to do for a change. I'm sort of on a fence as far as my personal feelings about that are concerned."

How did your right-wing leadership council get started?
"Around 1961, I went around and talked to all the right-wing leaders, everybody from Bob Welch in Belmont to Gerald L. K. Smith in Los Angeles. That was my first effort, and I came back very disillusioned. I found these people not at all the kind that were going to work together. Some of them gave me fairly sensible reasons why they weren't going to work together.

"Later on, Kenneth Goff and I tried to set up a national headquarters for a leadership council. We had an office, we hired a couple of full-time secretaries, we set up communications with other people, just on a friendly basis. But it fell through when I went to prison, and Ken Goff died when I was in prison. When I got out of prison, I thought, I don't want to have anything more to do with it. I had tons of literature in my warehouse in Norborne. My three sons were all there, working in the business. I said, 'Boys, get the truck out, we're going to haul this stuff to the dump.' We hauled tons of right wing literature out to the dump and we had it scraped under.

"But it was just a couple of weeks after that, though—I had been so much out of communication with the Minutemen organization that I thought it was just about dead. But slowly, you know, I'd get a phone call. Connecticut, maybe. And they'd say, 'Everything's waiting here in Connecticut, everything's set; in fact we've increased our membership and we're waiting for orders.' Then a letter from California, a letter from New Mexico, a letter from Oregon. And I realized, these people have worked hard. They've kept the faith, and this is no time to abandon ship. But I didn't want to go back strictly into the Minutemen type of activity. I didn't think it was any longer the most productive. I sent out invitations to just about every leader of every worthwhile right-wing organization I could think of.

"While I was in prison, I was no competition to anybody. Everybody spoke well of me then. I was a hero, I was a great guy that never did anybody harm. And that tended to continue for a while after I got out. So we had a meeting in Norborne of about eighty-five people who were leaders of different major or minor or medium-size right-wing organizations. I had only been out about four months, and, I'll tell you, that place was crawling with FBI agents and BATF agents. It was just crawling. Driving around with their cameras, jotting down license plates and everything.

"We sent a petition to Nixon. At the time, there was quite a bit of thinking that Rockefeller was going to be his new vice president, so we sent a petition against Rockefeller signed by about sixty-four different organizations. Which had no effect, of course, but it was a significant gesture in that it was the first time sixty-four leaders of sixty-four different organizations had ever done anything together, ever set their names to the same document. We had another meeting about a year later, and Bob Shelton and I were the initial nucleus of the thing.

"We started from the idea that we're going to work together and we'll see if we can find a third person who'll work with us. And we did; that was Jack Barlow of the National Alliance to Keep and Bear Arms. He came in about a year later. And the fourth person to come in was Artie McCreary, who was chairman of the U.S. Taxpayers' Union. It was seventy-five or seventy-six by the time we had McCreary in, and at that time the Taxpayers' Union was by far the dominant tax-revolt organization and the NAKBA was second probably to the National Rifle Association. So at that time we had four major organizations. There were others that we knew flat out would never join in any cooperative activity. Like the John Birch Society. Robert Welch would feel that his group is too big, it wouldn't need to join with anybody else.

"In 1977 we brought in a couple of other people, and we had about three hundred people for a meeting. We didn't insist that everybody had to be the top leader of an organization, but they had to be in a leadership position. We invited some people just because they gave enough money to an organization that they were listened to. We called these yearly meetings Patriots Leadership Conferences, and then within that the sponsor was the Patriots Leadership Council.

"In 1978 we traveled frequently, we had the Committee of Ten Million organized, and I personally participated in over two hundred meetings in two years, all around the country, mostly in the summertime. John Harrell and I traveled, Jack Barlow and I traveled, John Grady and I traveled. And some of them traveled on their own. Mostly we were speaking for the Committee of Ten Million. What we had agreed to do was to ask for a joint membership, so that a person could be a member of the Klan and a member of the COTM at the same time, for example.

"I felt that we were really going over the top. I thought we had it made. The COTM, we worked for Reagan in 1976, held some big rallies for him, and I think we won him the state of Missouri. When the delegates met in Springfield to vote for either Ford or Reagan, we had hundreds and hundreds of people there. When Ford came in, they had signs, WE'RE BORED WITH FORD or KISS OFF KISSINGER. And then the same people had different picket signs, boosting Reagan, when he came in. And those delegates that were out there meeting the two candidates couldn't help but notice that the crowd of maybe a thousand people at the airport was overwhelmingly ninety-five to five in favor of Reagan, and I think it made an impression. We did the same in other places.

"The irony is that Reagan would have won in seventy-six except for certain right-wing groups like Liberty Lobby, which published a book that really knocked him something terrible. Then there was a group out in California called the United Republicans of California, some of them hypercritical types that went way back to when he was president of the Screen Actors Guild. So the irony was that people like that on the right probably denied him the nomination in seventy-six, and that created even more of a split. It was one of the major dividing lines that opened up in the right at that time, and I was trying very tactfully to bring both sides together. Actually, not very successfully, but, I have to say, better than reason gave us a chance.

"In seventy-eight I think I made a couple of real tactical errors. We brought in about eight new members in a very short time. And this was a bad mistake because these eight people, they didn't know the long history of work that had gone into building this thing up gradually, and they somehow seemed to have the feeling that this leadership council had just started. I think that if we had continued to bring people in just one or two a year, and seen that they fitted into the cooperative philosophy, it would have worked.

"The same old maneuvering started. One of the new ones was John Harrell, and it put me in a bad position because I had personally endorsed him. John Harrell at that time was hardly known at all. He is a very dynamic and persuasive individual, and I feel that's where the problem lay. Once again we noticed this business of a guy trying to get somebody else's members fighting among themselves. And within two or three months, they were all fighting among themselves.

"Once again I resigned as chairman, and Artie McCreary was elected chairman, and that just made matters worse. So he resigned and John Grady was elected chairman. Grady complained that he wrote to the other leaders and they wouldn't even answer, and by that time it had fallen apart. Whether anybody will ever make another attempt is very problematical."

What is the influence of mainstream politics on the Radical Right? Does the movement thrive on adversity?
"No doubt about it. Right-wingers tend to be against instead of for things. A lot of the things they're against they need to be against, but they have a

hard time being *for* things. They don't have too hard a time, I think, articulating what they're for, but that doesn't really get them out fighting. But any threat to what they're for and they'll start fighting.

"One of the big problems comes from the fact that you have literally hundreds of organizations, and every one of them puts an emphasis on one single thing or another—tax strike, abortion—but they still have this core of things they all believe in, basically: a nationalist spirit, limited government, personal freedom from regimentation, belief in the free-enterprise system, a strong national defense.

"These few things we all had in common. That was the counterbalance, the things that we could all work for while we were working against other things. And we were too successful. We elected a president who campaigned on the very heart of this program, and was elected, and six months after his election had done far more than his fondest admirers felt he would actually accomplish, in realistic terms. So the tax-strike people can no longer say, 'Let's stop paying our taxes, because all of our money is being spent on welfare drones and given away as foreign aid and spent on CETA and so forth.' Because now the mainstream is saying we should bring the old battleships out of mothballs, and build a couple of new Trident submarines, and nobody thinks that those can be bought if we all quit paying our taxes.

"Government regimentation—being in the drug business, I know that the average FDA inspector has a different attitude than he had a year ago. He's knows he's being watched, and he knows a complaint against him is going to be taken seriously. OSHA inspectors, everybody is pulling in their horns. This has an effect on the small businessman, the right wing, what I call the true conservative. This has taken the wind out of the sails at the edge of this movement.

"Also, we have a very bad situation in that the very people who have always been the hard cutting edge, the highly tempered, who would never give up and never change, who had stayed in there through all the years of adversity, are now being left out in the cold. I don't blame the Reagan administration for leaving them there—there's no place for them. But now they are forced to take a more strident position, to cry that much louder, because they have nothing more that they can say to keep attracting their people. So the racists have to be ultraracist, the tax-strikers have to be more extreme. It's an ironic situation, because the pressure that's pushing them to the edge doesn't come from the left. So that brings us back to the situation where many organizations on the right are doing more harm than good. They're taking too extreme a position, and coming from me, boy, I'll tell you: That means something.

"A lot of the people that I'm talking about, if they ever read this, they're going to say, 'Well, obviously Bob has gone soft; he's gotten old and he's gone soft.' But if I was going to go soft, it would have been during those thirteen months that I spent in solitary confinement, not now when I'm free and I've got everything going for me. I think that I'm able to look at the situation from a fairly rational point of view, and see the dirt on my own nails, see the faults of my own movement, and say, 'I wish it was different, but I don't see how I can change it.' "

Do you feel you sacrificed a lot for the cause?
"I don't know. I'm still alive, still got my own business, still got my family. I was separated from my family six and a half years. Some of my kids, quote, grew up, unquote. I feel bad about it. Some of them had personal problems. Not everybody is kind to a kid whose father is in prison. Those things I regret very much. I ask myself many a time: Was it really worth it? I think it was. I've had to work twenty times as hard to get my business halfway back, and it'll never be what it was. My family will never be the same. I'll never be the same. From those points of view, I've given a lot. But I don't feel sorry for myself. I did it willingly and knowingly, and to some degree with a more hardhearted attitude than I like to admit.

"When I went into hiding, I had—it was a really raw deal. I know everybody who serves time in prison tends to feel that way. But I was indicted on one charge after another—some of them totally without foundation, tentative hearsay evidence. But every time I was indicted I had to go to the bank, put up a bigger and bigger share of my company, money to make bond. When I finally went into hiding, I jumped bond on $480,000. That was money that went down the drain, and I never saw another dime of it.

"When the indictments came down on this Washington State bank-robbery charge, it was as if two Catholics held up a filling station and they indicted the pope. That's how far removed I was. But I went out there to meet the lawyers, and they flew down to Oakland to talk with me. The arrangement was, I would talk with them, they would go back to make bond, and then I would go up there and turn myself in. I just didn't want to go to jail. I would always arrange to have my lawyers meet me at the courthouse, and we'd walk into the courthouse and make the bond that had been set by prearrangement, and then I'd walk out.

"At that time, it was hard for me to come up with more money, but they told me they thought they could get a bond for ten thousand each for me and Wally Peyson, who was my partner at that time, my second-in-command. I was really wondering whether I could do that or not, so I sort of semi went into hiding in Salt Lake, and we contacted my wife through three or four cutouts to find out how it was going. She got the word back to me that she had the twenty thousand and would wire it to our attorneys in Seattle. We were all ready to get on a plane in Salt Lake and fly to Seattle when we got word it was thirty thousand each, instead of ten.

"This time when my wife went to the bank she got a cold shoulder. So she kept working, trying to get the money, and we kept hiding out, and by that time we heard they had fugitive warrants out for us, and it just seemed like we'd reached the point of no return. So we went into hiding. But I'll have to confess that I expected that when I left home. I went out of that house without saying good-bye, a permanent good-bye, to my wife, my kids, anybody. And I really didn't expect that I'd see any of them again. So I say that maybe I did it with a little more hardhearted attitude than I like to admit. We all kind of get started down a certain road, and the further you get, the harder it is to turn back."

One of the worst effects of conflict is that it robs you of your peace of mind.
"I think that's one reason you find some of the people on the right wing that you do, that can deservedly be called kooks or far-out types. I've known some that I would now say, you know, the guy's a kook, yet he started out in the movement as a pretty squared-away individual.

"Of course, each of us thinks that we've escaped the problem, but at the same time I can be no more assured of knowing that I've escaped it than the next guy can. A lot of times I've wondered, How can I be right when all of my friends are crazy? Years ago, I was in my office in Norborne when I got a visit from a radiologist at the University of Tennessee hospital, a member of the Minutemen. He brought his wife and his kids in, and it was a beautiful family. If there ever was an all-American family, this was it. During the conversation, he asked me: 'Do you ever ask yourself how you can be right when most of people who agree with you are a little bit . . . flaky?'

"I laughed and I told him that I knew the feeling, but I told him that every once in a while, somebody like him and his family would come along, and I'd know I'm not alone. And in between times like that, I have to go back to the very, very basics, to remind myself that over in East Berlin there are people dying trying to get over that wall. Nobody is going the other way. There are people risking their lives trying to get from Cuba to Florida. There are people swimming shark-infested waters trying to get from China to Hong Kong. That is one of the few basic principles that we know, and it's undeniable. So you build your philosophy around a basic principle like that, and you know that you're right. Even if you're in a crowd of people that are acting crazy, you know that you're right, because you've built your philosophy on a foundation of things that are demonstrably true. So I think that if I have escaped the tendency to become paranoid—*if*—it's because every so often I do that.

"Now, my feelings as to whether I should take a different tack. I feel very strongly that the right wing is still a movement. Four years from now, Reagan may find himself in trouble. He may be dead. Sooner or later, the leftists are going to mount a vicious counterattack. And once again, it may be that the nuts are the only ones foolish enough to stand in their way. So I feel that we're needed. Whether I should, or need to be, there, is something that I'm beginning to wonder about. My decision is going to be entirely pragmatic. It's not going to be something I'll jump at. I think I've earned the right now to make my decision based on whether I'm going to do any good, rather than on whether it's a matter of principle. That's really the only change that's taken place in me in the last twenty years."

In late 1981, Bob DePugh sold both his printing business and Bio-Lab, the pharmaceutical company he had owned for twenty-five years. He was spending too much time on business these days, he said. Politics? "I have some plans," he said.

Some people will be watching with more than casual interest.

WITNESSING

Of Cross and Sword
(KERRY NOBLE, an instructor at the 1981 Christian-Patriots Defense League Freedom Festival, discussing the necessity for violence against the enemies of the Lord.)

"God created man to have dominion over the earth. He created man to subdue the earth, to put down and have total rule over everything else that was in the total creation. That word 'subdue' means to tread down, to subjugate, and to crumble. But right now we don't see all things under man, do we? Right now man is not in dominion of all things the way God created him to have it. The thing that is in dominion over the earth now is Babylon. The word 'Babylon' means confusion. Whenever anything is chaotic and out of order and not going the way God wants, that's Babylon. Babylon is what makes it possible to have race-mixing, to have pornography, the things that are going on with drugs in the schools. Everything that is out of order in the world is made possible by this confusion. And this confusion must be taken away somehow, made right.

"In Matthew chapter eleven, verse twelve, He tells us how this is to be. Jesus said, 'From the days of John the Baptist until now, the Kingdom of Heaven suffereth violence, and the violent take it by force.' Normally in the King James Bible, the word 'suffer' means to allow. Here the word 'suffer' literally means to force. In other words, the kingdom of heaven forces violence. This is saying that all the violence that is upon the earth is because of the kingdom of heaven. Why?

"If you're walking in the spirit of God, then you force violence upon the earth. Understand that? When good does what it's supposed to do, then what is evil going to do? Fight it, right? If you don't do what you're supposed to do, then God will punish you, but evil won't have to be all upset and get violent. There's nothing for evil to resist. But when the sons of God do what we're supposed to do, and move the way that we're supposed to move, then we force violence upon the earth. In the Scripture, anytime a man of God rose up, the forces of evil always came up against him. In history, the two times when you had the most demonic activity across the whole earth was when Jesus was walking the earth, and now. The more we do what God wants us to do, the more we walk in the power and spirit of God, the more violence will increase.

"You all know that not all of Israel is following God. There's only a certain remnant, and even out of the chosen there's only a few faithful. And it's the chosen and faithful that ride upon the white horses of Jesus, and it's the few faithful that cause the pressure, because they're learning to walk totally in the way of God. And as we grow stronger, violence is increased upon the earth.

"Jesus says, 'If any man has an ear, let him hear; he that lives with captivity shall go into captivity; he that kills with the sword shall be killed with the sword.' Now, the denominational churches of the world teach that that Scripture means we Christians are not to bear arms, we are not to resist, not to fight. That's their interpretation, and it's the opposite of what it really says. It means that because they use force, because they use weapons, because they put into captivity, then that gives us the right to use the same against them: The Jewish systems, the church systems, all the systems of Babylon suppress the white race, suppress Israel, and suppress the remnant of God. Whatever means they use to do that with, we have the authority to use those same means against them. If they use weapons against us, we're allowed to use weapons against them. If they use trickery, deceit, harassment against us, then we're allowed to do those same things against them. We are not commanded now to just take it, just sit there and not resist and let them trample all over us. Because then they have dominion over us. That's bondage, and God delivered us from bondage."

15

Hot night, summer night in rural Illinois. Three hundred people on metal chairs beneath an open canvas tent, big striped tent. Moths flutter around the bare bulbs overhead. Chairs and people face forward, to a podium on a raised platform. More lights there, spotlights that catch the podium in a bright white cross fire.

The man at the podium squints into the light. He looks nervous, looks as if he's peering out for faces that he knows, some contact, something to grasp. He grips the podium with one hand and he speaks.

"Anybody read the expanded version of Al Capone's notes?" he says. Not a movement in the crowd. But he's a gutsy little guy, short and feisty. He's not stopping now. "Go to a law library," he says. "Ask for the U.S. Code, Title Twenty-six, called the Internal Revenue Service Code."

That brings some laughter from beyond the lights. He shifts his weight from one leg to another and plunges on.

"It takes more than an act of Congress to get your hand in my pocket, folks. And I don't want to blame it all on Al Capone. He was an honest crook. He never tried to pass himself off as a government."

Now he's rolling. The people lean forward. They know him, him with his nicotine-stained fingers and his day's growth of beard and his white T-shirt peeking over the open neck of his cheap sport shirt. They sit with their feet rooted in the grass, their bottoms planted in the metal chairs, and they know he belongs to them.

So he flings his fighting words out into the white-lit night. He knows he's among friends.

"There's only one entity on earth that can qualify as a government," he says, "and that's the kingdom of God." Lots of applause for that; he has to stop to let it pass. "All others are lepers. They are despotic, they are frauds. Every government in the world is a despotism, as this one has become to us."

They listen, intent. Heads nod as the moths flutter around the electric bulbs. The man's voice is raspy and the speakers have a tinny, grating tone, but the people soak up the sound of the words. He's one of them. He knows.

"You can have a lot of things in this country if you're willing to pay the extortion fee," he says, and that makes some of them burst out grinning. This one, he knows, all right.

Behind all the words and the theories, behind the sociologists' numbers and the politicians' posturing and the newspapers' neglect, are these people. They sit on a hot summer night, beneath bare bulbs and a big striped tent owned by the Christian-Patriots Defense League. They are real and they know it, even if everybody else pretends not to.

"I don't care if they send me back to prison," he says. Now he's leaning over the podium, past the mike almost, but he doesn't need it anyhow. The words are going straight from his mouth into their hearts, nothing in between. "In prison, I'm converting men who already know how to kill somebody. And when they get their directions straightened out, when they get to find out that these people are anti-Christ, that they've made laws that have made them a part of this filthy system, I won't have to worry about giving them a training session on how to kill."

The real thing. Oh, yes.

"I'm converting some of these men. I'm looking forward to some of them getting out and being at these meetings."

Mad as hell? Chayefsky didn't know the half of it.

NOTICE
To all sincere Christians and/or Patriots Who are still under the illusion that all is well and that somehow we are going to make it through the coming energy, economic, military, political, social, Spiritual, moral, and foreign crises with relative calm, stability, safety, and security, and still preserve our CHRISTIAN HERITAGE and CONSTITUTIONAL FREEDOMS.
When you discover this simply isn't true
contact the
CHRISTIAN-PATRIOTS DEFENSE LEAGUE
or the

CITIZENS EMERGENCY DEFENSE SYSTEM
YOUR COUNTRY NEEDS YOU!!! IT IS LATER THAN YOU THINK!!!
Please keep this card for emergency use.

All John Harrell needs to know is that you're interested. A telephone call to the twenty-four-hour switchboard of the Christian-Patriots Defense League will do it. So will a postcard with a return address, *anything* that tells him you want to know more about what he has cooking there in Louisville, Illinois.

Then the envelopes start to arrive, some of them fat and heavy enough to stop a .22—something Harrell's instructors may want to remember the next time they lecture on SWAT tactics. Postage isn't a problem, since Harrell's church has nonprofit mailing privileges, so the envelopes come crammed with leaflets, newspaper reprints, broadsheets, booklets.

Among these is a pamphlet called *The Golden Triangle.* Carrying the by-line of Harrell himself, it claims in an introduction that it "may prove to be the most vital, life-saving piece of literature you shall ever hold in your hands outside of the Bible itself." It tells the story of a vision that came to George Washington while he was encamped at Valley Forge in 1777. Upon being visited by an apparition, the pamphlet claims, "he was held transfixed by a series of events flashing before him as on a modern-day projection screen." What he saw, no less, was the future history of the nation, culminating with a great war against America's world enemies, in which the forces of the Union withdraw to a triangular area with its points at the Great Lakes, southern Georgia, and mid-Texas.

That is one of Harrell's early publications. Later, he issued a map showing the "Mid-American Survival zone," in which the Golden Triangle is distorted into an irregular quadrangle that includes most of the Midwest and Midsouth. This, the map's notation explains, is the "major area for sustained and long-range survival through the anticipated coming crises."

Tone and messages are uniform. Virtually every page is a dour declaration that the country is headed straight to hell in a jet dragster, and that the rare wise man will bail out now while he can.

Every envelope from Harrell contains a broadsheet proclaiming the next Christian-Patriots Defense League freedom festival. What it is, is an outdoor convention for the Radical Right. Instruction in marksmanship, demolition and camouflage, guard-dog training, nuclear weapons and radiation, antiaircraft and antitank warfare, the Federal Reserve hoax. Only quality patriots wanted. Free attendance and camping privileges to all those of Caucasian race. Do not bring firearms or ammunition; Illinois has strict gun laws. Dress code is to be modest—no shorts by those over twelve, please. No alcoholic beverages or narcotics. Prepare for the obvious and inevitable.

Fill in the application at the bottom of the sheet, and in just a few days the return mail brings another envelope, this one containing—besides enough pamphlets, leaflets, booklets and reprints to heat the entire mid-American survival area for at least three nights—a certificate of admission to the estate grounds of the Christian Conservative Church in Louisville, Illinois, June 26 through July 2.

Louisville, Illinois, is exactly the way MGM used to portray Everytown, U.S.A. In the heartland of the heartland, 100 miles east of St. Louis, 225 south of Chicago; also 25 south of Effingham and 8 north of Flora, if that's any help. It is a town wrapped around a grassy city square, with a hardware store, a five-and-dime, a café, a grocery, a bank. Two blocks from the town center (but, by a quirk of zoning and jurisdictional lines, outside the city limits) are the fifty-five acres, once known locally as the Old Picnic Grounds, that John Harrell deeded to his Christian Conservative Church about twenty years ago.

Nice place. Open grassy fields, bordered by thick forest. The Wabash River flows through one end of the property. A stocked pond, a rolling lawn dotted with shade trees and arbors. Then there's the church headquarters, which used to be John Harrell's house when he was a businessman making a real pile selling mausoleums and real estate. That was before the IRS trouble, before he hid the Marine deserter, before the Holy Spirit paid a nine-hour visit to his hospital room at the Mayo Clinic, before the FBI compiled the first of its 3,000 pages about his doings, before he took it on the lam, before he served his stretch in federal prison. Before all that, when John Harrell was just another millionaire mausoleum salesman, he lived in this replica of George Washington's house at Mt. Vernon. There it sits, on a knoll overlooking the property. It is an identical replica, by John Harrell's account, except that it is scaled 10 percent larger than the original. So he says, and it could well be. The paint is fading and flaking now, but still: nice place.

By noon on Friday, June 26, 1981, they are already drifting in, some in cars and some in expensive mobile homes, but most with either little tag-along trailers or pickup trucks carrying piggyback camper shells. First there's a stop at the main gate—the very one that gave way to the rumbling half-track back in '61, when the government came to reclaim its marine. Now a T-shirted guard checks passes there and, with one hand on a hip, uses his semiautomatic rifle like a baton to direct traffic and to point out parking places.

The open end of his carbine sends me down a dusty road to a camping area, a clearing where the pickups and the trailers are parked. I find a place in the shade and unroll a little nylon backpacking tent, a serious and expensive jewel of tentwork that turns into a conversation piece.

First it attracts a stocky man who's been busy using jacks to level the rear end of what looks like a homemade camper shell. He praises the tent and then pops what will become the question of the weekend, the opener for serious talk.

"Well," he says, "what brought you here?"

"Decided to have a look."

"Yeah," he says. "Me, too, decided to have a look." It is a catchall, noncommittal answer here when you're trying to gauge a stranger.

We walk to his camper. He shows me his work inside: all his own, he says, and it really is nicer than you could buy.

Then, without prodding, he opens up.

"You aren't camera-shy, are you?" he says. " 'Cause I heard CBS, ABC, one of 'em, is coming down this evening. I don't need that. I'm a high-school teacher in Michigan. American history. God, what a mess. And I'm talking the suburbs, not Detroit. You couldn't pay me enough to teach in Detroit. You couldn't give me a big enough gun to teach in Detroit. Even the suburbs, white kids, Christ, they're all screwed up. And we're handing the country over to 'em in twenty years or so. We're in a mess, my friend, a mess. We have to do something."

A few minutes later, the tent pulls in a man of about twenty-five, hair cut close, tanned, looking like he can't be more than a couple of weeks out of a Special Forces camp. The clothes help the image: He's wearing combat boots, camouflage fatigue pants, an olive drab T-shirt.

"Nice tent," he says. "You take that back-country?"

"The desert. Sierras. Oregon coast."

"Keep you dry?"

"Every time."

He bends on one knee, rubs the fabric between thumb and forefinger, examines the stitching.

"Double-walled," he says. "Nice. No condensation, right? You got to keep dry. People don't realize that. Get wet and it just draws your body heat out. It'll chill you to death and the weather doesn't even have to be freezing. Am I right? You got to stay dry."

"You're right."

"How much a tent like that cost you?" he says.

"About three hundred."

"Three *hundred*? That's an awful lot of money for a tent."

"You have to stay dry," I say.

He grins and says, "For three hundred, I'd buy me a nice gun and some ammunition. And when the times comes that I need a tent that bad, I would go out and get about any one I wanted."

That evening, there's a meeting under the lights. First chance to see people in a group. They look like the people who live on your street, if you happen to live in a working-class suburb, or in a farm town. They are plain and simple people, most of them, and they dress that way. At least half of this crowd is over forty, many of them couples who look close to Social Security age, though there are a few young families, mom and pop and the kids lined up in metal folding chairs.

They are nice people. The Radical Right has a bewilderment of surprises for the ignorant outsider, and that may be the greatest of all: They are nice people, good and decent people who would probably make fine next-door neighbors if you happen to be white and Christian. Their kids behave. They do not intrude. That is an outrageous generalization, of course, but one that has stood up to a year of observation. It is their ideas, not they, which are strange and baffling.

There are perhaps 350 before him when John Harrell stands at the podium. A fine figure. Harrell would make a good southern senator with his longish white hair, his ease with the folksy manner, his strong voice, and his gift for oratory. He knows how to stretch syllables and bend vowels. John Harrell, to be blunt, knows how to work a crowd. He tells this one that the weekend is for learning, and for getting along.

"We are a grass-roots people that is interested in the preservation of this country. As we move down the road toward what we feel is a revolutionary period, we are trying to set a standard that will rally enough people to save this country. Many patriots think in terms of us and no more; we got our food and we're goin' to the hills. We are not even remotely thinkin' in those terms. We are thinking in terms of being moved in a way that we pray is spiritually correct, that we can amass twenty-five to thirty million of the most fierce patriots that's ever been seen in this country, that cannot be defeated, that cannot be whipped, that cannot be bent, that cannot be killed, that will preserve this country. We're headed for extremely difficult days."

They sit and take this stolidly. A few nod, yes; there isn't a rustle of impatience, not a hint of protest or disagreement. These people have come together, to be among strangers. They wouldn't be here if they didn't think they had a reason.

"We are a scripturally-oriented people, and I know we're going to win, because I've read the last chapter in the book and I know how it's going to turn out. I am deeply concerned about what lies between where we're at and where we're going to go. I sure think we're going to see some heavy storms, and I think we're going to go through some deep valleys, and climb some rugged mountains, and I think we're going to have to ford some rough and swift streams. But that's all right. We wasn't going to do anything anyway. Was any one of you going to do anything great, like be a king or a queen or a prince? A lot of people, when they start giving time to the patriotic effort, they act like they're wasting their time. I say, 'Well, what was you going to do with your life anyway? Did you have something great planned? Were you going to be a Thomas Edison, a Winston Churchill, a King Edward the Eighth? Well, you might as well make your time count for something.' "

He has that right. That one hits where they feel it. No, they wasn't planning anything great, and Harrell knows it. He knows what bugs them, too. When he starts talking about the press and how it has sided with the enemy, he gets murmurs of agreement, agitation out there in the metal chairs. They read the papers and watch TV. They know what's being said about them.

"I admonish 'em that they ought to try to do a little better, and I remind 'em that one day we may be a majority and they may be a minority and there may be a whole heap of trouble. Isn't there a song about be kind to those you meet on your way up, 'cause you may meet 'em on the way down? Of course, before this whole thing is over with, I expect to see a whole heap of treason trials in this country, and I'd like to participate in some of 'em. If treason is still givin' aid and comfort to the enemy, I think we ought to call some of these aiders and comforters up eventually and talk to 'em in a very frank manner and settle it as best we can for all the blood that they've caused to be spilled in this country. I don't see anything wrong with that at all. Call it to their attention in a rather firm and fixed manner as would befit the occasion and time."

Harrell is good at this. He knows he has a divided audience—some who know the message by rote, some newcomers and cautious conservatives and simply curious who are hearing this sort of thing for the first time. He manages to talk to them all, and when he's finished, after twenty minutes at the podium, I have a feeling that, like a carnival barker, he has wheedled and charmed the bystanders into his sideshow. They're with him now, ready for the half-dozen speakers stacked up behind him on the podium.

First off is the Defense League's military commander, a retired army colonel named B. F. M. von Stahl. He is a rumbling dreadnought of a man whose big belly stretches his brown khaki shirt to the limit. He moves slowly, ponderously, and speaks the same way. Harrell brings him forward to a prayer and the Pledge of Allegiance, but von Stahl launches into a lecture about capital punishment and then does an astounding segue into doomsday economics.

"The other thing I want to make sure that you're aware of, and never forget, is that we're the martial race. The Bible says, yes, you will turn your weapons into plowshares and whatnot, but before that, you shall turn your plowshares into swords and spears. So you better get to it. And don't bother stashing away gold and silver. Get ammunition, that's the best trading stock in the world. Nobody's going to trade food for gold and silver when food is scarce."

He is followed by another military man, another retired colonel now wearing the Defense League's brown uniform, but this one is a speaker. Jack Mohr has spent the last twenty-five years talking to Baptist congregations, to Birch Society meetings, to Kiwanians and Rotarians when they were in a mood to hear the hard line. Mohr plunges in with fists swinging and gets the distinction of being the first of many these five days who will talk in harsh terms about an absent enemy.

"We need men and women who are willing to talk back if necessary and fight if necessary against the international talmudic gangsters that are trying to control this world of ours under the direction of their father the devil."

And once more a few minutes later, this time even more plainly in case they missed it the first time.

"In the past months we have seen a vast Christian Conservative movement that has broken out in this country, like the Moral Majority. I don't have any quarrel against the Moral Majority. I wish them Godspeed in their battle against evil. But I will tell you that groups like the Moral Majority are nothing but skirmishes in the war, and they aren't going to make any headway until they quit trying to cut off the ends of the octopus's arms and get to the heart of the octopus and kill it. Once these fellows begin to realize that it's secular Jewish humanism that's destroying this country, and get hip to that angle, then they'll make headway against it.

"You're going to be hearing documented evidence of this threat. Some of you are going to be hearing this for the first time. You're going to be like I was a few years ago, that had come out of a conventional church where I'd heard the old hogwash for years and years, and I'd never been honest enough to check up on whether my pastor was telling the truth, and I learned some startling and frightening things. You're going to hear things you've never heard in your churches, some things you never hear from the news media, and some of you are going to refuse to accept it, and you're going to get mad about what you hear."

Couldn't be any clearer. Mohr throws it out there for all of them to catch: If you think Jerry Falwell is radical, and if you think the *National Review* has all the answers, you're probably not ready for what's going to happen in the next few days.

But nobody gets up to leave. Nobody gets mad. They're here for the rough stuff, and they get it a few minutes later when Ron Boggs walks to the podium. At first Boggs looks like he's ready to duke it out with the microphone; clearly, he's uneasy and unaccustomed to talking in public. But he substitutes pure passion for polish. He tells an abbreviated version of his fight with the IRS over his refusal to pay income taxes. It ends with his wife dying and with Boggs being sent to prison. When he gets to the part about recruiting convicted killers into the right wing, I look around. Two seats away is a woman literally slack-jawed with amazement. She is maybe sixty years old. On the bodice of her cotton print dress is an American flag pin made of rhinestones and glass rubies and artificial sapphires. To see the copies of *Human Events* on her coffee table, the levers that she pulled for Dick Nixon and Ronald Reagan and Barry Goldwater, maybe even the lapsed John Birch Society membership card in her purse, requires not so much imagination. She is a proud and stalwart patriot who has come here to save her nation. Now she is hearing this convicted criminal tell her about converting murderers to kill the IRS and she is very, very confused.

"I told the Internal Revenue Service that for the rest of my life I will follow the example they have set. They have shown me what they want me to do unto them. I do intend to see all of their wives dead. I do intend to see all of their possessions taken away from them. I'm so damn mad, I'm going to wait if I have to wait on the other side. I'm going to be patient, ladies and gentlemen."

Boggs finishes. Applause from the metal chairs. The lady with the American flag pin looks around, sees that all these patriots seem to approve, and begins to clap. Slowly and softly at first, then with more conviction. But the look on her face says that she has a lot of catching up to do in the next few days.

I catch up with Ron Boggs after his speech. Getting him alone isn't easy; he draws a crowd of backslappers and well-wishers wherever he goes here. Finally we sit together beneath an arbor on the grounds. It is dark and quiet; at the tent, somebody is talking over the loudspeakers about a foam-and-concrete survival igloo. Boggs lights a match that flares in the darkness, then he draws on his cigarette and talks.

It is a sad story about somebody who, after a lot of encouragement and persuasion, decides to buck his government and goes to jail for it, and loses his wife and all that he owns. Five years earlier he had been a machinist with a house and a family. Now he is alone, broke, and taking congratulations at a convention of right-wingers.

He talks for a long time. The last speaker finishes under the tent. The people leave, go to their tents and trailers and campers, and the lights go out. Ron Boggs talks some more. He's unrepentant and still angry, this casualty of the Radical Right's battle against the established order.

As he talks, I look around us. There is darkness, but I can see Harrell's security force patrolling the grounds, the gates, and the high fence with guns and dogs. One of them, with a rifle slung over his shoulder, sidles to within earshot of us and looks the other way.

Later, in the tent, it is some time before I can sleep. I feel an anxiety that isn't too far removed from fear, and I wonder why. I'm not in any jeopardy here, though I'd prefer not to have my sleep watched by strangers with guns. The ideas that I've heard don't frighten me, though they do seem, by turns, silly or repugnant or illogical or unlikely. I think of Ron Boggs and the way his life was changed by all this, and then I understand: I'm among rebels here. Some of them are ready to fight, to make huge sacrifices. The passion and the single-mindedness and the ardor are of a pitch that we don't see much anymore.

It is all just a little . . . disturbing.

The classes in survival and warfare run through the morning the next day, eight or ten of them running concurrently in different parts of the estate. After an hour, Harrell yanks the lanyard on a big bell and another set of classes begins.

Under one arbor, a man named Lawrence Smith is trying to get his listeners to support the Liberty Amendment. This was one of the classic right-wing causes of the Fifties, a proposed constitutional amendment that was supposed to end the federal income tax and get the government out

of any competition with private business. It has been a dead issue for years
(if it ever had any real life), but a few veterans still flog it for mileage.

Lawrence Smith is a veteran. His biography says that he cooperated
with the black nationalist Marcus Garvey in the back-to-Africa movement
of the Thirties, when some white segregationists were more than willing to
help blacks who wanted to leave this country. He has gray hair, bushy
eyebrows, and he is given to much gesticulating and arm-waving. He's
telling his audience that the way to get the Liberty Amendment passed is
to place lots of collect calls to congressmen to let them know that the
people are on the case. He says that he himself has recently made several
collect calls to New York representative Peter Rodino, and he announces
the number of Rodino's office for others who would like to do the same.
Several in his audience dutifully scribble down the digits.

About twenty yards away, the president of the company that plans to
manufacture the Atchisson Assault-12 "streetsweeper" shotgun is giving a
sales pitch to a couple of dozen people gathered around him in the grass.
He has been unable to bring the working prototype, he says, but he has
brought some spare parts for inspection. The most outstanding feature of
the gun, he tells his listeners, is a heavy bolt that reduces recoil to almost
nothing. This, he says, makes it a perfect self-defense weapon for those
who ordinarily wouldn't use a gun. He says that he certainly intends to
teach his family to use the gun.

"How small a child can fire the weapon?" a man in the crowd wants to
know.

The shotgun maker looks around, spots a boy the size of an average
seven-year-old, who is aiming down the barrel of a chrome cap pistol.

That boy, he says, could handle the weapon.

He passes around parts for the gun: a magazine, a bayonet, a spring.
Look at the workmanship, he tells the audience. Pay close attention to the
quality of the materials. At the front of the crowd is a big woman whose
gray hair is done in a bun. She has come with a man who brought a lawn
chair for her; she walks slowly, on swollen ankles, with the help of a black
wooden cane. Now, settled heavily into the chair, with the cane laid across
her knees, she takes the pieces of the gun as they make their way to her,
and she solemnly turns each one over in her hands. The gran'maw you
can imagine baking apple pies in her kitchen now listens attentively to
discussions of machining techniques and rate of fire, and checks the
bayonet for heft before she passes it on.

There's a big crowd gathered on the other side of the white house.
Three men in combat uniforms are demonstrating home-defense techniques. First rule: Buy a gun. Actually, this is so elementary that it is left

unsaid, but the implication is pretty strong because the three men do all their demonstrating with semiautomatic rifles and drawn .45s.

More rules: Sandbags are best for stopping bullets shot from outside the house, but if your supply of sandbags is low, you can get some protection from books. An open window above filled bookshelves makes a fine place from which to return fire. Walls won't stop a rifle bullet. Neither will doors, especially those of modern manufacture, which usually have a hollow core. So you can mow down your assailant without ever seeing him if you catch him behind a wall or a door. When going around corners, however, be sure not to let your gun precede you. Somebody could be waiting there to grab the barrel, wrest the gun away, and use it against you. And sometimes the house is just indefensible, so the best course is to vacate when the enemy penetrates, and then fire in from outside; let *him* try to find cover in your bookless, sandbagless home.

Under the striped tent, Harrell is having a press conference. I count three TV crews—from stations in Minneapolis, St. Louis, and Chicago—and more than ten reporters with notebooks and tape recorders. Harrell is at least 24,950,000 short of his goal of 25 million stalwarts, and the only way he can find sympathizers beyond the closed system of the Radical Right, out where the real numbers are, is to welcome the media and hope for the best.

Occasionally this means problems, like the young woman from the St. Louis paper this morning who keeps trying to nail him down on some sticky questions about the nonprofit status of the Christian Conservative church. He keeps pitching the same message, in the same orotund style he used the night before, and most of the reporters are happy to let him grind on. When they ask about the possible presence of Klansmen on the grounds, he answers by saying that there's everything here from a turtle-dove to a turkey buzzard, that his organization admits everybody, not only Klansmen but also Democrats and Republicans. They're happy with that; he gives them what they want. The woman reporter from St. Louis interrupts a couple of times to ask about finances; he answers in a few short words, his face looking as if he has bitten an unripe persimmon. Then he is off flying again, keeping the pencils jumping over the notebooks.

"We set up the mid-America survival zone so that people can concentrate their efforts to save this country if it's required. The American people are an extremely weak, marshmallow, fragmented, humored, pampered, babied people. You turn off the electricity, turn off the gas, turn off the water, take away their can opener and send them to an outdoor toilet, and they will sign almost any kind of a surrender. Our cities are already in shambles. You can't even walk safely down the street."

Later, I chat with a couple of the reporters. I get the impression that they look on Harrell as a daft and silly eccentric whose good sense has taken an extended sabbatical. Myself, I can't forget a story about Harrell that appears in Harry Jones's book, *The Minutemen*. The story is that Bob DePugh needed $15,000 to make final payment for a $25,000 shipment of dynamite. This was before Harrell's tax troubles, when he still had a personal fortune, but at a time when Harrell's long personal dialogues with the Creator were already legendary on the right. Jones writes that DePugh called Harrell to ask for the money, and that the conversation went something like this:

DePugh: John, something's happened to me. I've been born again.

Harrell: Bob, I'm glad to hear it.

DePugh: That's right. In fact, I had a long talk with the Lord last night.

Harrell: You did? And what did he say?

DePugh: Well, he said that I should ask John Harrell for the fifteen thousand dollars we need, and he'll probably give it to me.

Harrell (after a long pause): I think I'll have to hear it from the Lord myself.

The festival is, among other things, a bazaar, with several rows of tables bearing goods and books and wares. The literature tends to be anti-Jewish, apocalyptic, religious. Two Identity pastors, Sheldon Emry and Dan Gayman, have tables with books and tracts. Harrell's own church has a table, distributing mostly reprinted articles from the mainstream media. Three different vendors are hawking collections that include the *Protocols*. Identity jargon floats through the air: ". . . and I said to him, 'Do you know who you are? You're Israel,' I told him. . . ."

". . . it's the anti-Christ Jew who's behind the bankers. This is their dictatorship, it ain't in the Constitution. . . ."

". . . the preachers just won't tell it to you straight. They're the worst, 'cause they know we're Israel and they won't tell us, they're so afraid somebody is going to call 'em anti-Semitic. . . ."

A company from Oregon seems to be doing a good business with a stack of manuals on surviving nuclear war; the books lie beneath a map of the United States with plastic overlays showing primary, secondary, and tertiary nuclear targets.

At one table is a hand-lettered sign advertising "Patriotic Fly Swatters." These are black and ugly pieces of scrap metal, thick steel straps bent to fit around the heel of the hand, welded to short, stubby bars.

"Carry it in your car, call it a tire iron," says the man behind the table. He shows how it fits in the hand, how it can be brought up into an attacker's jaw or swung down into the skull. "You can put somebody's lights out real quick with one of these."

Later in the weekend, he marks his goods down to half-price. "They just aren't moving," he complains. "I did good business here last year. This time, the people seem awful peaceful, know what I mean?"

There are two tables selling knives, surplus camouflage clothes at highly inflated prices, and accessories for the popular Ruger Mini-14 rifle.

"I've heard these bullets go so fast they go right through somebody," says a teen-age girl to a man at one of the tables.

"The .223, you mean," he says. "Not if you use soft points. When they hit, they explode. They make a big hole. It's called 'hydrostatic damage.' I've seen deer killed with this bullet here."

A second man interjects: "I'd like to see the army go back to the old .308, if you ask me." He holds up an assault rifle manufactured by the Belgian Fabrique Nationale. "This is a .308," he says.

"Oh, my," says the girl. "That looks official."

Late in the afternoon, there's a minor contretemps when a woman notices that two National Socialists have set up a table and are displaying Nazi literature. She finds Harrell and complains: "This is terrible, just terrible. Here we're supposed to be patriots and you allow something like that."

He tells her that there has to be some room for disagreement, that he doesn't endorse everybody here; but when she persists, he promises that he will speak to them. He strolls over to their table, looking almost courtly in his blue suit. He bends over the table, puts on glasses to examine the books and pamphlets they're selling; the two Nazis are sullen and silent.

Finally, Harrell shakes his head. "People don't like this," he says. "The swastika does something, you know that. You can sell what you want, but anything that's got the swastika on it has to be covered up. Turn it over, whatever you want to do, but don't show the swastika."

The Nazis pout. One of them says something, too low for me to catch. But I can hear Harrell's reply.

"It ain't a-gonna work," he says. "Don't you know that? Wearing that swastika, it ain't a-gonna get you what you want. It's like the Klan—there's too much that's happened, too much that people remember. You can sell your books if you want, but keep that swastika covered up."

He walks away. An hour later, the Nazis are packed and gone.

Under the big striped tent, an old Southern Baptist minister holds forth on the subject of race-mixing.

"I wouldn't give the Red Cross one drop of my blood to be injected into some nigger's veins. And I certainly don't want to use nigger blood, that's for sure. If you want blood from your race, you demand it from your doctor and he'll get it from a blood bank, otherwise you'll just get what comes off the shelf. No nigger is ever going to get any blood from me, and no Jap, either, but if you need blood, and I've got your type, I'll help you.

"Any colored race and a white, say a nigger and a white, they mate and have a baby, what is it? It's not white. And a nigger could say it's not black. Then what is it? It's something different. It's a half-breed. In past years, when I was growing up, it had to go over to the black side. Even down through ten generations, even if that blood stayed on the black side, it still has a fraction of our blood in it. Most of you have prob'ly seen, I know I have, seen a nigger going down the street with a big splotch of pink skin on his face. In Montgomery, Alabama, I've seen what I call an 'albino nigger' with terrible-looking eyes—they weren't gray, they weren't blue, a terrible mixture. And his skin was pink and slippery. He looked terrible to me, a disgrace to both races. Down in North Carolina, you'll see people with skin as white as you or me, but you get up close and you'll see a little nigger look in their eyes. The way I consider it, it's too bad they didn't get dunked three times and pulled out once."

By Saturday afternoon, the outhouses on the property are rank and fetid. Somebody mentions this to Harrell, and he replies with infinite patience: "We're going to have to learn to put up with some inconveniences. We've got trying times ahead of us before we get where we're going, and it's time we started getting used to a little hardships."

In four days, I hear only two things that really frighten me.

One comes from a man in a camouflage uniform who teaches a course called "Why Christians Should Fight." He stands before his audience with a Bible in his left hand and a .45 holstered on his hip.

"Only by violence will Babylon be cast down," he tells us. "They are out to destroy the white race, and the only way to stop them is by violence."

That's one. The other comes from a young man who tells of the Anti-Defamation League: "The ADL has people so brainwashed, you can't argue with them about six million people dying in the Holocaust. So instead, you should try to explain why it had to happen."

The festival program has words about the burghers of Louisville, Illinois, warnings roughly similar to those that tourists in Yellowstone Park get about feeding the bears.

"It is requested that all attending the Freedom Festival be wise and cautious with local citizenry," the notice begins. "As Patriots, you already know the feeling of lethargy among the general public of America; and it is similar here, if not a bit worse."

Still, by Sunday afternoon the church estate has begun to inspire claustrophobia. I can take only so much of talmudic Jew gangsters and impending battles with the antichrist. A little political lethargy sounds appealing. I decide to feed the bears.

I have an iced tea at the café, walk across the square to a shop, and get a lesson in political reality, another example of the unease with which the Radical Right nestles down among the nation's ordinary citizens. You would believe—if you happen to accept the cultural stereotypes—that John Harrell's church and his followers would find ardent support in a town like Louisville. And what kind of town is that? It is a town where a newcomer who walks into a shop gets spotted for the stranger that he is, and also a town where the lady at the check-out counter will hesitate before she gets up the courage to ask him:

"You one of them people out at the church grounds?"

"I'm out there looking around."

She looks closer at me and asks, "Are there any snakes out there? My girlfriend lives right across the road from there and she says she saw a truck drive in there that said 'snakes' on it."

I tell her that I've seen the truck, too, with a sign that claims the truck is being guarded by poisonous snakes.

"But they aren't handling snakes out there or anything crazy like that?" she asks.

"None that I've seen."

She shakes her head slowly; she's still not pleased.

"Let me ask you," I say. "What do people in Louisville think about living so close to the church grounds?"

She looks me straight in the eye and says, "We don't like it. Especially those that are right across the road from him. They don't like it at all. They don't have any idea what goes on there. They hear shooting sometimes, and they don't like it. It scares them, but the church grounds are right outside the town, so there's not much Louisville can do about it. We just don't know what got into Johnny Bob."

"Johnny Bob?"

"Johnny Bob Harrell. He used to be a businessman, made himself a lot of money. People around here liked him and respected him. We all belonged to the Methodist church, and sometimes when the pastor couldn't be there, Johnny Bob got up and gave the sermon, and did a right nice job of it, too.

"But it all went bad when Johnny Bob started talking to God. He'd get up in his airplane and fly around by himself and talk to God. That's what he told people. He left and the Methodist church broke up and there's been hard feelings against him about all the things that have happened since then."

A customer, another woman, comes to the counter, looks at me, and says to the saleslady, "Looks like they're powwowin' over at the church again."

The saleslady tips her head toward me and says, "He's been over there watching."

"That right?" says the customer. "I hear they don't allow any black people over there, that right?"

"That's right."

"That doesn't seem like the Christian thing to do," she says. "I don't believe in race-mixing or marrying out of your kind, but it's not right just to keep the blacks out like that. I don't believe the things they stand for out there are Christian, you understand?"

She leaves; I talk with the clerk for a few more minutes and as I'm ready to leave she says: "I sit here and I watch those cars and trucks go in there, and I look at 'em, and they've got money, they look normal, just like you and me, and I wonder, Why in the world do they believe the strange things they do?"

It feels good to be on the other side of the fence again.

There it was in miniature: the angry and suspicious minority cloistered behind a fence, surrounded by people uncomprehending, untrusting, but ultimately disinterested in them. The salesclerk hadn't been curious about nuances of philosophy; she only knew that she didn't understand those people and that they were strange. And she really only wanted to know whether they were a danger to her.

In that way, Louisville was like the rest of the nation. If only figuratively, the Radical Right in this country has retreated behind a high fence. But its ominous sounds reach our ears sometimes, and they worry us. And we want to know: Do we have to worry about what they're doing?

The easiest answer to that question is that they are more dangerous to each other than they are to us. Their rhetoric of violent action can be truly frightening, but it should be heard with the knowledge that the Radical Right's threats are rarely accompanied by action. And we should know from the record of infiltration that the harsh talk does not go unnoted by our police. Somebody is peeking through the fence and taking names. That does not mean that the Radical Right—or, more precisely, some individuals who fall within its purview—will never act violently. They have in the past, and they will again. But massive and concerted armed action is probably out of the question, for it is beyond the capability of the Radical Right in more than one way.

That leaves change through the electoral process. The Radical Right's paltry headcount is obvious, which would seem to preclude real change through ballot-box politics. Some of those who search history for answers would say that Germany's Nazis started with far fewer than we have today on the Radical Right. But Germany had no Nazis in its past; we now have Hitler and his evil to anchor us against any precipitous plunge into racist extremism. Can the Radical Right, as Bob DePugh suggests, slowly chip away at us with its ideas? It could, if it were the only faction doing that. But there are dozens of others, vagrant strains of political movements that work on us just as assiduously, so that our collective political consciousness is a likeness of none.

A year of intimate contact with the Radical Right, shuttling between its confines and what still seems like the real world outside, does suggest that there are two possibilities for the Radical Right to become a real force in our nation. One is a severe economic depression accompanied by political and social upheaval. The nation spurned extremist solutions the last time it endured economic misery. This time, there are many on the Radical Right who have shown that they are willing to exploit national weaknesses, and they might prove persuasive to large numbers. The second of these nightmare scenarios is a war in the Middle East, in which we fight on the side of Israel. Such a conflict might be unpopular here, and those who shout their anti-Jewish messages of hate into empty halls today might suddenly find eager, receptive audiences.

So the danger does exist; there is always risk in freedom. We could purge ourselves of the extremists if we really wanted. But in doing so we would wound our liberties and ourselves more grievously than the Radical Right ever could.

Sources and Index

By far the greater part of the material in this book was gathered firsthand, through observation, interviews, and study of material not generally available to the public. The library card files, bibliographies, and indexes of newspapers that any journalist or researcher would consult first yielded little beyond facts of public record: arrests, convictions, bombings, demonstrations. In the usual published sources, there was scarce mention—let alone explanation—of the Radical Right's complexities and contradictions.

This means that an orderly collecting and arranging of published information is a poor way to approach a serious book about the Radical Right today. The alternative is less systematic: weeks upon weeks of observation, close contact, careful study of the internal literature—in short, virtual immersion in the subject. That method makes for vivid impressions and deep understanding, but it does not lend itself well to a strict comprehensive listing of sources in textbook style. It would be impossible, for example, to cite the source that first led me to understand the important differences between the rather conservative John Birch Society and a racist group like the Ku Klux Klan. It might have been a JBS tract, a remark during an interview, maybe some cue even more subtle. Whatever it was, though, became reinforced dozens of times by observation, more tracts, more interviews, until the fundamental differences between the two groups became as natural, comprehensive, and unquestionable as principles of geometry are to a surveyor. They were the rules by which this world functioned.

In that way, the ultimate source became the people of the movement themselves, through their often arcane and narrowly circulated writings, and through conversations that ranged from formal interviews to brief chats to back-fence gossip. Where I have drawn on accessible published material for facts that may be subject to dispute or inquiry, those sources are noted below. I have also tried to name more-general sources, both within and without the movement. Some of those Radical Right publications are so obscure and ephemeral that to list them all would be an exercise in scholarly vanity.

The listing of those I interviewed during research for the book is incomplete, in part for that same reason. Those who contributed significantly are already cited in the text, where they are quoted. Beyond those people, however, are many dozens of others who either wished to remain anonymous or whose identities are meaningless for the purposes of the book or whose names I never asked. For it should be noted that "research" for this book often amounted to what an anthropologist might call "fieldwork," often conducted under circumstances in which personal curiosity would have been a gross indiscretion.

1

1. *New York Times,* "The Klan Has More Crosses to Bear Than Burn," July 30, 1978, p. IV, 5.
2. *New York Times,* "More Than a Dozen Klan Factions Compete for Membership and Feud Over Predominance," July 11, 1977, p. 14.
3. Interview with Bill Wilkinson, July 1981.
4. *New York Times,* July 11, 1977, p. 14.
5. Interview, anonymous, June 1981.
6. *Jackson* (Miss.) *Capital Reporter,* "Separatist Elmore D. Greaves Would Love To Be Governor," Oct. 23, 1980.
7. "Hugh Morris in Stoner Case," and "Time Runs Out for Lame Duck Baxley," reprints in the *Thunderbolt,* Oct. 1978, of articles originally appearing in *Atlanta Journal,* Feb. 7, 1978, and *Atlanta Journal,* Oct. 11, 1981.
8. The *Thunderbolt,* Jan. 1981.
9. *New York Times,* Dec. 1, 1978, p. 19.

10. The *Thunderbolt,* Oct. 1980.

11. *Mother Jones,* April 1980.

12. Ibid.

13. *Minneapolis Star,* "Crusaders Gear Up for War of Words," Feb. 5, 1981.

14. *Minneapolis Star,* "Pro-Nuke Army Waging Puzzling War for Power," Feb. 2, 1981.

15. *New York Times,* "One Man Leads USLP on Its Erratic Path," Oct. 8, 1979, p. D19.

16. Ibid.

17. Gregory Rose, "The Smarmy Life and Times of the NCLC," *National Review,* Mar. 20, 1979, p. 409.

18. Ibid.

19. *The Public Eye,* Spring 1981.

20. Ibid.

Lyndon LaRouche, the U.S. Labor Party, the National Caucus of Labor Committees, and their various front groups probably have received more critical scrutiny from mainstream media in the last four years than any other group espousing a Radical Right ideology. The *National Review* article by former USLP member Gregory Rose, cited above, is the most complete and damaging in its treatment of LaRouche's overtures to the right. Other articles have included a five-part series by George Johnson in the *Minneapolis Star,* Feb. 2–6, 1981; a two-part series by Howard Blum and Paul Montgomery in the *New York Times,* Sept. 7 and 8, 1979; a ten-part series by Dennis King in the New York weekly *Our Town,* to which LaRouche responded with a $20-million lawsuit; "The U.S. Labor Party's Radical Crusade," in *Business Week,* Oct. 2, 1978; an article by Chip Berlet, "What Is This Man Afraid Of? Nearly Everything," in the Chicago weekly *Reader,* Mar. 7, 1980; and "Is LaRouche's Cult Collapsing?" in the *Village Voice,* Nov. 11, 1981.

Additional material for other portions of this chapter include publicity releases and broadsides published by the Southern National party; numerous issues of the *Thunderbolt* for the last five years; back issues of Liberty Lobby's *Spotlight;* the multitude of tracts and pamphlets published by the Christian-Patriots Defense League; publications of the USLP and the NCLC, including *Investigative Leads,* and back issues of the *Campaigner* and *New Solidarity;* articles in the *New York Times* during the late 1960s reporting on the long series of legal difficulties of Bob DePugh and the Minutemen; and various pieces of Nazi literature published during the 1970s.

2

1. John Birch Society *Bulletin* No. 208, July 1976.
2. Ibid.
3. Gary Allen, *None Dare Call It Conspiracy,* Concord Press, 1971.
4. JBS *Bulletin* No. 261, Dec. 1980.
5. JBS *Bulletin* No. 219, June 1977.
6. *Conspiracy Digest,* Vol. IV, No. 2, Spring 1979.

There are numerous sources for numerous offshoots of the right-wing conspiracy theory. The JBS *Bulletin* has described different aspects of the theory over the years. The issues cited above are two of many that have dealt with the conspiracy. Gary Allen's book, cited above, is probably the most comprehensive. The Sept. 1970 issue of the United Klans of America's newspaper, *Fiery Cross,* contains an article that deals in detail with the conspiracy as it is supposed to relate to the assassination of Abraham Lincoln. Two somewhat obscure monthly publications, *Conspiracy Digest* (Alpine Enterprises, Dearborn, Michigan) and *Conspiracies Unlimited* (St. Paul, Minnesota) have published numerous articles about the right-wing conspiracy theories.

3

This chapter is based on interviews and correspondence with Hillman Holcomb in spring and summer 1981, and on material from his privately published works, including *G.I.F.T.*

4

1. Interview with Bill Wilkinson, July 1981.
2. Earl Shorris, "The Hollywood Right," *Harper's,* Sept. 1980.
3. *Reno Evening Gazette,* Sept. 10, 1980.
4. *Nevada State Journal,* July 23, 1980.

Additional sources for this chapter included publications of the Christian Crusade and fund-raising letters by Billy James Hargis; publications of the

Christian Anti-Communist Crusade; an open letter by Bob DePugh; correspondence with Bill Wilkinson; *An Introduction to the United Klans of America,* distributed during the Sixties; numerous issues of the Reverend Ron Branson's published critiques of conservative churchmen; numerous issues of the Moral Majority newsletter; the publications of the Eagle Forum; and interviews with Janine Triggs, Michael Triggs, and other members of the Oliver Hansen family.

5

1. *Oakland* (Mich.) *Press,* Aug. 30, 1981.
2. *From the Mountain,* July–Aug. 1980.

An interview with the Reverend Clyde Edminster, as cited in the text, originally provided much of the background for the explanation and interpretation of the Identity belief. However, other sources treat the faith in more detail. Pastor Sheldon Emry has written at least ten books and several dozen tracts and pamphlets dealing with different aspects of the Identity faith. Much of that material is included in a series of tape cassette sermons, and was used as background material for this chapter. So, too, were some of the taped sermons of the late Dr. Wesley Swift. Clyde Edminster's several books, which originally appeared in different issues of his monthly publication *Christ Is the Answer,* deal with both the historical implications and the End Time aspects of Identity theory. Several issues of the newsletter *From the Mountain* describe the theory of dualism as preached by Robert Miles. An information packet distributed by the Aryan Nations Church of Hayden Lake, Idaho, describes the racial theories of Richard Butler.

6

The observations about the Renegade Right that are the main substance of this chapter are, perhaps more than any other segment of the book, highly subjective and personal. They are based in part on the angry writings of right-wing rebels like Robert Miles, and in part on the nuances and impressions gained from personal interviews. The material on tactics used by Illegal Tax Protesters is based on interviews with tax rebels and on confidential sources.

7

1. *Seattle Times,* "Are They the Good Guys or the Bad Guys?" Part Three of a series by Peter Arnett of the Associated Press, Mar. 4, 1981.
2. Ibid.
3. The *Public Eye,* Spring 1981.
5. *Sacramento Bee,* Sept. 1, 1976.
6. Ibid.
7. The *Oregonian,* Portland, Oregon, Aug. 27, 1976.
7. "Every Man a Sheriff," the *Nation,* Dec. 20, 1975, p. 659.

Biographical information on John Harrell, and information about his arrests, his tax difficulties, his life as a fugitive, and his reputed miraculous recovery, are from a variety of sources. They include Harrell's own comments during an interview in June 1981; his writings, including an autobiographical section of a Christian-Patriots Defense League orientation booklet; and pages 100–103 of Harry J. Jones's the *Minutemen* (Doubleday, 1968). Further information about the Defense League was obtained from the group's literature; from the numerous articles that the Defense League's "freedom festivals" have generated during the last three years (including "In Illinois: Festival of the Fed-Up," *Time,* Nov. 5, 1979; "The Guns of Fear," the *Arizona Republic,* April 19, 1981; and "Preparing for the Worst," *Sunday Courier-Press,* Evansville, Indiana, May 31, 1981); from "Armies of the Right," a documentary film produced by WCCO-TV, Minneapolis, Minnesota, broadcast Dec. 1981; and in large part from personal observation and interviews with present and former members of the C-PDL. Information about the Christian Survivalist Militants (CSA) was obtained from interviews with CSA members and from a brochure advertising the group's survivalist courses.

Much of the background for the segment dealing with the Posse Comitatus is from personal contact, from letters and petitions sent by Posse members to selected public officials in California, and from conversations with one of those officials and with members of a sheriff's department and a district attorney in that state.

The section dealing with the Radical Right's tastes in firearms is, again, a product of personal knowledge, combined with references from gun magazines, catalogs of firearms accessories, and conversations with gun-store owners.

Joseph Kerska's comments are from an interview. Additional background is from several of the tracts he has published through the Sons of Liberty.

8

This chapter is a synthesis of a myriad of sources. Some of the most important were the writings of Bob DePugh—issues of *On Target* from the 1960s and also from 1979 to 1981, *Blueprint for Victory, A Short History of the Minutemen, Principles of Guerrilla Warfare,* and others. Material written about Bob DePugh that was helpful in this chapter included nearly fifty articles published about DePugh, the Minutemen, or their activities between 1963 and 1972. Harry Jones's study of the Minutemen, cited above, was important in interpreting DePugh's intentions and his state of mind during the first seven years that the Minutemen existed. Laird Wilcox supplied not only details of his relationship with DePugh, beginning in the mid-Sixties, but also an interview taped with former Minuteman Jerry Brooks and a file of newspaper clippings that dealt with DePugh's criticism of student radicals at the University of Kansas and with the allegedly forged issue of the *Kansas Free Press.* Finally, conversations with DePugh during summer of 1981, including the interview that is reproduced in chapter 14, were crucial in understanding the man and what he had done.

9

As noted in the text, there is no reliable single source for membership figures on the Radical Right. The section that deals with those figures is, as noted, highly speculative and based on personal observation balanced against commonly accepted estimates that have never been refuted. Therefore, the sources for those speculations are too numerous to list.

The segment on *The Duck Book* is derived from an interview with Bob White, from issues of the magazine published through December 1981, and from White's advertising and promotion letters.

As elsewhere, most of the material on Liberty Lobby is from the publications of the group itself, including issues of the *Spotlight* from 1978 to 1981. Probably the most critical study of Willis Carto as a conservative is from the Sept. 10, 1971, issue of the *National Review.*

Some of the most important background on the John Birch Society and its attitudes is in the JBS *Bulletin,* of which I read most of the issues published between 1970 and 1981 before writing this section. Also significant are the dozens of pamphlets, many written by Robert Welch himself, that deal with specific issues like race and religion, and which are sold in American Opinion bookstores. Often they are the key to understanding the JBS philosophy. Information on the JBS's policy of disavowing racism can be found, among many sources, in "John Birch Leader Raps 'Hate' Groups," *Atlanta Constitution,* Aug. 21, 1969; in the *Peoria* (Illinois) *Journal Star,* Jan. 16, 1979; and in the *Thunderbolt,* March 1979. Bill Murray's privately published *Belmont Syndrome* gave some insight into the Birch system of front groups, as well as the organization's approach to marketing and recruitment and the frustrations that approach seems to have caused among some Birch members. Also of some use were *The Radical Right,* by Benjamin Epstein and Arnold Forster (Random House, 1966); *The Fear Brokers,* by Thomas J. McIntyre with John C. Obert (Beacon, 1981); *The Radical Right: The New American Right,* edited by Daniel Bell (Doubleday, 1964); and Robert Welch's *The Politician,* privately published in 1963.

10

The segment on current disunity on the Radical Right is culled from impressions and facts collected during more than a year of research. Among the sources that can be positively cited are Bob DePugh's series on Willis Carto, published in *On Target* and cited in the text; various issues of the *Thunderbolt,* including those dealing with Bill Wilkinson's FBI connection; numerous issues of the Invisible Empire's newspaper, the *Klansman,* and the United Klans of America's *Fiery Cross;* an open letter from Bob DePugh to Ed Fields; and several of a series of circulars written by Harold Covington in 1981.

The recounting of the disintegration of the Patriots' leadership council was corroborated by two former members of the council.

Information on the Libertarian party and its positions is from sources that include *National Review* articles published June 8, 1979, and party publications.

11

1. *Washington Star,* "Eight Arrested in Klan Bomb Plot," May 22, 1981.
2. *Greensboro Record,* July 16, 1980, et al.
3. *Washington Post,* Nov. 22, 1981.
4. *Columbus Dispatch,* Dec. 16, 1979.
5. *Columbus Citizen-Journal,* Dec. 17, 1979.
6. *Speak Up,* Aug.–Sept. 1978, p. 1.

7. *Washington Post,* "Crackdown in Poland Raises Fears of Increased Anti-Semitism," Dec. 26, 1981.
8. Column released through syndications, week of Dec. 28, 1981.

Though the issue of paranoia as a component of right-wing psychology has probably been overworked in the popular media, concern about infiltration—in general, concern that people or organizations may not be what they seem to be—is widespread through some quarters of the Radical Right. The "Deguello Communication," cited and quoted in the text, demonstrates that this fear exists. So does the furor that followed the release of that communiqué. The *Thunderbolt* often is a voice for such concerns; the issue of April 1981 carried an article, accompanied by a reprint from the *Chicago Sun-Times,* claiming that the FBI helped Polish intelligence agents to spy on Polish nationalists in this country. The Feb. 1979 issue of the *Thunderbolt* carried a story titled "Deprez Misleads Louisville Patriots," claiming that an antibusing organization in Louisville, Kentucky, was actually a front group for the Anti-Defamation League of B'nai B'rith. And the U.S. Labor party has claimed in a pamphlet entitled *Wall Street Fabians in the Conservative Movement,* published by the *Executive Intelligence Review,* that William F. Buckley and his family have manipulated the conservative cause for the ends of a great conspiracy. A complete list of citations in this vein would be endless.

The issue of Communist disinformation efforts was popularized by the publication of the best-selling novel *The Spike,* by Robert Moss and Arnaud de Borchgrave (Crown, 1980). Among recent material on the subject is de Borchgrave's "Bum Tips and Spies," *New York Times,* Aug. 12, 1981; Moss's testimony before the U.S. Senate Subcommittee on Security and Terrorism in July 1981 about a link between Communists and neo-Nazi groups in Europe; William Parham's "Soviets Embark on New Campaign of Anti-American Lies," *Norwich* (Conn.) *Bulletin,* April 14, 1981; and John Barron's *KGB: The Secret Work of Soviet Agents* (Reader's Digest Press, 1974).

12

Material on the Ku Klux Klan was derived from a variety of sources, including newspapers published by the three leading Klans of the last decade: the *Klansman* of the Invisible Empire, the United Klans of America's *Fiery Cross,* and the *Crusader* of the National Knights of the Ku Klux Klan. Of special interest is Vol. 16, No. 3 of *Fiery Cross,* which constitutes almost a crash course in the rivalries among those Klans.

Bill Wilkinson's conflicts with legal authority are chronicled in articles appearing in the *New York Times* from 1976 to the present. The careful and astute reporting of Wayne King in the *New York Times,* on the subject of the KKK, deserves mention. Cf special interest is King's overview of the Klan appearing in the Dec. 7, 1980, issue.

Hooded Americanism: The History of the Ku Klux Klan by David M. Chalmers (Franklin Watts, 1981) provided historical background.

13

Publications of the various Nazi groups, including *White Power* by the National Socialist White People's party, the National Socialist White Workers' *Stormer,* and *Carolina Action,* the bulletin of the National Socialist party of North Carolina, supplemented research for this chapter. The figures on membership numbers are common estimates within the Radical Right. There has never been any evidence to make it less credible. The material on homosexuality among the Nazis is presented unabashedly as speculation and popular rumor. The sexual aspects of the National Socialist League are documented in party publications, including *NS Mobilizer,* Vol. III, Nos. 35, 36, and 37.

INDEX